Identifying
Avon
Jewelry

Sandra Sturdivant

Schiffer Publishing Ltd

4880 Lower Valley Road Atglen, Pennsylvania 19310

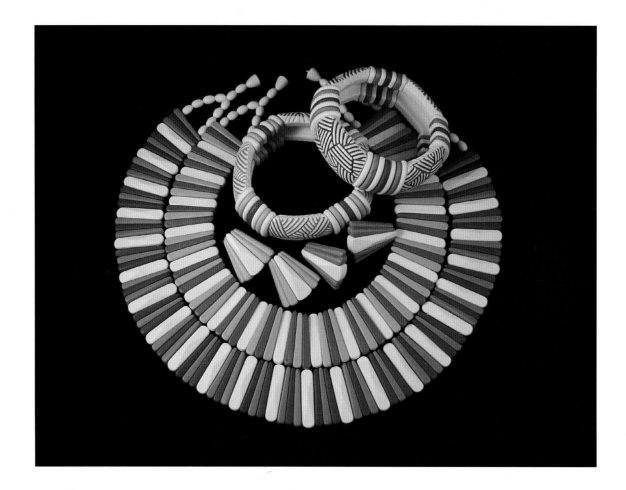

Designed by "Sue"
Type set in Caslon224 Bk BT/NewsGoth BT

ISBN: 978-0-7643-3061-2
Printed in China

Schiffer Books are available at special discounts for bulk
purchases for sales promotions or premiums. Special
editions, including personalized covers, corporate imprints,
and excerpts can be created in large quantities for special
needs. For more information contact the publisher:

Published by Schiffer Publishing Ltd.
4880 Lower Valley Road
Atglen, PA 19310
Phone: (610) 593-1777; Fax: (610) 593-2002
E-mail: Info@schifferbooks.com

For the largest selection of fine reference books on this and
related subjects, please visit our web site at:
www.SCHIFFERBOOKS.COM
We are always looking for people to write books on new
and related subjects. If you have an idea for a book please
contact us at the above address.

This book may be purchased from the publisher.
Include $5.00 for shipping.
Please try your bookstore first.
You may write for a free catalog.

In Europe, Schiffer books are distributed by
Bushwood Books
6 Marksbury Ave.
Kew Gardens
Surrey TW9 4JF England
Phone: 44 (0) 20 8392-8585; Fax: 44 (0) 20 8392-9876
E-mail: info@bushwoodbooks.co.uk
Website: www.bushwoodbooks.co.uk
Free postage in the U.K., Europe; air mail at cost.

Dedication and Acknowledgments

The author wishes to dedicate this book
To Jim Sturdivant, husband and best friend
To Jackie Paul, who started this project
To Shirley Crabtree, who donated all her mother's jewelry
To the wonderful folks at Apertures Photo, especially Jeff Park
To the Avon jewelry collector who made this book necessary

Photography by Sandra Sturdivant
   The jewelry shown is from the author's private collection.

The values in this book represent a guide and will vary according to supply and demand, condition of items, packaging, and geographical location. They are not intended to set prices and should not be used in that fashion. Both the author and the publisher assume no responsibility for any losses that might incur by consulting this guide.

Preface

The idea for this book surfaced over the Thanksgiving holidays of 2002. My mother, Jackie Paul, was the keeper of the family jewels, inheriting all the jewelry from both sides of the family. Having a footlocker full of Avon, plus several jewelry boxes with loose pieces, she asked if I could name and date the collection for her. *Piece of cake*, I thought. When I got home, I began searching for Avon jewelry on the Internet. To my chagrin, I discovered plenty of photos of the jewelry, but literally NO documentation or provenance for anything Mother owned. To make a long story short, she and I began to research her jewelry the hard way: brochure acquisition. This turned out to be every bit as difficult as we expected. Over the course of the next year, we had enough information to identify her jewelry, plus formulate plans for a book. Four months later, Mother died, but this book is her legacy.

My friend Shirley Crabtree scoured flea markets, craft fairs, and the Internet for additional pieces, many of them unmarked, some of them unboxed, and all of them in collectible condition. She also interviewed many of the long-time sales representatives for additional information, and she personally knows Lena Vaughn, who received an award for the longest time served by any Avon sales representative.

Not every piece of Avon jewelry could be found, but I am confident that 97 percent of the jewelry line is represented in this book. I had to end it somewhere, and I chose July 2005, since that is where my brochures end, but there are also a smattering of items from 2006 and 2007. I trust everyone will find this book useful.

Contents

Introduction

This guide to Avon jewelry includes more than 3,200 individual items, each identified with its proper name and date-of-release, as provided by Avon company brochures. None are unidentified. There are no watches in this book, but you will find hundreds of striking necklaces, bracelets, earrings, pins, rings, sets, gift sets, children's jewelry, special occasion pieces, and items from the fabulous designers and Smithsonian Institution. Provenance comes directly from the Avon brochures; there is no guesswork. Also included is a value guide compiled by several current antique jewelry appraisers.

Locating Avon jewelry is fairly simple --- it is sold worldwide and collectors live in every corner of the Earth. Knowing what you find is extremely difficult. There are no books on Avon jewelry with adequate information for the serious collector. Unless you find someone with a large collection still in the original boxes, or you locate old brochures, you are out of luck in identifying what you have. Critics complain there is too much of it for the serious collector, but women scarf it up like hotcakes. In Avon's desire to provide women with trendy jewelry at affordable prices, they created an astonishing array of sizes and colors. There are thousands of exquisitely beautiful items, some of such elaborately fine craftsmanship that they could easily pass as museum pieces. Avon used precious metals, materials, and faux stones of high quality in size and appearance, as well as synthetics of every color and shape. Avon made frivolous and fun items, but always they had fashion in mind.

The Beginning

Avon did not spring into existence overnight. David Hall McConnell was a successful door-to-door book salesman before it dawned on him that people bought his books because of the little vials of rose oil perfume that he gave away to his customers. Forming the California Perfume Company in New York in 1886, his first product was the Little Dot Perfume Set --- Violet, White Rose, Heliotrope, Lily-of-the-Valley, and Hyacinth --- sold by men. He already knew the direct market approach was the key to success, but it was Mrs. Persis Foster Eames Albee of Winchester, New Hampshire, his General Manager, who pioneered the method by recruiting women as well as men.

McConnell built his first laboratory and printed his first catalog in 1897. He published his first ads in the nation-wide *Good Housekeeping Magazine*, in 1905.

He lost his California office in the 1906 San Francisco earthquake, went International to Montreal, Canada, in 1914, and incorporated in 1916. By 1920, sales had topped $1,000,000.

Avon Products Is Born

The name Avon became associated with the company in 1928 in honor of McConnell's favorite playwright, William Shakespeare, who lived in Stratford-upon-Avon, England. The first items offered under that brand name were a toothbrush, talcum powder, and a vanity set. By 1939, the company was officially known as Avon Products, Inc. The rest, as the say, is history.

The phenomenal success of Avon is clear. They increased their sales and general interest by going into the home instead of competing with the corner drug and department stores. They started with perfumes and expanded to include a long line of great cosmetics, keeping up with the ever-changing fashion trends and colors. In 1964, the company was listed on the New York Stock Exchange, and the company expanded to include giftware, clothing, videos, music, books, puzzles, games, collectibles, and a host of other interesting items.

The Jewelry Line Begins

Avon jewelry entered the Avon family in 1965, with a stylish locket pin called simply Solid Perfume Jewel Pin. It came with an individually wrapped, small round tub of solid perfume, called a *glacé*, which simply means a solid perfume, and this was the original intention of the pin. The idea was to place the tub in the pin and throughout the day, open the pin, rub your finger across the perfume, and apply it to various pulse points, such as your neck or wrist, for an uplifting and invigorating whiff of wonderful scent, but the pin had versatility. When not being used to hold the *glacé*, the pin could be used to hold a favorite photograph, locket of hair, or other memorabilia. This was ingenuity at its finest. The jewelry quickly caught on, rings and two pendants were immediately added, and Avon was off and running in the jewelry business with their perfume *glacé* designs.

The First Collections

Avon jewelry officially became a reality in May, 1971, with the stylish and versatile Precious Pretenders Collection. It consisted of a pin, necklace, bracelet, and clip earrings all in the same design and gold wash. Avon followed this success with the Evening Creation Collection two months later, which included two different styles of rings, one for day wear and one for an evening out on the town. By 1974, Avon was adding about 25 new pieces each year, and by the end of 1976, this had mushroomed to about 10 new pieces each month. Today, Avon adds about 250 new pieces each year, making it the number-one jewelry company in the world.

Most of Avon's jewelry incorporates a selection of sizes and colors for each design. Some pieces are rare, having been sold during only one campaign, while others are carried over several years. Some of the popular early designs are now back under new names, an indication of the staying power and versatility of the designs.

The Perfume Connection

Avon even made special items to honor top-selling perfumes, such as the Bird of Paradise ring, the Sonnet necklace, and the Bold Starring pin and earrings. In 1986, they created an entire collection of necklace, bracelet, pin, ring, and earrings, plus a glamorous gold jewelry case, to honor their 100th jubilee. They continue this trend to this day with items like the Mesmerize pendant and the Far Away necklace set, to name but a few. The last necklace issued in honor of a perfume was the Crystal Aura in 2006.

Some perfumes used to spawn jewelry items:
Back: Patterns, Sonnet, Bold Starring;
Front: Far Away, Bird of Paradise Skin Softener and Perfume

Packaging

The first packaging was functional, but somewhat ordinary and plain. Avon was not in the jewelry business at this time; they were selling cosmetics, so the package lid lifted off to reveal the contents, as is the case of the Solid Perfume Jewel Pin. By the time the perfume *glacé* rings arrived, the packaging had changed to replicate the perfume container. Thus, it was possible to tell at a glance that the Patterns Fashion Perfume ring of 1969 was based on the Patterns perfume by the zebra look of the box.

Packaging for the Daisy Pin and Solid Perfume Jewel.

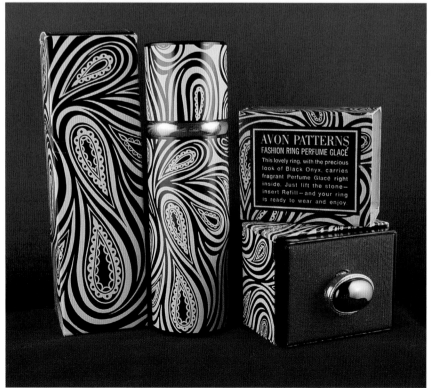

Patterns Perfume and Patterns Ring packaging

8

When Avon officially entered the jewelry industry in 1971, its packaging was still in its infancy. Most items were carefully mounted on blue inserts inside a gold bottom with a solid royal blue lid. This was inserted inside a white outer sleeve imprinted with the name and date of the item. If the sleeve became separated from the internal box, and many did, the only way to identify the item was to use the brochure. Eventually the molded insert was discarded and replaced with cotton, but Avon kept this general configuration right up through 1980, making changes only from a solid royal blue lid to a swirled blue lid.

In 1980, Avon brought some great changes to the packaging. The first change was to switch from the gold bottom and blue top to a cream container with a cream outer sleeve. It was still possible to lose the outer sleeve, so the tan flip-top box arrived. With this configuration, the box identified the contents, since there was no outer sleeve to become lost. Cardboard inserts were also used as mounting material to keep the jewelry from moving around in the cotton and becoming scratched. The tan flip-top box evolved to the black flip-top box in the 1990's with black sponge inserts, and this changed to the gold flip-top box in 2000 with gray inserts. Things changed again to a light blue fold-over box with blue sponge inserts, and this evolved to the silvered blue fold-over box with blue sponge inserts to the silvered brown fold-over box with black sponge inserts in use today. Along the way, Avon used a wide variety of special occasion boxes to cover a variety of events, such as holidays and children's items.

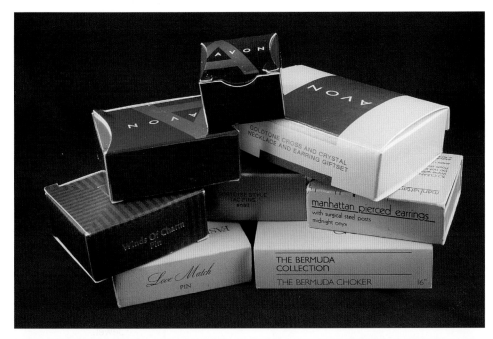

Examples of Avon packaging through the years, from the white and cream outer sleeves on the bottom to the flip-top boxes in the middle to the fold-over boxes on top.

Examples of special occasion packaging

9

More examples of special occasion packaging

Avon stamped markings

Originality was always Avon's goal with consumer demand the target, but trend-setters were abundant with all jewelry companies, and it is impossible to know who came first with many of the designs. To keep from becoming anonymous in a world filled with hundreds of jewelry makers, Avon began to stamp their jewelry. Most Avon pieces bear its name on the back of the item or on the clasp, or they carry a small hangtag for identification. This is not true for most Avon bead necklaces, pierced earrings, most of the bangle bracelets, and several of the rings, which bear no mark whatsoever, making these pieces difficult for collectors to locate. In fact, about the only way to know that these pieces are from Avon is through this book.

Avon of Belleville, Canada

It has been postulated --- inaccurately --- that Avon jewelry sprang into existence by purchasing the Avon of Belleville, Canada, company in 1971. This is not true. I took this directly to Avon Products in New York, and they assured me that they did NOT force Avon of Belleville out of business nor did they purchase the Canadian company. Avon of Belleville was the brainchild of Abe Mazer in 1945. His company made hundreds of pieces that were beautifully designed using goldtone, silvertone, and sterling silver, with brilliantly faceted clear and colored

rhinestones, crystals, and pearls. It is simply coincidental that it went out of business in 1971. What is confusing is the trademark 'AVON' stamped on the Avon of Belleville jewelry. Avon of Belleville used AVON in capital block upper case letters, or *Avon* in script, followed with a four-digit code number. Some items may contain CANADA in block letters or BELLEVILLE in block letters or a combination of all. They did not cease in 1971 because of a trademark infringement on the use of the hallmark, and Avon Products did not take offense at the use of the name. Avon of Belleville simply decided to go out of business.

Avon Products marks

Unfortunately, it is possible to find Avon Products jewelry stamped AVON in capital block upper case letters, which causes some people to confuse the two jewelry lines. The Brick Chain necklace of 1996 is a case in point. I once saw it sold as Avon of Belleville because of the mark, but it is an Avon Products piece.

All Avon jewelry is versatile. The pieces are as adaptable as possible to lifestyles and wearers with creations ranging from casual to formal wear. There are pieces utilizing sterling silver and karat gold with real diamonds, pearls, and precious gemstones, but the vast majority of pieces are composed of non-tarnishing goldtone or silvertone metals with simulated gemstones, including faux pearls, coral, ivory, and turquoise.

Designer Series

In 1976, Vice President of Package Design, Seymour Murray Kent, began what is termed by collectors as the "Designer Series." He was one of the foremost names in the world of design, but his interest and experience took him into all areas of fashion. In November of 1976, he introduced The Collection, creating a series of 25 unique pieces spanning the next four years. Avon described it as the most exquisite jewelry in the world. It was Kent's belief that "jewelry is as important to a woman's wardrobe as her clothes. Each and every piece must work for the wearer. It must be her statement, reflect her personality." The pieces were not cheap and not every woman could afford them, which gave the lucky wearer the feeling of owning pieces designed exclusively for her. These pieces had the added distinction of allowing her the ability to create a new fashion statement while still enhancing her own personal style.

By 1983, the company was using world-famous designer Louis Feraud of Paris, France, who brought jewelry, perfume, and clothing to Avon. Kenneth Jay Lane soon followed, when Gloria Fiori, a jewelry buyer for Bonwit Teller in New York City, joined Avon and brought Lane with her. Lane's trademark as "Jeweler to the World's Most Admired Women" does not disappoint. His jewelry incorporates shiny goldtone and silvertone studded with sparkling rhinestones and crystals in a rainbow of glorious colors. Other designers soon followed: Celia Sebiri, Coreen Simpson, Jose Maria Barrera, Shaill Jhaveri, Akoya Culture Pearls, and Technibond, to name a few. Avon also began to replicate pieces found in the collections of Elizabeth Taylor and the Smithsonian Instiution museums. None of the designer pieces were for the faint of heart. They were all expensive and rare, making them among the most highly sought pieces in the collecting world today. An example is Elizabeth Taylor's Shah Jehan necklace of 1993, which was then and continues to remain the most expensive piece of jewelry in the Avon line.

Gift Sets

As early as 1987, Avon started making Gift Sets. These were usually a choker necklace and matching pair of earrings, but there are some sets with other combinations. The gift sets enabled customers to acquire a full collection without having to purchase the pieces individually. They had the added advantage of holding costs down, since gift set items could be packaged together. The Gift Sets were all inspired and unique, most using shiny metals with quality gemstones and pearl accents. By 2000, they had evolved to using burnished brass for the antique or vintage look. Most gift sets today come in a variety of metals for individual tastes

The Three Truths About Avon Jewelry

In conducting the research for this book, three "truths" were discovered that the collector should keep in mind when searching for Avon jewelry:

1) In the early years, Avon seldom used the same name twice, which makes it easy for collectors to locate a specific piece from that time period, providing it is still in its original packaging. Around 1986, Avon began to repeat names fairly frequently. It is now possible to find Windchimes earrings dated 1972, 1987, and 1992. All three are distinctly different. Beware when doing your shopping.

2) Avon released several of their pieces under two separate names several years apart. An example of this is the Creation-in-Blue ring from 1972, which was released again in 1987 as the Regal Style ring. Another example is the Christmas Tree Pin, originally released in 1992 and re-released in 2004. Some later items had only a simple clasp change, with everything else being identical to a predecessor. It is not possible to know how often this happened, but the trend continues today, making it difficult for collectors to know the exact vintage of an item not in its original packaging.

3) Many Avon boxes bear one date on the box, yet have a different release date in the brochures. This practice started around 1976 and continues today. This book uses only the release dates found in the brochures, since all items have been verified against the brochures for exact spelling and their original release date. If you have a box with a date that disagrees with this book, it means that Avon did not officially release the item until the date indicated in this book.

Quality Above All

Today, Avon has closed most of its jewelry plants in Western countries to concentrate manufacturing in Asia. Thereby, Avon can offer more complex designs at competitive prices. Avon continues to offer top-of-the-line, affordable, high-quality jewelry that reflects modern trends with quality metals and gemstones. It is not sold in stores, but has entered the age of technology by being available from many sales personnel who maintain Internet web sites. If David Hall McConnell were to see his company today, he would not recognize it. It has evolved from a perfume company into an International mega-conglomerate with more than 5 million people in the sales force in more than 100 countries!

Chapter One
Designers

Today, much of Avon's revenue is in jewelry, and of the jewelry line, many of the exquisitely beautiful early pieces came from the imaginations of a small handful of creators known as The Designers. These artisans had vastly different styles, which made their pieces attractive to Avon's customer base. Most of Avon's jewelry bears a hallmark, which is a technical way for gold- and silver-smiths to annotate the quality and purity of the metals used, but today the term is used interchangeably with stamping to mean the design manufacturer or craftsman of the piece. It is normally incised, stamped, or punched on the piece, but it may come in the form of a metal or paper hangtag attached to the item, or a designer stamp on the back of the piece, or even initials carved into the item. Nearly all of Avon's jewelry, including those of The Designers, bears the name Avon or AVON.

S. M. Kent, "The Collection"

In 1976, Avon's Vice President of Package Design, Seymour Murray Kent, began what is termed by collectors as the "Designer Series." He was one of the foremost names in the world of design, but his interest and experience took him into all areas of fashion. In Campaign 24, he introduced The Collection, creating a series of unique pieces spanning the next four years. Avon described it as the most exquisite jewelry in the world. It was Kent's belief that "jewelry is as important to a woman's wardrobe as her clothes. Each and every piece must work for the wearer. It must be her statement, reflect her personality." The pieces were not cheap and not every woman could afford them, which gave the lucky wearer the feeling of owning pieces designed exclusively for her.

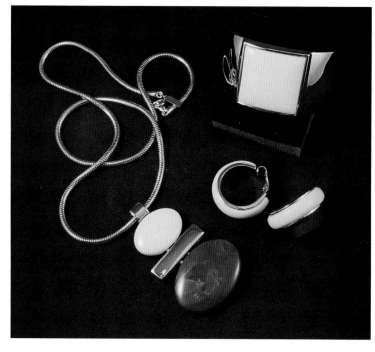

Polished Ovals Necklace, 1976, $35 – ivory and tortoise ovals joined with polished gold center bar; **Hoop Earrings**, 1977, $25 – ivory hoop clips with polished gold setting to match necklace; **Cuff Bracelet**, 1977, $35 – ivory insert with polished gold sides to match necklace

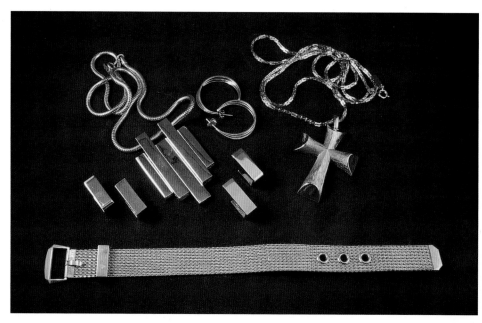

Geometric Collection, 1976, pendant necklace, $40, c/p earrings $30 – gold and silver design inspired by the New York City skyline with finely polished outer surfaces and Florentine-styled sides. The earrings came in gold or silver. **Sterling Silver Triple Hoop Pierced Earrings**, 1978, $25 – came in either 14k gold-filled or sterling silver; **Goldtone Mesh Bracelet**, 1976, $30 – flexible mesh with highly polished tongue and buckle; **Florentine-Finish Cross Pendant Necklace**, 1976, $50

14k Gold-Filled Rose Collection, 1980, pendant necklace $40, pierced earrings $45 – rare rose blossom design; **Cultured Pearl Collection**, 1978, pendant $45, pierced earrings $45 – rare 14k gold-filled pendant and earrings with genuine pearl and diamond accent; **14k Gold-Filled Box Chain** with **14k Gold-Filled Ball Earrings**, 1977, necklace $50, pierced earrings $45 – extremely rare designed to compliment the other pieces in this series

Sterling Silver Heart Pendant Necklace, 1980, $40 – sterling silver heart on sterling silver chain; **14k Gold-Filled and Sterling Silver Kiss Necklace**, 1980, $50, gold-filled chain and sterling silver kiss motif

Square Cut Lead Crystal Collection, 1977, pendant necklace $35, c/p earrings $30 – real lead crystal in gold-washed setting; **Tiger Eye Collection**, 1978, pendant necklace $45, pierced earrings $30 – 14k gold-filled pendant and earrings with real tiger eye stone

Diamond Loop Necklace, 14k Gold-Filled with Genuine Diamond, 1978, $50, 14K gold chain and loop with genuine .01 carat diamond; **Precious Ruby Pendant Necklace**, 1978; $65 – extremely rare real rubies in 14k gold; **Precious Sapphire Pendant Necklace**, 1978, $65 – extremely rare real sapphires in white gold

Louis Feraud

The House of Feraud is one of the twenty-one remaining true Haute Couture houses in existence today. Dressing the French Elite, Louis Feraud established himself as one of the great designers whose faithful clientele included Brigitte Bardot, Kim Novak, Ingrid Bergman, and Danielle Mitterrand, wife of the late French president Francois Mitterrand. He specialized in black and white fashion, making it a basic staple in the fashion world. In 1983, he created several perfumes for Avon, as well as a line of jewelry that was as brilliant and beautiful as the fashions that made Paris famous. He died at his Paris home in 1999, at the age of seventy-eight, after a four-year battle against Alzheimer's disease.

Caviar Bead Necklace, 1983, $100 – rich color of hematite caviar beads of glass with gold links; **Couture Collection**, 1983, necklace $100, c/p earrings $45 – rich faceted black beads enhanced with faceted gold accents

Blossoms of Spring Collection, 1984, necklace $65, c/p earrings $30 – French inspred white flowers with gold leaves. **Classic Collection**, 1983, choker necklace $45, pierced earrings $35 – large hematite bead set in gold

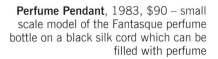

Perfume Pendant, 1983, $90 – small scale model of the Fantasque perfume bottle on a black silk cord which can be filled with perfume

Celia Sebiri

At the time Celia Sebiri made her creations for Avon, she had already been a prominent jewelry designer for three decades, selling in high-end department stores and boutiques. In 1973, she won the prestigious Coty Award for her designs. She died in April 2006 at the age of 93.

Rose Quartz Collection, 1987, pin/pendant $45, c/p earrings $45 – rare rose quartz surrounded by enamel accents and set in rich silver plate, shown with **Genuine Rose Quartz Necklace** from 1987, which Avon suggested to accessorize it

Jose Maria Barrera

Jose Maria Barrera designs couture jewelry for sophisticated women all over the world. In 1989, he began contributing upscale jewelry designs with a Spanish influence for Avon. Each piece is innovative and imaginative, and they prove that costume jewelry can be as beautiful as the 'real thing.'

Spanish Style Collection, 1989, necklace $65, clip earrings $50 – elaborate metal art with a pierced leaf design in gold or silver.

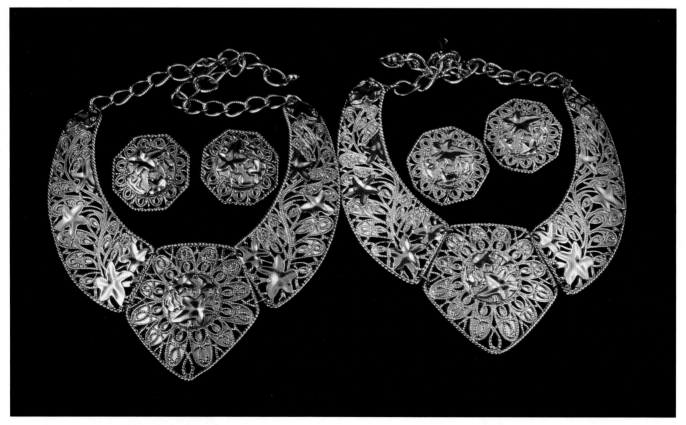

Granada Collection, 1990, necklace $50, earrings $35 – gold swirl choker studded with crystals and black cabochon inserts and has the unusual distinction of being able to hook in the front or in the back.

Venetian Mist Collection, 1990, necklace $70, clip earrings $35 – the necklace is composed of two 40-inch-long strands of light gray chips resembling quartz which can be worn in a variety of ways as well as twisted into a torsade. The vine motif pendant drop can be removed and worn separately as a pin. The earrings are clips only

Marbella Collection, 1992, necklace $75, earrings $50 – very ornate gold filigree studded with lavender, pink, and purple moonstone accents

Below, left:
Florentine Style Collection, 1994, pin $65, clip earrings $50 – large gold scrollwork pin studded with jewels and 3 large blue marble cabochons. The earrings have blue marble drops; **Roman Holiday Collection**, 1993, pin/pendant $55, clip earrings, $40 – large starburst pin in blue enamel with center pearl and studded with turquoise beads and crystal accents can be worn as a pin or a pendant. The earrings have a fantastic blue drop.

Below, right:
These earrings came in clip style only. **American Style Earrings**, 1991, $30 – elegant long dangle earrings came in either turquoise with silver filigree or coral with gold filigree; **Versatile Elegance Earrings**, 1993, $45 – elegant earrings came in both gold and silver and the dangle can be removed; **Holiday Splendor Earrings**, 1993, $40 – dramatic crystal drop in elaborate gold setting; **Imperial Elegance Earrings**, 1991, $45 – crystal-studded long dangles came in antiqued gold or antiqued silver

Fashion Flower Collection, 1994, pin $45, clip earrings $70 – the pin is a large metal flower covered in pink and green enamel and studded with rhinestone accents. The earrings can be worn without the oval drop; **Corinthian Collection**, 1989, cuff bracelet, $80, c/p earrings $40 – Greek inspired hammered gold swirls set.

Antoinette Collection, 1992, necklace $45, clip earrings $40 – ornate gold filigree with crystal accents

Adriatic Collection, 1991, necklace $100, earrings $40 – elaborate antique gold medallions. The necklace included large circular moonstones in pink, blue, and green on a light pink bead chain

Mayan Style Collection, 1994, necklace $80, clip earrings $50, ring $50 – The necklace can be worn with or without the center motif, and all pieces are done in antiqued gold

Coreen Simpson

While best known as the creator of The Black Cameo jewelry line in 1990, Coreen Simpson is a multi-media artist acclaimed in numerous fields of expertise, especially that of photography, where she has been represented throughout the world. In 1994, she signed her first licensing agreement with Avon to create exclusive designs for their African American market. Today, she is recognized as one of the most successful jewelry designers in the fashion world.

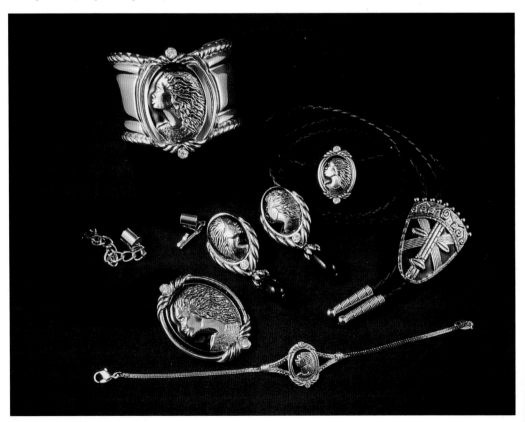

Regal Beauty Collection, 1994, cameo pin/pendant, $45, chain bracelet $25, cuff bracelet $45, c/p earrings $40, ring $50 – magnificent black Americana cameo design on all pieces. The necklace can be a pin or pendant and comes on a black velvet cord, and the earrings have a removable black teardrop bead; **Shield of Honor Bolo/Pin**, 1997, $35 – convertible gold African mask bolo/pin with black enamel accents

Kenneth Jay Lane

Winner of the prestigious Coty Award, Kenneth J. Lane's trademark is "Jeweler to the World's Most Admired Women," and he does not disappoint. His exquisite haute couture creations are displayed in the finest stores of Paris, London, Tokyo, and New York. He incorporates shiny goldtone and silvertone, studded with sparkling rhinestones and crystals in a rainbow of glorious colors.

He began his career in the Art Department of New York Vogue in 1954, but he decided to head out on his own in 1963 after designing for Hattie Carnegie. He came to Avon with the Society Collection in 1986 and continues to produce for Avon today. Most of his jewelry is big, bold, and dramatic with the use of fine stones that he personally developed with his sources in Germany.

Society Collection, 1986, necklace $45, earrings $35 – double strand of pearls with lion head clasp having matching gold lion's head doorknocker earrings

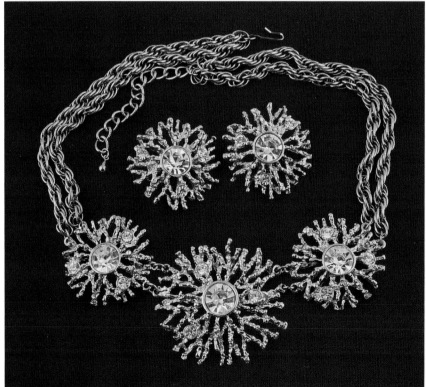

Regal Riches Collection, 1992, necklace $55, clip earrings $40 – golden starbursts with sparkling crystals

Lustrous Bow Collection, 1993, pin $55, clip earrings $45 – elaborate gold bow studded with crystals. **Camelot Collection**, 1987, necklace enhancer $35, c/p earrings $35 – elegant black bow on gold. **Lustrous Bow Collection**, 2001, pin $55, clip earrings $45 – elaborate silver bow studded with crystals. This set is identical to the gold, only it is in shiny silver

Caprianti Collection, 1993, necklace $85, clip earrings $40 – this set is undeniably one of the most brilliantly-colored, dramatically-shaped, jeweled-cabochon creations in existence. The earrings are blue cabochons.

Midnight Rose Collection, 1989, necklace $55, c/p earrings $30 – This collection came in a double strand of black pearls with white blooming rose clasp and white rosebud earrings or white pearls with black rose accents, both in shiny gold trim.

Undersea Collection, 1989, necklace $100, c/p earrings $35 – double strand of shell beads in oranges or whites with crystal accents. Both colors were sold separately, and no two necklaces were alike in color. According to the instruction sheet that came with the necklace, it can be worn six different ways. Both colors use the same clasp and earrings.

Papillon Collection, 1988, necklace $75, c/p earrings $35 – double strand of pearls with a translucent butterfly medallion having matching earrings of translucent butterfly wings with crystal accents; **Perfect Pansy Collection**, 1995, necklace $45, c/p earrings $40 – carved pink flower with crystal accents on a double strand of lustrous pearls

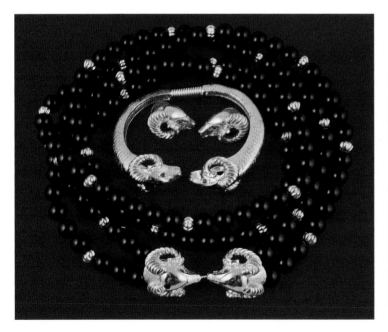

Sophisticated Lady Collection, 1986, necklace $60, bracelet $45, earrings $40 – a gold ram's head with rhinestones and emerald green eyes is the central theme of all three pieces. The necklace is 32-inches of black beads with shiny gold spacers and ram's head closure. The bracelet is a gold cuff with ram's head knobs at each end. The earrings are the same ram's head design as the necklace.

Clockwise from top left: **Royal Elephant Pin/Pendant**, 1995, $45 – golden elephant with ivory inserts and crystal accents; **Serpent Pin**, 1995, $50 – magnificent golden serpent studded with rhinestones and lapis and ruby cabochons; **Glittering Crown Pin**, 1988, $40 – golden crown studded with crystals; **Earring Wardrobe**, 1986, clip only $35 – rhinestone centers with red, green, and black jackets; **Bee Pin**, 2004, $50 – exquisitely detailed gold bee pin with crystal accents; **Nature's Treasures Dragonfly Pin**, 1990, $45 – beautiful dragonfly with enamel wings in pink and white and having rhinestones body; **Color Attraction Convertible Earrings**, 1987, c/p, $40 – tiny magnets back rich stones of lapis, pearl, and onyx in gold rope frame; **Antique Impressions Pin**, 1990, $45 – heirloom look of marcasite and pearls; **Feather Pin**, 2003, $50 – giant silver feather encrusted with crystals

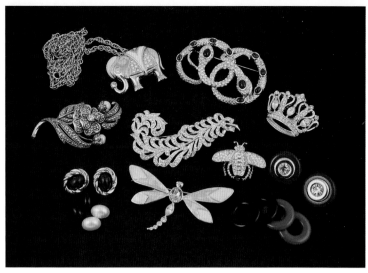

Renaissance Collection, 1989, pin/pendant $40, necklace $45, c/p earrings $35 – large gold diamond-shaped pendant studded with pearls and rhinestones. It can be worn by itself as a pin or attached to the baroque pearls with accent beads for a stunning look

New York Collection, 1991, necklace $50, clip earrings $30 – single strand of pearls with onyx and gold accents

Pearlesque Choker Necklace, 2003, $55 – luscious pearl necklace with crystal-studded center medallion; **Dome Hoop Pierced Earrings**, 2003, $40 – silver hoops with crystal accents to match the medallion of the necklace; **Chandelier Pierced Earrings**, 2003, $40 – delicate silver filigree chandelier earrings studded with crystals to match the necklace

Poetic Romance Collection, 1994, necklace $75, clip earrings, $40 – beautiful cameo on pink background in gold leaf frame with pearl accents. The chain is 24-inches and also has pearl accents; **Modern Silhouette Collection**, 1986, necklace $50, c/p earrings $35 – this set came in gold with silver accents or silver with gold accents

25

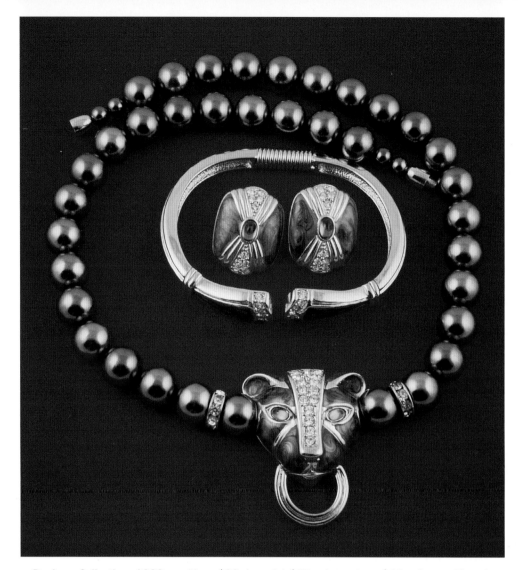

Duchess Collection, 1988, necklace $80, bracelet $55, c/p earrings $40 – the necklace is hematite black beads with a magnificent panther head enhancer. The panther is studded in crystals and has emerald green eyes. The bracelet is a gold bangle with black tips and crystal accents. The earrings are black cabochons with emerald green centers and crystal accents.

Medallion Collection, 1994, pin/pendant, $100, clip earrings $46 – the medallion of the necklace is surrounded with pearl accents and has a unique clasp so it can be removed and worn as a pin. **Royal Sea Collection**, 1992, necklace $80, earrings $40 – magnificent gold sea life charms with the starfish of the necklace having a center pearl accent. The earrings have a center pearl accent on the sand dollar and have oyster shell dangles.

Panther Collection, 2002, torsade necklace, $75, clip earrings $40, pin $50 – the necklace is 8 strands of jet black glass beads with a crystal accented silver panther clasp having emerald green eyes. The pin is a crouching panther studded in crystals with emerald eyes, and earrings are doorknocker style.

26

Shaill Jhaveri

Shaill Jhaveri was born in India and came to America to study art. He got into jewelry art while attending the Parsons School of Design in New York City because it was something he had never tried before, and the school offered a class in it. When he was 22-years-old, he began collaborating with Elizabeth Taylor, creating her versions of the Shah Jehan Pendant, the Sea Shimmer, the Elephant Walk, and the Egyptian Collections for Avon. That same year, he designed a jewelry set for Avon under his own name. It was based on the crown jewels of India, and if created today, using real gems and gold, the estimated cost would be about $5,000. In 2000, he formed his own company, Shaill New York, using primarily 18k gold and precious stones. His creations are not for the faint of heart. A stunning 3-strand bracelet of sapphires, diamonds, and rubies set in white gold was offered at Neiman-Marcus for $21,670. He calls New York City home and continues to collaborate with other designers and jewelry corporations, including a line of jewelry for Barbie dolls. His jewelry can be found in exclusive markets around the world.

Imperial Elegance Collection, 1993, necklace $85, clip earrings $60 – elegant design in amethyst, pearls, rubies, and clear crystals

Elizabeth Taylor

Academy Award-winning actress Elizabeth Taylor is world famous for owning some of the world's most magnificent jewelry, included the 33-carat Krupp Diamond, the Duchess of Windsor diamond brooch, the Grand Duchess of Russia emeralds, the LaPeregina Pearl, and the fabulous pear-shaped 69-carat Burton-Cartier Diamond that husband Richard Burton gave her in 1969, which she auctioned in 1979 to fund a hospital in Botswana. She began her association with Avon in 1993 with the introduction of the Shah Jehan pendant, the most expensive piece of jewelry Avon has ever offered. Over the next several years, she offered an astonishing selection of pieces based on originals in her own collection. Every piece is dramatic, down to the smallest detail.

Shah Jehan Pendant, 1993, $350 – one of the most magnificent pieces in Elizabeth's private collection is the Shah Jehan diamond, a 40th birthday present from husband Richard Burton. In 1628, this priceless heart-shaped diamond was inscribed with the name of the Maharani Noor Jehan and the date of Emperor Shah Jehan's accession to the throne. Shah Jehan built the magnificent Taj Mahal for his beloved bride. The Avon recreation is a brilliantly faceted crystal heart and bears the same inscriptions as the Shah Jehan diamond. The intricate setting is embellished with faux rubies, a jade-green inlay, and is set off with crystal accents. The back is a checkerboard of jade and gold. On the adjustable ornate gold cord are ruby glass bead tassels. It continues to be the most expensive piece of jewelry in the Avon line. Front and back are shown.

Love Blooms Collection, 1995, bangle bracelet $75, clip earrings, $50, ring $70 – sculpted roses and crystal hearts in gold circlets of extraordinary beauty; **Sparkle Kiss Collection**, 1995, pierced earrings, $55, ring $80 – earrings came in both large or small hoops of gold X's kissed with crystals. Ring is a large sapphire stone set in X-shaped 22k gold overlay band with pave crystal accents.

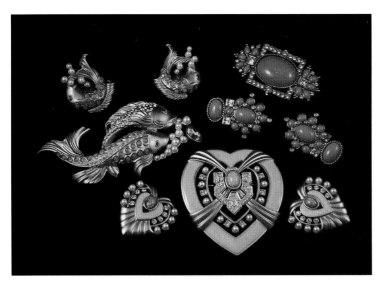

Sea Shimmer Collection, 1994, pin $150, clip earrings $80 – with gracefully flowing fins, opalescent and rhinestone scales, these fish breathe out bubbles of pearls and pursue a sapphire water drop; **Coral Sea Collection**, 1995, pin $100, clip earrings $100 – coral-hued cabochons set in gold with sparkling rhinestone accents; **Heart of Hollywood Collection**, 1994, pin $120, clip earrings $80 – draped in swirls of matte gold, these openwork hearts with pearly inlays, pearls and crystals embrace fiery opals

Katharina Cross Collection, 1994, pin/pendant $180, pierced earrings, $80 – the lavish jewelry Elizabeth wore in The Taming of the Shrew was the inspiration for this splendid collection of Renaissance style crosses of gold with pearls and artfully flawed rubies and emeralds. The necklace came in two sizes, a 4-inch large cross and a 2-inch small cross, on adjustable black cords. The earrings are pierced gold hoops with removable cross charms.

Evening Star Collection, 1995, necklace $225, bracelet $150, clip earrings, $120, ring $150 – necklace is a fantastic pearl choker with crystal slide. The bracelet is a tennis bracelet design with clear crystals. The earrings are half hoops. The large cubic zirconia ring is designed to look like real diamonds.

Radience Collection, 1996, CZ necklace $130, pierced earrings $85, ring, $130 – the necklace is a fantastic 6-carat total weight cubic zirconia on a 19-inch 22k gold chain. The earrings are 6-carats of sparkling cubic zirconia, which are also set in 22k gold. The ring is 3.5 carat weight in 22k gold

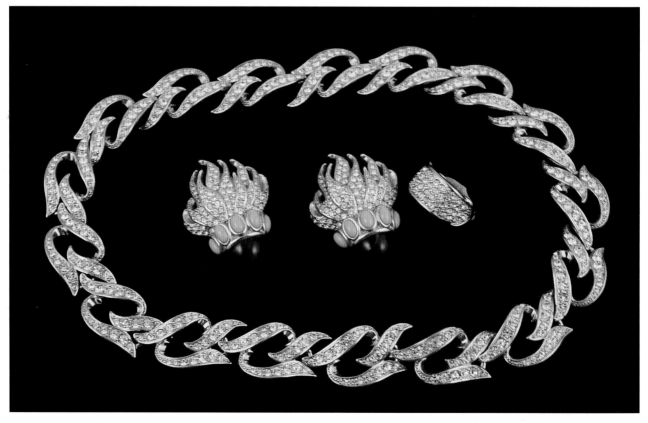

Eternal Flame Collection, 1994, necklace $275, clip earrings $200 – breathtakingly beautiful necklace of openwork gold flames studded with crystals. The earrings have ruby cabochons and turquoise accents to enhance the crystal-studded flames; **Brilliance Ring**, 1995, $120 – pave crystals surrounded by a gleaming band of 22 k gold overlay

Forever Violet Collection, 1994, necklace $200, clip earrings $120 – 8 strands of amethyst glass beads are held by a clasp that combines crystal violets, tourmaline green leaves and pearl cabochons set in latticed gold. The earrings match the clasp.

Signature Gold Coast Collection, 1994, necklace $150, bracelet $80, earrings $60 – inspired by the antique coins Elizabeth collects, these artfully linked hammered medallions are plated with 22 k gold and inscribed with an "E" in a lovely script selected by Elizabeth herself; **Taylored Style Collection**, 1995, necklace $80, earrings $45 – large adventurine cabochon set in gold

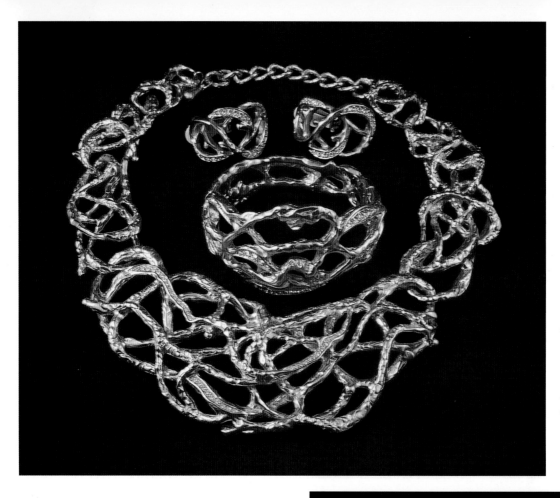

Treasured Vine Collection, 1994, necklace $225, bracelet $130, clip earrings $90 – crafted of openwork heavy gold, the intricately twined collection glitters with dustings of crystals

Pave Crystal Rose Collection, 1995, pin $100, clip earrings $80 – gold open-work rose studded with crystals; **Hearts in Tandem Pin**, 1994, $100 – the talent of Elizabeth's daughter, Liza Todd Tivey, was called upon to create this exquisite pin. Dramatically sculpted in gold with jet-black eyes and rhinestone collars, the piece bears three baroque pearl teardrops beneath a square-cut crystal; **Passion Flower Collection**, 1994, pin $100, clip earrings, $90 – softly glowing matte gold rose rests amidst textured leaves with sparkling crystal dew drops

Elephant Walk Collection, 1993, pin $225, earrings $200 – elaborately detailed gold elephant studded with crystals and sapphires and having purple bead dangles

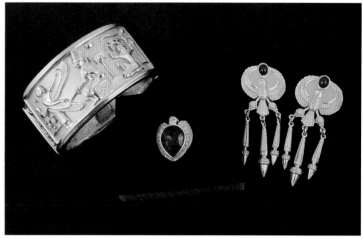

Gilded Age Collection, 1994, ring $100, clip earrings $90 – gold cherubs bear impressive cabochons simulating the look of artfully flawed rubies; **Zebra Stripe Collection**, 1994, bracelet $80, clip earrings $55 – boldly striped in gold and black, these circular hoops bear gold motifs embossed with zebra faces and rimmed with sparkling rhinestones

Egyptian Style Collection, 1993, bangle bracelet, $150, clip earrings $100, ring $120 – inspired by Elizabeth's most spectacular role…that of Cleopatra…the cuff bracelet is matte gold inscribed with hieroglyphic figures all around the bangle. The earrings represent an imperial plumed falcon with turquoise inlay and rich beads. The gold ring is the same plumed falcon with turquoise glass accents and amethyst.

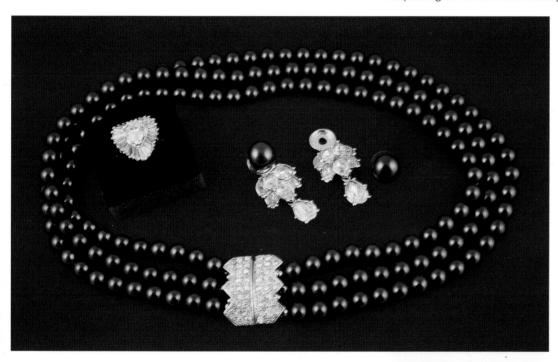

Midnight Romance Collection, 1996, necklace $130, pierced earrings $100, ring $125 – black glass pearls with ornate crystal accents. The earrings can be worn without the rhinestone burst dangles, and the center cubic zirconia of the ring is 6.6 carat diamond weight set in silver surrounded by a cluster of cubic zirconia.

The Smithsonian Institution

In 1996, Avon began a series of exclusive jewelry designs based on items found in the Smithsonian Institution museums in Washington, D.C. Each of these items is rare and highly collectible.

Key to the Castle Set, 1996, necklace $50, **Sunburst Earrings** $40, **Sunburst Stickpin** $35 – Often called the "Castle" on the Mall, the Smithsonian Institution's first building was constructed around 1850 in a medieval revival style. The original 1855 brass key to the Castle has been used for ceremonial purposed for over 40 years. Just as the Castle has come to be a symbol of the entire Smithsonian, the sun emblem was taken from the Smithson coat of arms. This has come to symbolize the Smithsonian's original charge of serving as a center "for the increase and diffusion of knowledge." Now you can share in the Smithsonian's mission with this shining work of gold and frosted cabochon jewelry.

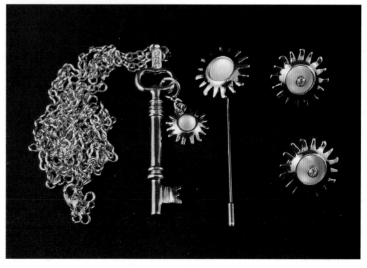

33

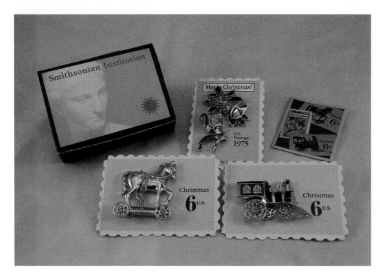

Angel Pin, 1996, $30; **Toy Horse Pin**, 1996, $30; **Toy Train Pin**, 1996, $30 – among the over 16 million U.S. and foreign stamps in the National Postal Museum are these festive Christmas stamps. The first US postage stamp designed for use on Christmas cards was issued on 1 November 1962. It was so popular that the Postal Service began the tradition of offering special holiday stamps every year. These pins are based on actual stamp designs in the Philatelic Collection of the Smithsonian

Cameo Medallion, 1997, $55, **Flower Earrings**, 1997, $45, **Jeweled Ring**, 1997, $50 – During his brief reign, Charles X of France acquired a splendid jewelry cabinet from the royal porcelain factory of Sevres. Guided by the prevailing taste for neoclassical ornamentation, the richly ornate 1826 Jewel Cabinet is covered with delicately painted and gilded porcelain plaques depicting gods, goddesses, flowers, and jewelry popular in the period. The abundant detailing on this magnificent piece inspired our opulent jewelry collection. From the porcelain cameo on one door depicting Psyche, beloved of Cupid, comes the gilt-framed pin with faux pearls. The painted florets that border each panel are echoed in the pearl drop earrings set in matte gold with faux pearl and faux gem accents with lever-back ear wires. A ring depicted on the cabinet is recreated in matte gold with Austrian crystal center and beautifully simulated pearls and faux gems.

Queen Elizabeth I Pierced Earrings, 1996, $40 – Among the rarely viewed antiquities in the Smithsonian's collection is an exquisite miniature of Queen Elizabeth I of England. It shows her dressed for court wearing a pair of ruby and pearl earrings in the Renaissance style. Our reproduction of these regal earrings features removable drops of crimson Austrian crystal and luminous pearl surrounded by floral gold. **Mary Todd Lincoln Bracelet**, 1996, $80 – Mary Todd Lincoln's lavish style of dress and entertaining was the talk of Washington. Although criticized for her extravagance during the Civil War, Mrs. Lincoln's fine taste is shown in an exquisite Swiss bracelet watch of gold, blue enamel and diamonds, which according to family lore, she wore during her years in the White House. It is today a permanent part of the First Ladies Collection. Our reproduction is beautifully crafted in gold with glossy blue inlay and sparkling Austrian crystals. **Akua'ba Fertility Goddess Set**, 1997, pin $50, pierced earrings $40 – As legend has it, a woman named Akua from the Ashante culture of Ghana was barren, until a healer instructed her to carry and care for a doll as if it were a child. Villagers jeered, but her faith was rewarded with the birth of a daughter, the "ba" or child in the name. With a large moon-shaped head and skinny stick figure, she represents a life form yet to have arrived. Now recognized all over Africa as a symbol of fertility, the Akua'ba versions of a Madonna and child are displayed in the Smithsonian.

Gellatly Cross Collection, 1997, necklace $90, earrings $45 – most wealthy American collectors of European art purchased foreign treasures simply for their own personal joy of possession. John Gellatly was different. In 1929, he generously donated his extensive collection to the Smithsonian. Among the objets d'art is an Italian-painted and champleve-enamel gold cross pendant of the 17th century. This pendant is recreated in gold with blue and white glaze on one side reversing to an ornately engraved golden design on the other. Our earrings replicate the floret in the center of the cross.

Marie Antoinette Collection, 1996, necklace $120, earrings $80 – one of the most remarkable objects in the Smithsonian is a pair of diamond earrings said to have been taken from Louis XVI's imperious queen, Marie Antoinette, upon her arrest during the French Revolution. The earrings, with the pear-shaped stones, became the possession of Russia's Grand Duchess Tatiana Yousupoff sometime in the early 1800's and remained in her family for over a century. In 1928, they were purchased from a London jeweler by an American heiress, and in 1964, her daughter presented them to the Smithsonian. Our recreation of these fabulous earrings is an ensemble of exquisitely faceted Austrian crystal with matching necklace.

Below:
Juliette Gordon Low Swallow Pin, 1996, large $55, small $45 – In the Smithsonian's distinguished National Portrait Gallery hangs Edward Hughes's masterful portrait of a remarkable woman. Born to a prosperous southern family and married to the wealthy William Mackay Low, Juliette Gordon Low is best known for founding the Girl Scouts of America. In Hughes's elegant 1887 likeness, Mrs. Low wears three diamond-studded swallows, part of a set of five brooches, which could be worn in a variety of ways in glorious flight. Our magnificently sculpted adaptation of the swallow brooch is pave with genuine Austrian crystals and embellished with a sapphire eye; **Openwork Bow Pin**, 1997, $45 – Best known as the inventor of the telegraph, Samuel F.B. Morse was also a noted portrait painter and founder of the National Academy of Design. In his charming oil-on-wood painting The Goldfish Bowl, Morse's sister-in-law and her children are depicted in the comfort of their parlor. Among the details of the early 19th century dress chronicled in the scene is the large bow-shaped brooch, which secures the mother's shawl. The distinctive design of Mrs. Richard Cary Morse's pin has been recreated by Avon in intricate gold filigreew with crystal accents; **Hummingbird Birthstone Pin**, 1997, $40 – The son of head gardener at Windsor Castle, John Gould became a curator at the Zoological Society of London in 1827. With the assistance of accomplished artists, Gould produced 15 folio works on birds and mammals with a total of more than 3200 plates. A complete set of Gould's masterpiece, *A mongraph of the Trochilidae, or family of humming-birds* (five volumes, 1849 -1887), which provided the inspiration for these dainty pins, is in the Special Collections Department of the Smithsonian. See how the hummingbird's iridescent beauty is captured in this golden pin set – the larger pin is pave with Austrian crystals in a choice of twelve birthstone colors, the smaller has a clear crystal eye. The one shown is the September sapphire; **Pave Pansy Set,** 1997, pin $50, earrings $40 – Victorian women delighted in their flower gardens and on bleak winter days, eagerly awaited the arrival of the latest seed catalogs. In the late 1800's, seed companies spared no expense in preparing catalogs filled with colorful lithographs of flowers and vegetables illustrated by master artisans. Today, these 'paper gardens' are valuable collectors' items. The cover of the 1895 Alneer Bros' Catalogue of Everything for the Flower and Vegetable Garden from the Archives Center in the Smithsonian depicts one of the period's most popular flowers – the pansy. The appealing form of this flower is captured in a pin and earring set of pave Austrian crystals.

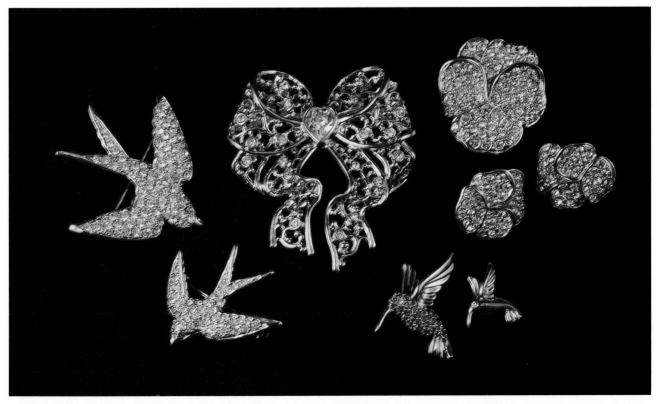

Chapter Two
Sets

In jewelry vernacular, a parure is three or more matching pieces to a set. A full parure is a necklace, bracelet, earrings, pin, and ring, and a demi-parure is a combination of any two of those items. Cameo and intalgio are two words meaning basically the same thing, but in reverse of each other. Cameos are molded or carved in shell, gems, coral and other materials and generally depict a scene or portrait. They sit on top the shelf of the piece, whereas the intalgio cameo is carved or molded into the shelf itself. Some intalgio cameos are carved into the shelf from the backside of the material, making it a reverse intalgio. Enameling is the firing of melted glass, which can be in any color, and cloisonné is a form of enameling. In cloisonné, the base metal forms cells (cloisons), which are then filled with enamel with each compartment being held separate from each other by the metal cloisons. The term faux literally means 'false light,' which is a way for gems and gemstones to reflect a false light where the brilliance is achieved by highly faceted glass and foil backing. It's possible to have faux turquoise, rubies, emeralds, and sapphires, as well as pearls, coral and other materials. Avon used all these methods in their jewelry

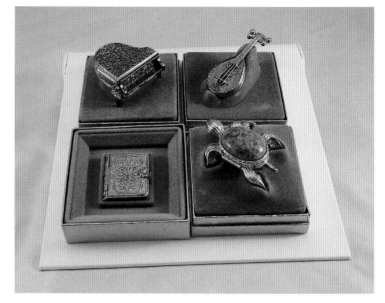

Table Top Jewelry Collection, 1971, valued at $50 each. They are all metal miniatures finished in antique gold and held a perfume compact. The Tortoise has a green stone cabochon shell. **Baby Grande Perfume Glace**; **Mandolin Perfume Glace**; **Memory Book Perfume Glace**; **Tortoise Perfume Glace**

Bird of Paradise, 1969, $55 – this is a complete set of pin, bracelet, and clip earrings in textured gold with turquoise accents used to promote Avon's top-selling Bird of Paradise perfume. It was never offered for sale to the public and is extremely rare.

Precious Pretenders, 1971, necklace $40, bracelet $20, clip earrings $20, pin $30 – Avon's second complete collection of designer jewelry was introduced four months after the Evening Creation Collection and is all gold washed

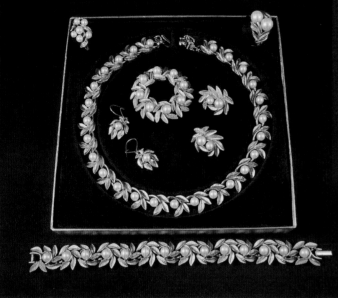

Evening Creation, 1971, necklace $55, bracelet $30, clip earrings $25, pierced earrings, $50, pin $40, Duet ring $50, Cluster ring $50 – Avon's first complete collection of designer jewelry came with two types of earrings and two styles of rings. All pieces are brushed golden leaves with luxuriant pearls. The pierced earrings use 14k gold wires and are extremely rare. Cluster ring is studded with rhinestone leaves

Starflower, 1972, pin $15, bracelet $20, clip earrings $15 – gold starburst design; **Azurene**, 1972, pin $25, clip earrings $20 – gold starburst design with turquoise accents

Mirabella, 1974, necklace $25, clip earrings $20, ring $25 – hematite and turquoise in antique silver; **Mayan Pendant** with **Swirlcraft Earrings**, 1974, necklace $25, clip earrings $30 – rich textured silver design. The earrings have a pearl accent and are extremely rare; **Sierra**, 1973, necklace $25, bracelet $25, ring $25 – antique silver with turquoise accents. There are no matching earrings

37

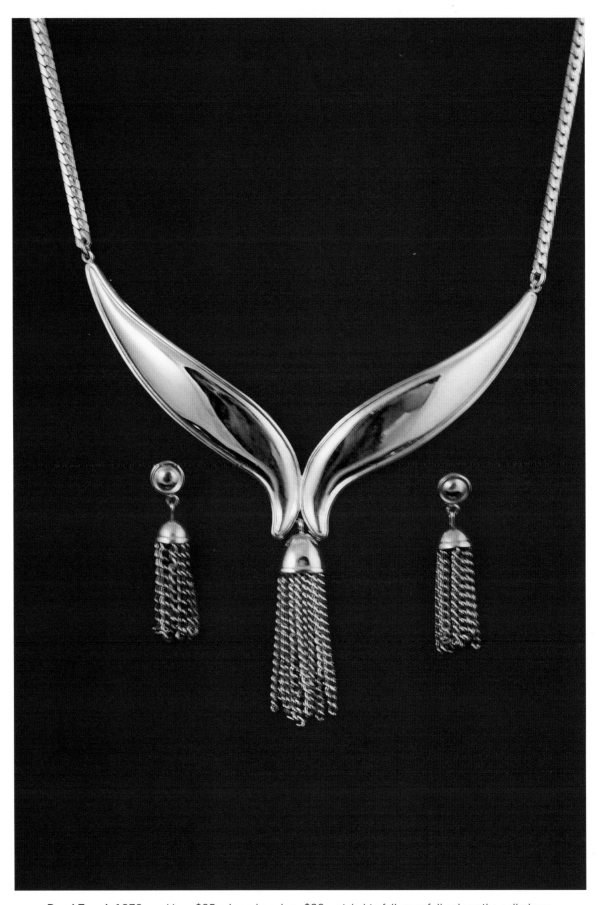

Royal Tassel, 1972, necklace $25, pierced earrings $20 – styled to fall gracefully along the collarbone

Private Collection, 1986, necklace $25, c/p earrings $20 – dramatic gold motif highlighted with sparkling rhinestones with Avon Centennial dates on the back; **Sculptured**, 1981, pendant $25, pierced earrings $15 – graceful dogwood blossom in gold and silver; **Love Blossoms**, 1972, convertible necklace/pin $25, c/p earrings $20 – plastic blue flowers with center rhinestones

Castillian, 1974, necklace $20, c/p earrings $15 – orange agate and coral in gold; **Florentine Flowers**, 1974, pendant $20, c/p earrings $20 – black oval disc with elegant mosaic flowers; **Feather Flurry**, 1980, lariat necklace $20, c/p earrings $15 – textured gold feathers

Creation-In-Blue, 1972, necklace/pin $60, pierced earrings $45, ring $45 – large faceted sapphire surrounded by crystals which simulated diamonds. The necklace can be worn as a pin, and the extremely rare earrings can be worn as a crystal stud without the sapphire drop. The ring was released again in 1987 as the Regal Style with a different style earring

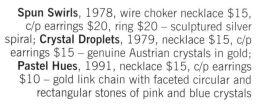

Spun Swirls, 1978, wire choker necklace $15, c/p earrings $20, ring $20 – sculptured silver spiral; **Crystal Droplets**, 1979, necklace $15, c/p earrings $15 – genuine Austrian crystals in gold; **Pastel Hues**, 1991, necklace $15, c/p earrings $10 – gold link chain with faceted circular and rectangular stones of pink and blue crystals

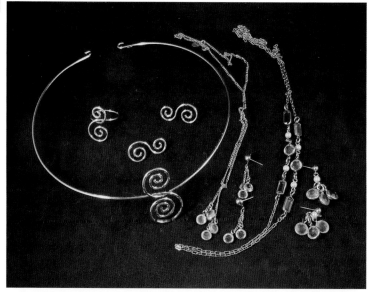

Viennese, 1976, pendant $15, c/p earrings $15, ring $25 – lapis and pearls in antique gold; **Baroness**, 1973, pendant necklace $15, bracelet $15, c/p earrings $15, ring $25 – magnificent simulated jade in gold flower design

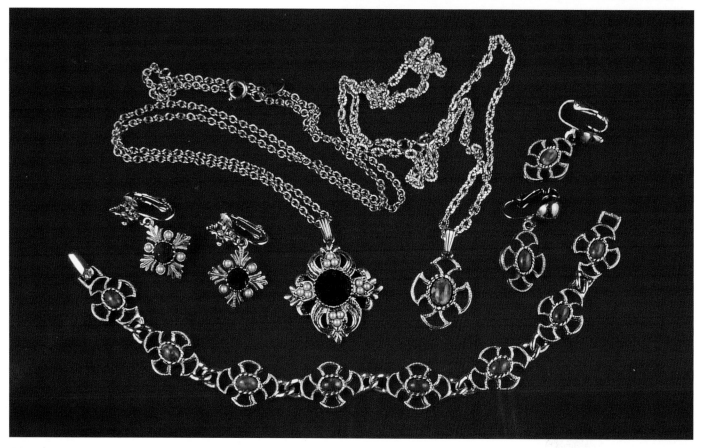

40

Porcelain Pastel, 1981, 30-inch rose necklace $30, 24-inch dusty blue necklace $25, 18-inch lavender necklace $20, ring $25 – quartz beads accented with gold fluted beads have no matching earrings. The ring only came in rose quartz; **Tri-Toned Bangle**, 1997, bracelet $20, doorknocker pierced earrings $20 – gold, rose gold, and silver. **Accent-in-White**, 1972, bracelet $20, pin $15 – magnificent white cabochon in shiny gold have no other matching pieces

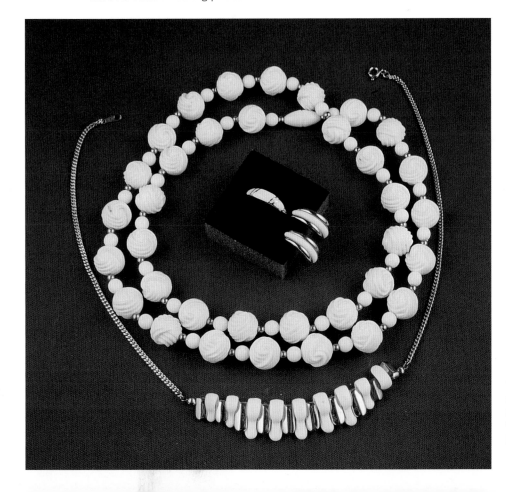

The Bermuda, 1983, beads $35, choker necklace $20, c/p hoop earrings $20, ring $25 – dainty white plastic petals with look of enamel and gold accents; beads and ring are extremely rare

The Single Cube, 1976, necklace $10, pierced earrings $15 –
versatile cube in gold or silver. **Sculptured Cube Pierced Earrings**,
1982, $15 – slightly smaller cube earrings in gold or silver;
Flowerlace, 1979, necklace $10, bracelet $10 – flowers and lace in
gold or silver with no other matching pieces

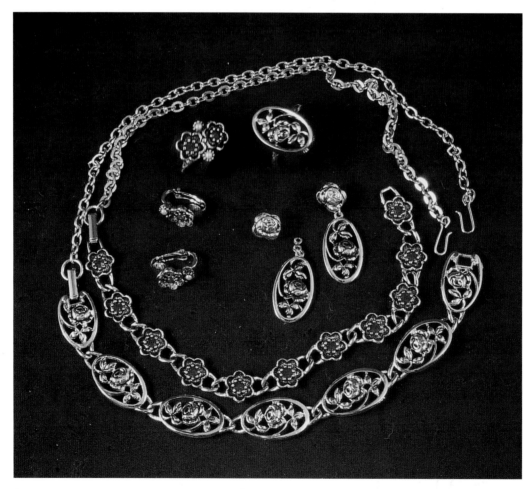

Rosegay, 1974, convertible necklace/bracelet $20, c/p earrings $15, ring $25 – rose stone centers in
antique silver – the necklace can be worn as an 8-inch bracelet by removing the 9-inch chain extender;
Rosamonde, 1975, convertible necklace/bracelet $20, c/p earrings $15, ring $20 – rose in silver
filigree. The necklace can be worn as an 8-inch bracelet by removing the 9-inch chain extender

Versailles, 1976, pendant $20, c/p convertible earrings $20, ring $25 – sparkling emerald stone surrounded by seed pearls in antiqued gold filigree frame with earrings that can be worn without the pendant drop; **Delmonico**, 1976, necklace $15, c/p earrings $15, ring $20 – simulated onyx with rhinestone accent in gold

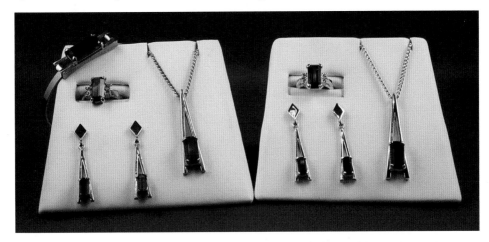

Plaza IV, 1975, necklace $15, bracelet $20, c/p earrings $15, ring $25 – simulated amethyst in gold A-frame setting. Ring has four rhinestone accents; **Park East**, 1976, necklace $15, c/p earrings $15, ring $25 – simulated emerald in silver A-frame setting. There is no matching bracelet

Catch A Star, 1978, bracelet $10, pierced earrings $10, ring $15 – brilliant clear crystal and delicate gold. The bracelet was released again in 1979 as Catch a Birthstone Star with Austrian crystal birthstones for each month; **French Flowers Locket**, 1975, bracelet $10, ring $20 – floral design on glass cabochon. Both pieces are a locket and open to hold your favorite photograph; **Sun Brilliants**, 1974, pendant/pin $20, clip earrings $20, ring $30 – stunning simulated olivine and yellow-green stones with gold leaves accents

Moonspun, 1975, necklace $25, c/p convertible earrings $15 – extremely rare set of luscious pearls and gold with earrings that can be worn without the pearl drops; **Burnished Roses**, 1975, pin/pendant $20, bracelet $20, pierced earrings $15, ring $25 – two gold finishes create a beautiful burnished effect; **Eclipse**, 1975, pin $10, clip earrings $15, ring $20 – dark and light pearls in silver; **Kensington**, 1979, stickpin $10, pierced earrings $10, ring $20 – antique gold design with rhinestone accent

Frostlights, 1977, pendant $15, ring $20 – frosted pink glass with delicate rhinestone. **Frosted Sparkle**, 1990, necklace $15, pierced earrings $10 – frosted pink glass with rhinestone accents; These two necklaces are often confused

Victorian, 1983, reversible pendant $25, c/p drop earrings $15, ring $25 – simulated onyx with rhinestone. The pendant reverses to gold; **Sculptured Heart**, 1975, necklace $15, c/p earrings $15 – highly polished dimensional silver heart. Matching **Heart-to-Heart Ring** is in the Ring chapter

Burgundy Wine, 1979, necklace $15, c/p earrings $10, ring $35 – circle of amethyst rimmed with gold. The ring is a very large faceted stone; **Royal Occasion**, 1973, pendant $15, pierced earrings $10, ring $25 – large faceted amber crystal in gold rope frame with rhinestone accents

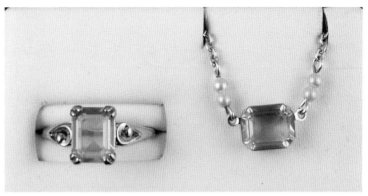

Blue Ice, 1983 pendant $20, 1981 ring $25 – silver with aquamarine stone

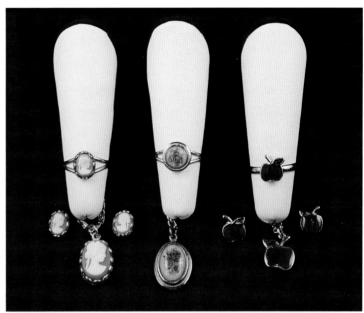

Cameo Princess, 1975, pendant $15, pierced earrings $15, ring $20 – traditional cameo on blue background in gold frame for children; **Secret Garden**, 1975, necklace $15, ring $20 – plastic cabochon flowers in gold setting for children, no matching earrings; **Candy Apple**, 1979, pendant $15, pierced earrings $15, ring $20 – enamel red apple with green leaf set in gold for children. All sets are extremely rare.

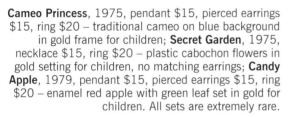

Bamboo Magic, 1972, pin $10, clip earrings $10, pierced earrings $30, ring $15 – shiny and textured gold bamboo set. The pierced earrings are extremely rare; **Porcelain Petals**, 1987, pin $20, c/p earrings $20 – genuine bisque porcelain roses and leaves in pink or white; **Sweet Violet**, 1983, pin $15, pierced earrings $15 – plastic frosted crystal set with simulated pearl centers; **Bold and Classic**, 1992, pin $15, c/p earrings $10 – bold amethyst cabochon in silver filigree or amber cabochon in gold filigree

Abalone, 1978, pendant $15, bracelet $15, c/p earrings $15, ring $25 – genuine abalone shell in silver and no two are alike; **Queensbury**, 1974, pendant $20, bracelet $30, convertible pierced earrings $20, ring $25 – magnificent amethyst and pearls in elaborate gold with earrings that can be worn without the drop. Bracelet and earrings are very rare

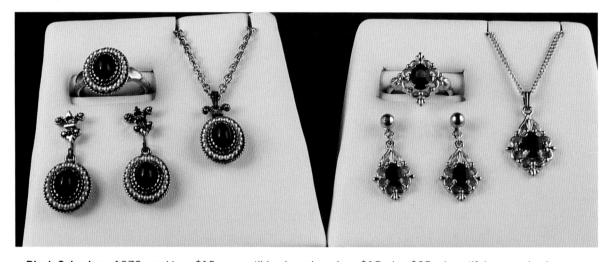

Black Cabochon, 1973, necklace $15, convertible pierced earrings $15, ring $25 – beautiful onyx cabochon in gold frame surrounded by seed pearls and earrings that can be worn without the dangle drop; **Venetian Lace**, 1977, pendant necklace $20, c/p earrings $20, ring $25 – simulated amethyst in gold lace frame

Perfect Pear Color CZ, 2004, necklace $20, pierced earrings $20 – this set came in pink, yellow, or clear stones; **Sunny Star**, 1975, choker necklace $10, bracelet $10, pierced earrings $15 – shiny gold or silver star; **Pink Ice**, 2003, necklace $20, pierced earrings $20 – faceted 4-carat pink ice crystal in sparkling silver

Dear Heart, 1974, pendant $20, pierced earrings $25 – pink sapphire heart stone with rhinestone accents surrounded by seed pearls. The earrings are extremely rare in pink sapphire hearts with pearl and rhinestone accents; **Radiant Leaf**, 1978, pendant necklace $15, c/p earrings $15 – gold leaf with rhinestone accent; **Blue Teardrop**, 1972, convertible pendant $20, clip earrings $15 – silver rope and leaf design with large turquoise cabochon can be worn four different ways

Color Go Round, 1977, bracelet $10, ring $15 – bracelet came in five colors: Vanilla White, Ice Blue, Ice Green, Cherry Red, and Mocha Creme. No two are alike, as shown by the two Mocha Creme bangles. The 1977 ring set was composed of marbleized plastic in white, green, cream, beige, and coral held in a shiny gold band. **Color Go Round**, 1979, bracelet $10, ring $15 – bracelet came in solid pastel colors of white, coral, green, blue, and yellow. The 1979 ring set has pastels in yellow, white, coral, and green held in a shiny gold band

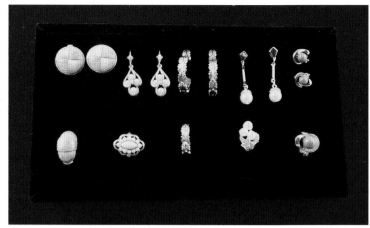

China Fantasy and **Longevity**, 1982, necklace $15, pierced earrings $15, bangle bracelet $10 each, rings $10 – this is one collection with two names. The necklace is a gold longevity knot with interchangeable motifs in ivory, jade, and cinnabar. The earrings match the longevity knot of the necklace and came in gold or silver. The bracelets came in ivory, jade, or cinnabar, and the rings were a set of stack rings in ivory, jade, and cinnabar

These are all ring/earrings collections with no other matching pieces: **Tailored Classics**, 1976, earrings $15, ring $20 – timeless look of woven strands of gold in a lovely dome design; **Touch of Beauty**, 1972, pierced earrings, $25 with **Serena** ring $30 – this is another collection with two names having angelskin coral and seed pearls in 14k gold setting. The earrings are extremely rare; **Laurel Leaf**, 1979, c/p hoop earrings $15, ring $25 – overlapping leaf design in antique silver; **Evening Splendor**, 1973, pierced earrings $25, ring $25 – pearls and rhinestones in silver setting. The earrings are extremely rare; **Spindrift**, 1975, c/p earrings $15, ring $25 – nice coral pearl in sweeping gold

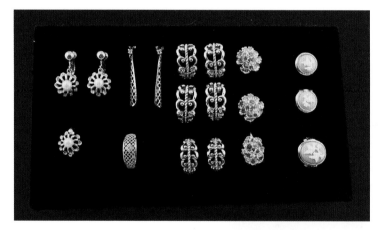

These are all ring/earrings collections with no other matching pieces: **Flowerburst**, 1974, clip earrings $15, ring $25 – pearl in gold petals; **Lattice Lace**, c/p dangle earrings $15, ring $25 – gold lace with rhinestone accent; **French Filigree**, 1977, c/p earrings $15, ring $25 – elaborate filigree set in gold or silver; **Flowerblaze**, 1976, c/p earrings $15, ring $25 – gold carnation with rhinestone dew drop; **Cameo Silhouette**, 1983, c/p earrings $15, ring $25 – white birds on a blue background

Soft Blush, 1984, necklace/ bracelet $35, pendant choker necklace $20, pierced earrings $15 – bead necklace of pink plastic with gold accents can be used with the bracelet to make one long necklace or split apart into two pieces. The choker is a gold leaf motif with pink cabochon accents; **Moon Magic**, 1974, necklace $20, ring $25 – pale blue glass stone surrounded by blue sapphires, no other matching pieces

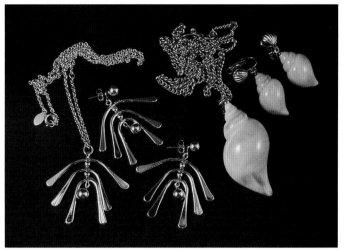

Windchimes, 1972, pendant $15, c/p convertible earrings $15 – shiny silver chimes that move. The earrings can be worn without the chimes dangles; **Sea Swirl**, 1975, pendant $15, c/p earrings $15 – marbleized conch shell in gold

Gatsby, 1981, necklace $15, c/p earrings $15 – plastic white swirls with the look of enamel and gold accents; **Come Summer**, 1975, necklace $15, c/p convertible earrings $15 – dramatic green and white plastic beads with earrings that can be worn without the green drop

Summer Brights, 1984, stretch bracelet $10, convertible pierced earrings $15 – stretch bracelet in multi-colors or white with basic white earrings with interchangeable red and blue jackets; **Gracious Tulips**, 1982, stretch bracelet $10, pierced earrings $10 – the look of carved ivory in plastic

Pale Fire, 1974, pendant $25, pierced earrings $25, ring $35 – pink coral cabochon surrounded by crystals

Summerset, 1977, necklace $15, c/p earrings $15 – bright white plastic with shiny gold accents; **Summer Set**, 1994, necklace $15, c/p earrings $15 – lustrous pearls with gold rosette accent

Color Impact, 1987, necklace $20, c/p earrings $15 – this set is golden flecked plastic in fiery red/ivory or cobalt blue/black

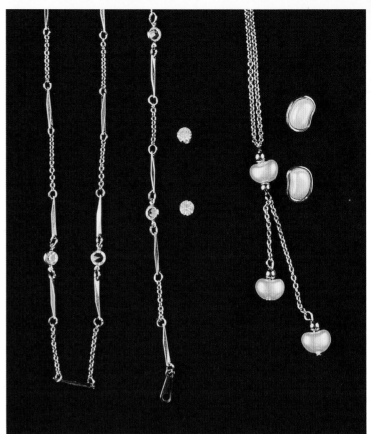

Simulated Diamond Accent, 1984, necklace $25, bracelet, $20, pierced earrings $15 – gold or silver with sparkling Austrian lead crystal accents; **Seashine Drop**, 1980, necklace $15, pierced earrings $15 – simulated freshwater Biwa pearls in gold

Mediterranean, 1986, necklace $25, c/p earrings $20 – marbleized Capri blue or light coral plastic beads alternating with ivory and gold accents

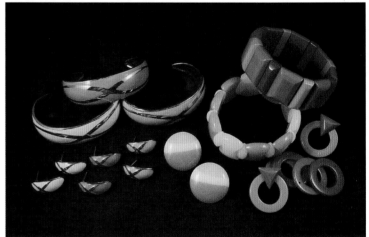

Fashion Pastel, 1987, bracelet $25, pierced earrings, $20 – magnificent look of enamel with gold accents in ivory, coral, or turquoise on gold. Matching ring shown in ring chapter; **Pastel Parfait**, 1988, bracelet $10, c/p earrings $10 – plastic stretch bracelet in blue, purple, and pink with white accents; **Color Schemes**, 1986, bracelet $15, convertible pierced earrings $15 – geometric plastic stretch bracelet in blue, fuchsia, and green. The earrings are graphic blue triangles with interchangeable colored circles

Bold Romance, 1991, pin $15, clip earrings $15 – large marcasite set; **Gilded Glory**, 1981, pin $10, c/p earrings $10 – antique gold blossom bar pin with matching blossom earrings; **Paisley Colors**, 1986, pin $15, c/p earrings $15 – gold with enamel-like accents; **Chesterfield**, 1980, pin $15, convertible pierced earrings $15, ring $25 – simulated mother-of-pearl pin with marcasite and rhinestone center having interchangeable onyx and mother-of-pearl cabochon earrings. Oval ring set with marcasites and tiny rhinestones

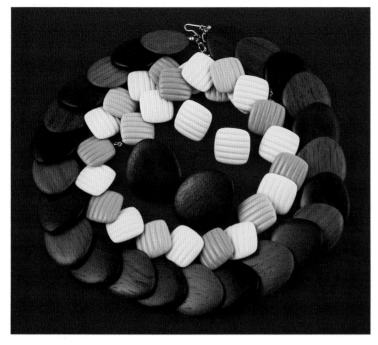

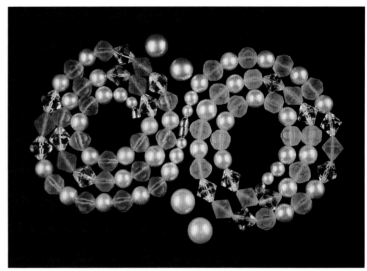

Icy Pastels, 1987, necklace $20, c/p earrings $15 – multi-faceted beads in either frosted lavender or aqua

Summer Sands, 1985, necklace $15, c/p earrings $10 – ribbed plastic beads in tan or all white; **Subtle Hues Wood**, 1989, necklace $20, c/p earrings $15 – three alternating natural wood disk colors polished to a soft glow;

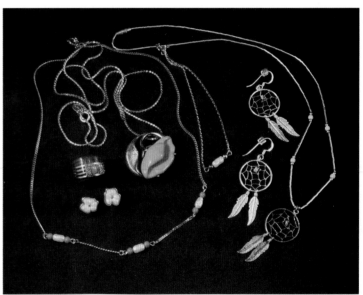

Zebra Stripe, 1987, bracelet $10, c/p earrings $10 – plastic stretch bracelet with pink/white or black/white; **Iridescent Fabric**, 1988, bracelet $10, c/p earrings $10 – fabric set with iridescent swirls

Sea Treasure, 1981, choker necklace $15, convertible pendant/pin $20, ankle bracelet $10, c/p earrings $10, ring $20 – this multi-piece gold set uses simulated Biwa pearls and coral beads. The ring has rhinestone accents; **Sterling Silver Dream Catcher**, necklace (1998) $25, pierced earrings (1997) $20 – sterling silver with genuine turquoise stone

Sun Medallion Pin (1994) with **Aztec Sun Earrings** (1992), pin $15, pierced earrings $15 – matte finish gold sun with rhinestone accents; **African Mask**, 1993, pin $30, pierced earrings $25 – antiqued gold mask with red, green, and topaz crystals in African artwork design

51

Dazzlessence, 1985, necklace $15, pierced earrings $10 – gold or silver chevron motif with sparkling diamond-like accents; **Galaxy of Color Collection**, 1982, necklace $15, c/p earrings $15 – chevron necklace and waterfall earrings in color combinations of crystal/ruby, crystal/sapphire, crystal/emerald, or clear crystal Austrian stones. There were matching tennis bracelets in all color combinations; **Majestic**, 1990, necklace $15, pierced earrings $15 – simulated diamonds in gold also came in ruby or sapphire

Fiery Opalesque Ring, 1989, $25 with **Radient Opalesque Earrings**, 1989, c/p, $25 – brilliant opal in gold oval frame. There is a matching pendant necklace on 18-inch gold chain, and all pieces are extremely rare; **Iceflower Set**, 1979, bar pin $10, pierced earrings $10 – elegant four-petal shaped rhinestones with gold center; **Fireglow Teardrop Pendant**, 1977, $20, opal and rhinestone pendant often sold with Radient Opalesque Earrings; **Fiery Glow**, 1984, pendant necklace $15, c/p earrings $15 – simulated opal in a fiery fantasy of color set in gleaming gold

Touch of Spring Necklace (1989) with **Blush Hoop Earrings** (1987), necklace $25, c/p earrings $15 – the look of real rose quartz with an exquisite flowered center bead in the necklace. Although sold in separate years, Avon put this together as a set in their brochures; **Indian Summer**, necklace (1990) $20, c/p earrings (1989) $15 – Avon released the earrings in late 1989 and the matching necklace in early 1990. Set is composed of thin disks of multi-colored beads

Desert Sands, 1988, necklace $35, c/p earrings $20 – magnificent peach and tan marbleized beads with silver accents in graduated sizes

Midnight Brilliance, 1987, necklace $20, clasp $10, c/p earrings $15 – necklace is 60-inches of black beads with removable clasp. The clasp and earrings are square motifs with rhinestone accents

French Countryside, 1989, choker necklace $25, long bead necklace $25, c/p earrings $15 – wonderful pastel beads with the luster of pearls having gold accents. The choker came in blue only, but the long bead necklaces came in amber or blue

Fashion Essentials, 1987, choker necklace $35, long necklace $30, c/p earrings, $20 – magnificent light and dark tortoise-toned beads with black and gold accents

Sea Swept, 1989, necklace $20, pierced earrings $15 –frosted plastic beads in aqua, lavender, and green; **Fresco Colors**, 1989, $25, c/p earrings $15 – marbleized and copper-colored plastic beads

Pastel Lily, 1983, lariat necklace $15, c/p earrings $15 – frosted lily bell flower with gold stamen came in blue, pink, or white

Sparkling Rope, 1989, necklace $40, c/p earrings $25 – magnificent crystal beads with gold accents and frosted drops

Gilded Links, 1976, necklace $10, bracelet $10 – interlocking, textured gold links are perfect for every outfit; Polished Links, 1995, necklace $10, bracelet $10 – smaller highly polished links add an updated, dramatic effect

Lotus Blossom Pendant with Tenderdrop Dangle Earrings, 1978, pendant $10, c/p earrings $15 – simulated rose quartz with rhinestone accents; Quilted Fashion Heart, 1987, necklace $20, c/p earrings $15 – gold heart with crystal accents; Pave Ombre Heart, 2005, necklace $25, pierced earrings $20 – rose-shaded crystals set in gold

Soft Knot Convertible Necklace, 1985, with Soft Twist Earrings, 1982, necklace $20, pierced earrings $15 – necklace has both gold and silver flexible chains that could be taken apart and worn individually. Matching earrings came in gold or silver loops; Woven Beauty Convertible Necklace, 1980, with Shimmering Cord Bracelet, 1979 – necklace $20, bracelet $15 – mesh chain with removable polished bar having rhinestone accents

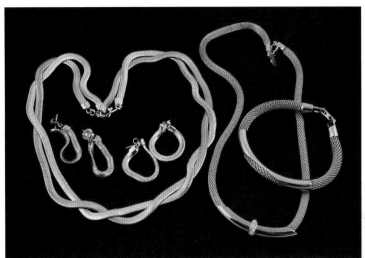

Sunsations, 1987, choker necklace $25, c/p earrings $15 – white with contrasting spectator yellow, spectator black, or spectator red in an interlocking design

Snow Fantasy, 1980, pendant necklace, $15, c/p earrings $15 – heirloom-look gold snowflake design on black onyx; Pink Sparkle, 1985, necklace $20, pierced earrings $15 – vivid pink and clear rhinestones with the look of real gems set in gold; Victorian Delicate, 1983, pendant necklace $15, pierced earrings $15 – delicate antique gold frame with seed pearl accents; Aurora Borealis, 1981, necklace $15, c/p earrings $15 – borealis crystal in a gold setting.

55

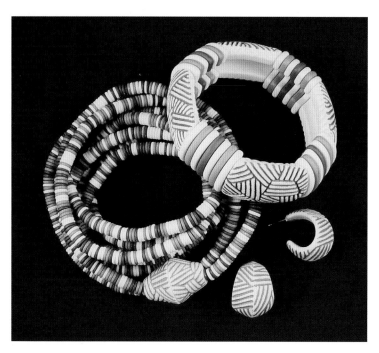

Sirocco Rope, 1988, necklace $25, stretch bracelet $20, pierced hoop earrings $15 – necklace is 36-inches composed of thin disks in taupe tones. The bracelet is handsomely detailed to resemble old carved ivory.

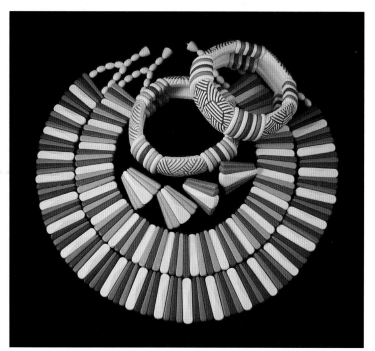

Sirocco Stick, 1988, necklace $25, stretch bracelet $20, c/p earrings $15 – innovative flat stick collar choker echoes the natural colors of sand, earth, and stone in taupe tones or peach tones

Colorworks, 1987, necklace $20, c/p earrings $15 – choker necklace in black disks with white beads or red/white disks with blue beads. The earrings are black with white bead or red with blue bead

Raj, 1986, necklace $15, c/p earrings $15 – emerald, ruby, sapphire, or multi-color beads with pearl and gold accents

Polka Dots, 1987, bracelet $10, c/p earrings $10 – sparkling white plastic with dots of red, black, or yellow; **Art Color**, 1986, stretch bracelet $20, pierced earrings $15 – stunning interlocking stretch bracelet in fuchsia/black/blue or ivory/taupe/black

Sunbleached Colors, 1987, choker necklace $20, stretch bracelet $15, c/p earrings $15 – marbleized tubular beads of lavender/blue/tan or peach/mint/gray alternate with colorful rondelles and wheel-like beads

Modern Heart, 1988, choker necklace $15, c/p earrings $15 – pearlized heart necklace with coral or black tubular beads

Pearlessence Cluster, 1987, necklace $15, bracelet $15, c/p earrings $15 – elegant gold set with clusters of creamy grape pearls

Jeweled Classics, 1983, convertible pearl necklace with detachable gem-studded clasp/pin $55, pendant necklace $15, c/p earrings $15 – this elegant set came with a single strand of pearls, 47-inches long, extremely rare, and a multi-jeweled clasp/pin, which can be worn separately. The rest of the collection consists of a Mabe pearl pendant necklace and Mabe pearl earrings; **Caviar**, 1988, beaded necklace $20, clasp $15, c/p earrings $15 – magnificent beads in hematite with colorful ruby bead accents and gold spacers having removable clasp that can be worn as a pin

Burst of Spring, 1988, necklace $25, c/p earrings $15 – plastic set in apple jade or pink coral; **Ivoryesque Patterns**, 1989, necklace $25, c/p earrings $15 – plastic set in ivory with taupe accents of rounds, rondelles, and teardrops bead

Color Waves, 1987, necklace $20, c/p earrings $15 – ivory and black or green onyx and black plastic

Newport, 1982, necklace $15, convertible pierced earrings $15 – plastic disk set in skipper blue/sail white, flag red/sail white, or sail white. The earrings are gold with interchangeable plastic disks in blue, white, or red

Key Biscayne, 1989, bracelet $20, c/p earrings $15, ring $30 – enamel-like turquoise or ivory in gold setting; **Tropical Splendor**, 1991, bracelet $20, c/p earrings $15 – fuchsia flowers of epoxy enamel on gold leaves

Dramatic Beauty Choker, 1981, necklace $15, motif $10 each – reversible gold chain which uses the **Classic Accent Motif**, **Amber Accent Motif**, or **Deep Azure Motif**; **Tender Memories Set**, 1990, necklace $15 - convertible gold chain with rhinestone accents which hold the memory-making charms, **Tender Memories Charm**, 1990, $5 each (Lantern, Present, Bells) not shown: Key, Clover, or Heart Charm

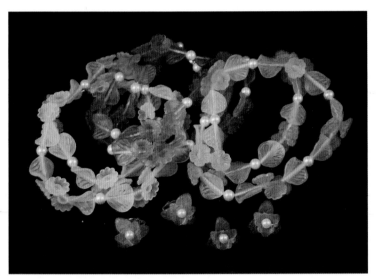

Pastel Blossoms, 1986, necklace $25, c/p earrings $15 – delicate lalique-look of plastic petals with pearl centers in frosted pink, blue, or white

Glossy Style, 1994, bracelet $20, pierced earrings $15 – bold gold ripples; **Serena Rose**, 1973, mirrored pendant $25, ring $30 – the necklace has a carved rose stone framed in black onyx in a wreath of gold leaves which reverses to a mirror on the back. Two necklaces are profiled so both sides can be seen. The ring is a carved rose to match the necklace. No two carved roses are alike. There are no matching earrings to this set

All of these are genuine stone necklaces from 1987, available in various lengths, and can be worn with the silver clasp and earrings as a complete set. **Genuine Amethyst Quartz Pierced Earrings**, $15; **Genuine Rose Quartz Pierced Earrings**, $15; **Genuine Hematite Hoop Pierced Earrings**, $30; **Silver-plated Fluted Chevron Set**, clasp $15, c/p earrings $15 – seashell motif used as a perfect adornment to the genuine stone necklaces; **Genuine Pink and White Coral**; choker, $35, bracelet $30 – two strands of finely cut coral nuggets intertwined to create a lace-like effect; **Genuine Sodalite and White Coral Choker**, $45; **Genuine Amethyst Quartz Necklace**, $45; **Genuine Onyx and Mother of Pearl Necklace**, $45 – the chips in this necklace are separated at intervals by matching round beads; **Genuine Rose Quartz Necklace**, $45; **Genuine Howlite Necklace**, $50; **Genuine Crystal Quartz Necklace**, $45; **Genuine Hematite Necklace**, $55

Metallic Lustre, 18-inch beads $15, 30-inch beads $20, c/p earrings $15 – gold or silver pearls in metallic finish; **Fashion Lustre**, 1980, 17-inch necklace $15, 28-inch necklace $20, c/p button earrings $10 – ivory or jade beads

Timeless Elegance Necklace, 1988, with **Pearly Hoop Earrings**, 1992, necklace $25, pierced earrings $15 – although released in different years, Avon recommended these as a set. The necklace is 36-inches of round pearls accented with oblong beads of jet or carnelian and the earrings have a lustrous pearl drop in a gold ring.

South of France, 1988, $35; pierced earrings $30 – a blue and green bead beauty with pearl accents. Earrings are extremely rare.

Better Breast Care Ribbon Pin, 1993, large $5, small $5; **Pink Ribbon Key Ring**, 1994, $5, **Pink Ribbon Earrings**, 1996, c/p, $5 – pink enamel and gold. All items, except the key ring, were released several times, and each box bears a different date

Pave, 1984, choker necklace $15, pendant necklace $15, c/p earrings $15 – pave plaque of rhinestones on gold create the rich look of pave diamonds. There is also a stickpin in the collection; **Golden Reflections**, 1987, necklace $15, c/p earrings $10 – faceted gold beads; **Art Deco Style**, 2004, necklace $20, c/p earrings $15 – clear rhinestones in silver with black accents in a chevron design

Romantic Portraits, 1988, necklace $20, c/p earrings $15 – beautiful cameo on pink background in gold frame with pearl accents; **Romantic Poet Necklace** with **Dangling Cameo Earrings** and **Sentimental Cameo Ring**, 1994, necklace $20, pierced earrings, $15, ring, $25 – white cameo on pink background in gold frame with pearl and rhinestone accents

Capitol Style, 1989, necklace $25, bracelet $20, pierced earrings $15 – necklace and bracelet are two strands of pearls held by a pearl and gold clasp. Clasps and earrings match with large cabochon pearl set in gold frame

Cubic Style, 1987, necklace $30, pierced earrings $15 – extremely rare plastic cube beads with gold accents in ombre shades of taupe, blue, or pink

Tourmaline Impressions, 1982, pendant necklace $20, bead necklace $30, c/p earrings $15 – rose quartz, amethyst, and light jade with rhinestone accents

Dramatic Kiss, 1989, necklace $30, cuff bracelet $25, c/p earrings $20 – gold kiss on black braided cord

Each bracelet is a wide plastic bangle, $15, with c/p earrings, $10:
Tropical Beauty, 1987;
Color Collage, 1988;
Color Contrast, 1989;
Passion Flowers, 1989

64

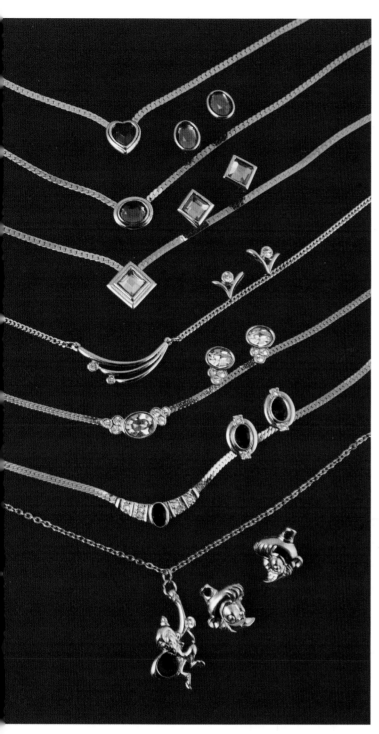

Sparkle Connection, 1987, necklace $15, bracelet $10, c/p earrings $15 – amazing diamond-look rhinestones set in gold

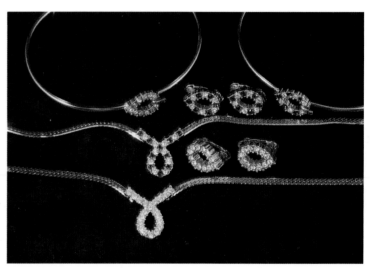

Plaza, 1988, necklace $15, bracelet $10, c/p earrings $15 – the look of real diamonds in gold in sapphire/crystal, ruby/crystal, emerald/crystal, or clear crystal

Dazzle Dots, 1985, necklace $15, pierced earrings, $15 – highly polished gold cobra chain with sparkling stones. Shown are the ruby heart, pink diamond oval, and aquamarine square, but there is also a topaz circle and clear diamond triangle; **Sweeping Sparkle**, 1985, necklace $15, pierced earrings $15 – graceful sweep of gleaming gold accented by Austrian lead crystals with the look of diamonds; **Pastel Facets**, 1990, necklace $15, pierced earrings $15 – elegant light rose or aquamarine gemstone with crystal accents in gold setting; **Royal Stones**, 1985; necklace $15, pierced earrings $15 – glamorous center stone surrounded on either side by dazzling crystals came in sapphire, topaz, or diamond; **Abu**, 1994, necklace $15, pierced earrings $10 – Aladdin's monkey Abu with ruby rhinestone in gold

Color Shapes, 1987, necklace $15, c/p earrings $10 – swirls wrap around plastic ovals in turquoise or amber

Classic Lines, 1989, choker necklace $20, bead necklace $25, stretch bracelet $15, c/p earrings $15 – the choker necklace is chevron-shaped in red/white or black/white. The long necklace has barrel-shaped beads with thin wafer spacers. The bracelet is white with colored spacers, and the earrings are two-toned sculptured buttons

Classic Lines set in black/white

Carved Accent, 1988, necklace $25, c/p earrings $15 – magnificent look of carved ivory

Turquoise Impressions, 1983, torsade necklace $25, bead necklace $20, c/p button earrings $10, c/p swirl earrings $15, ring $20. The torsade necklace, swirl earrings, and ring have simulated turquoise and pearl. The bead necklace has round and oval simulated turquoise beads with gold accents

Marble Hues, 1986, necklace $25, pierced earrings $15 – great look of marbles in cool white or soft coral

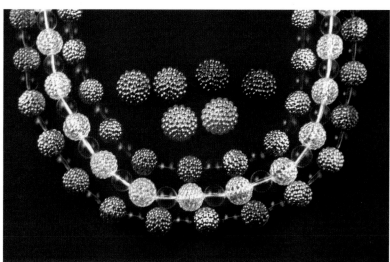

Summer Berries, 1987, necklace $20, c/p earrings $15 – shimmering iridescent plastic berries in redberry, blueberry, or iceberry

Frosted Pastel Bead, 1998, necklace $15, pierced earrings $15 – frosted and matte beads in gold; **Gilded Strands Necklace** with **Mother-of-Pearl Convertible Earrings**, 1978; necklace $15, pierced earrings $15 – necklace is a gentle cascade of 3 gold chains of different lengths enhanced by two oval beads of genuine mother-of-pearl on the center strand. The matching earrings can be worn as a stud or as a teardrop of genuine mother-of-pearl in gold. Both are extremely rare.

Color Dash, 1988, cuff $20, pierced earrings $15 – stunning chevron design in raspberry, blue, or black on shiny gold repeated in the half-hoop earrings; **Touch of Blue**, 1989, bangle bracelet $20, pierced earrings $20 – classic look in shiny gold or silver with blue stripe accent

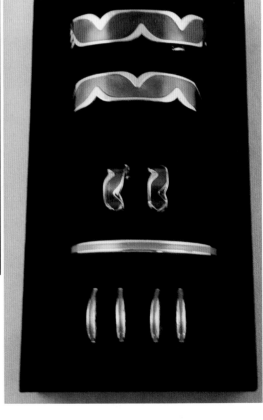

Polished Spectrum, 1986, necklace $25, pierced earrings $15 – classy look in polished disks of agate, amber, jade, and ebony with earrings in either amber or jade

Autumn Glow, 1982, necklace $20, convertible pierced earrings $15 – twisted beads in carnelian or onyx with gold accents and earrings with interchangeable disks; **Frosted Petals**, 1982, necklace $15, c/p earrings $15 – frosted plastic petals in rose or aqua with gold accents

Fifth Avenue, 1986, necklace $30, c/p earrings $20 – pearls with faceted black beads, gold beads, and tiny black bead spacers

Purple Dawn, 1987, necklace $20, c/p earrings $15 – baroque crystal beads with look of amethyst

69

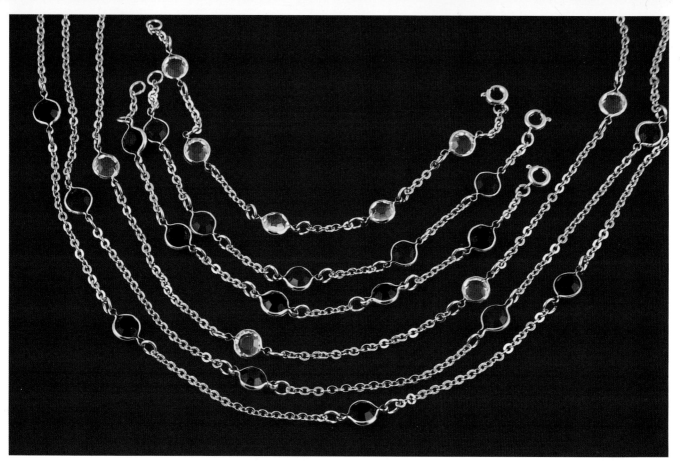

Elegant Expressions, 1989, necklace $15, bracelet $10 – faceted stones on a gleaming gold chain came in sapphire, ruby, or diamond

Sand Pebbles, 1986, necklace $25, c/p earrings, $15 – sea blue or sea sand plastic disks with tiny bead accents; **Seashore**, 1987, necklace $20, pierced earrings $15 – wonderful scallop shell motif in Malibu blue or Tahitian tan

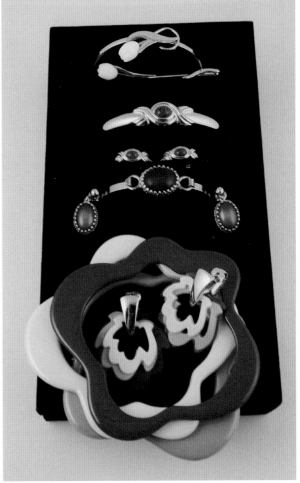

Versatile Elegance, 1989, necklace $15, bracelet $10 – creamy pearls with hidden clasp; **Pearly Drop**, 1990, necklace $15, bracelet $10, c/p earrings $10 – lustrous pearl charms on gold chain

Graceful Tulip, 1980, bracelet $15, pin $15 – ivory tulip in a gold setting; **Blue Iris**, 1990, bracelet $15, c/p earrings $15 – gleaming gold with an impressive sapphire, matching ring shown in the Ring Chapter; **Oval Classic**, 1974, bracelet $15, pierced earrings $20 – shiny gold set with large lapis stone. The earrings are extremely rare and can be worn without the lapis dangle; **Color Curves**, 1987, bracelet $15, pierced earrings $15 – scalloped-edge plastic in wave upon wave of royal blue, aqua, teal or coral, red, pink

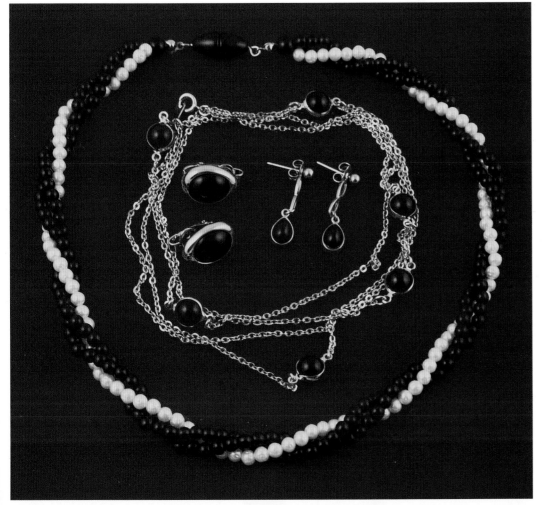

Opulent, 1981, cabochon chain necklace $20, torsade necklace $20, chain convertible pierced earrings $15, cabochon c/p earrings $15, ring $35 – a stunning collection of cabochon garnets, pearls, and gold accents. The chain convertible earrings can be worn without the drop. Both earring styles also came in golden topaz.

71

Decorative Tassel, 1989, pin $15, c/p earrings $15 – twisted golden rope with fixed tassels; **Birthstone Heart**, 1992, pin $10, heart drop pierced earrings, 1993, $10 – gold heart with birthstone accent; **Free Form**, 1987, pin $15, pierced earrings $15 – silver or gold lightning bolt

Dancing Stars, 1985, necklace $15, pierced earrings $10 – 3-dimensional gold stars with crystal bead center; **Silvertone Snake Fringe**, 2003, necklace $10, pierced earrings $10 – shiny silver fringe set; **Sea Swirls**, 1985, lariat necklace $15, c/p earrings $15 – white plastic seashell motif; **Ocean's Dream**, 1995, necklace $10, c/p earrings $15 – lustrous pearl set in gold sea shell with rhinestone accents

Tea Rose, 1987, translucent pink necklace $20, frosted pink necklace $25, transparent pink necklace $30, c/p earrings $15 – magnificent beads of different lengths with transparent pink earrings

Winter Pastels, 1987, necklace $25, c/p earrings $15 – magnificent plastic leaves in green or pink ombre

Cosmopolitan, 1987, necklace $25, c/p earrings $15 – multi-strand beaded necklace in amber/ivory or red/black with earrings to match

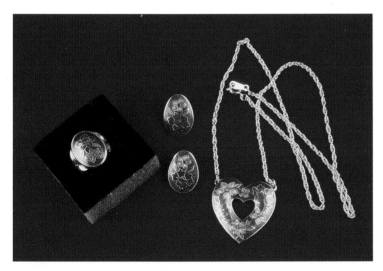

Genuine Cloisonne Heart Pendant Necklace, 1988, with **Romantic Cloisonne**, 1989, necklace $20, pierced earrings $20, ring $35 – this is a set with the necklace bearing a separate name and date from the rest of the set. All pieces are genuine cloisonne in shiny gold

Allegro, 1983, Maltese cross pin $15, stone chain necklace $15, stone c/p earrings $15 – large gold cross pin with amethyst or topaz stone. The stone necklace has amethyst, light amethyst, topaz and tourmaline stones set in gold; **Spectator Style**, 1980, necklace $10, c/p earrings $10 – gold chain with plastic stations in black or white with traditional button earrings

Pearlized Lace Gift Set, 1987, $20 – pearl lace collar and earrings

Ice Facets Necklace with **Crystalique Drop Earrings**, 1985, 18-inch necklace $25, 30-inch necklace $30, c/p drop earrings $15 – elegant crystal beads, swirl-faceted and graduated in size, accented with rondelles of silver set with rhinestones

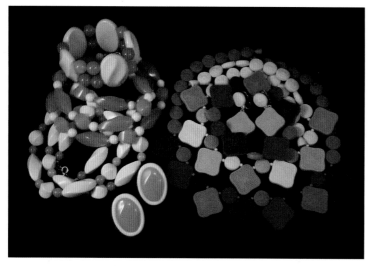

Shades of Spring, 1990, necklace $15, stretch bracelet $15, c/p earrings $15 – pink/purple or ivory beads with pastel accents with pink swirl earrings having ivory trim; **Summer Resort**, 1988, choker necklace $15, bracelet $15, c/p earrings $15 – the look of raffia done up in plastic in turquoise/fuchsia or ivory/pink

Fashion Waves, 1987, necklace $15, pierced earrings $15 – clear, crystal-like shape enlivened with bright colors in heat wave pink or cool wave blue

Arabesque, 1989, necklace $25, c/p earrings $15 – simulated lapis and carnelian beads with gold and pearl accents having carnelian inset earrings rimmed in gold with lapis blue border

Blue Marble Art with **Golden Splatter Earrings**, 1986 –
necklace $15, bracelet $15, c/p earrings $15 – blue plastic
with a gentle marble effect; **Fashion Bead Necklace**, 1987,
$15 – two alternating bead sizes in royal blue or matte gold

**Modern Art with Golden Splatter
Earrings**, 1986, necklace $15,
bracelet $10, c/p earrings $15 –
black or white abstract beads with
matching bangle and complimentary
earrings

Color Flash Necklace with Golden Splatter Earrings, 1986, necklace $25, c/p earrings $15 – baroque beads came in crimson red or cobalt blue with gold bead accents and complimentary earrings

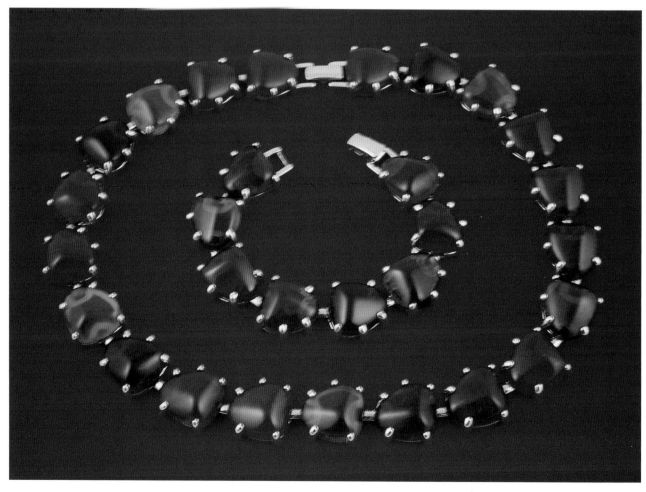

Jewelesque Nugget, 1988, necklace $95, bracelet $75 – extremely rare multicolored nuggets set and linked in gold. There are no matching earrings.

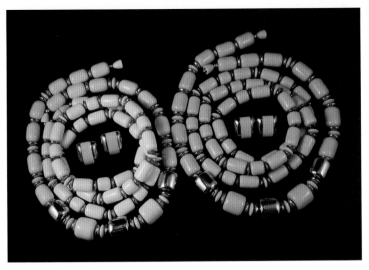

City Sleek, 1986, choker necklace $20, long necklace $30, c/p earrings $15 – barrel-shaped beads in either seaessence or ivoryessence with silver accents

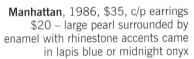

Manhattan, 1986, $35, c/p earrings $20 – large pearl surrounded by enamel with rhinestone accents came in lapis blue or midnight onyx

Ribbon Curl, 1989, necklace $15, c/p earrings $15, pin $10 – textured scalloped motif in silver or gold

Scrollwork, 1989, necklace $15, bracelet $20, c/p earrings $15 –
gold chevron scrollwork with marbleized enamel accents

Autumn Harvest, 1989, necklace $20, c/p earrings $10 – wonderful collection of brightly colored chip-type
beads of purple, teal, burnt orange, brick red, yellow ochre, and black mingled with large round beads

Dramatic Style, 1988, necklace $25, c/p earrings $15 – center motif available in red or black with gold and rhinestone accents; **Whispering Leaves**, 1991, necklace $25, c/p earrings $20 – graceful gold leaf design entwined on elegant black braided cord with matching gold leaf earrings

Precious Bee, 1989, lariat necklace $15, c/p earrings, $10 – artistically crafted bee with pearl body; **Golden Shell Convertible Necklace**, 1983, with **Scallop Shell Earrings**, 1986, necklace $15, c/p earrings $15 – gleaming gold shell pendant can be worn without the pearl in the shell; **Endless Heart Necklace**, 1985, with **Dangling Heart Earrings**, 1983, and **Heart Hoop Earrings**, 1985, necklace $15, pierced earrings $15 – polished gold hearts in all pieces; **Autumn Leaves Necklace**, 1990, with **Falling Acorn Earrings,** 1990, necklace $20, c/p earrings $15 – necklace has gold leaves with pearl accents, and the earrings are gold acorns hanging from gold leaves. Avon put this together as a set in their brochure

Frosted Coolers, 1989, bracelet $15, c/p earrings $15 – frosted plastic with the look and feel of glass in melon with gold accents or blueberry with silver accents; **Candy Colors**, 1986, stretched bracelet $15, c/p earrings $15 – colorful cotton candy colors. The earrings only came with blue stripes; **Textured Luxuries**, 1988, bracelet $15, c/p earrings $10 – exotic bangle with leather appearance in teal or burgundy

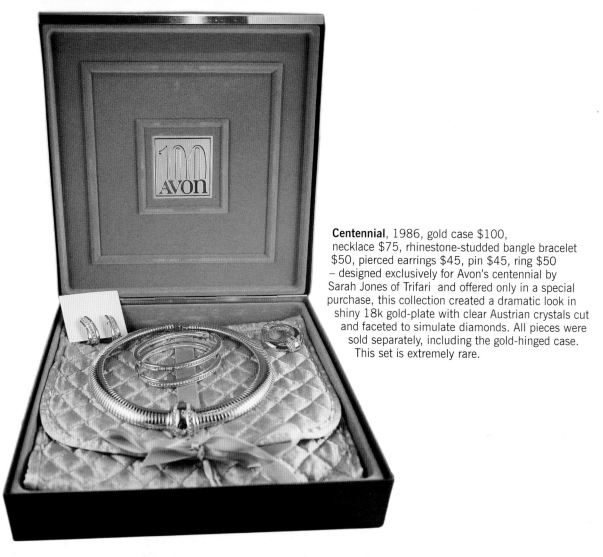

Centennial, 1986, gold case $100,
necklace $75, rhinestone-studded bangle bracelet
$50, pierced earrings $45, pin $45, ring $50
– designed exclusively for Avon's centennial by
Sarah Jones of Trifari and offered only in a special
purchase, this collection created a dramatic look in
shiny 18k gold-plate with clear Austrian crystals cut
and faceted to simulate diamonds. All pieces were
sold separately, including the gold-hinged case.
This set is extremely rare.

Close-up of the
Centennial jewelry to
show more detail

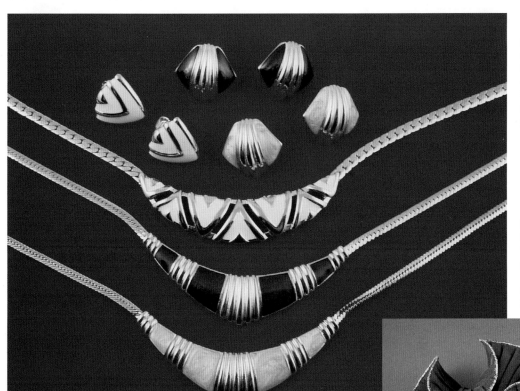

Abstract Style, 1988, necklace $20, c/p earrings $15 – white or blue enamel chevrons on gold; **Classic Crescent**, 1987, necklace $15, c/p earrings $15 – classic design of gold crescent with sapphire or mother-of-pearl inserts

Ruffle, 1988, pin $10, pierced earrings $10 – black ruffle ribbon with delicate gold trim. There were also matching shoe clips. **Black Tie**, 1986, $10 c/p earrings $10 – elegant dress-up tie with matching rhinestone studded earrings

Charm Bracelet, 1973, bracelet $20, each charm $10, 14k gold washed and 3-D in appearance. **French Telephone, Precious Owl, Sweet Shoppe, Fashion Boot, Country Store Coffee Mill, Victoriana Pitcher and Bowl**. The bracelet is extremely rare; **Seaside**, 1987, bracelet $15, c/p earrings $10 – iridescent finish on white metal; **Fashion Waves**, 1978, bracelet $15, ring $30 – two silver bands border a band of gold to create an interlocking scalloped bangle. The ring comes apart into five different scalloped bands of gold and silver and is extremely rare.

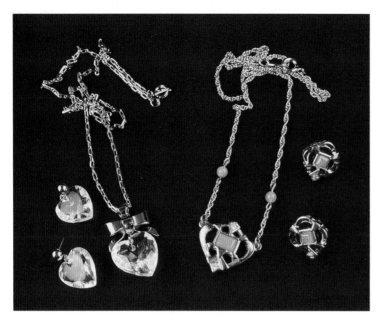

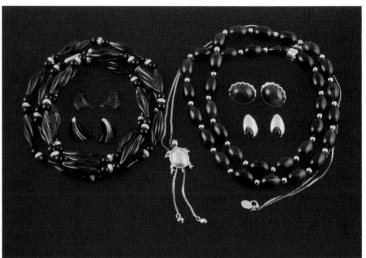

Romantic Facets, 1985, necklace $15, pierced earrings $15 – faceted heart with the glowing look of crystal in clear, aqua, or rose; **Genuine Adventurine**, 1993, pendant necklace $15, c/p earrings $15 – genuine adventurine in gold filigree frame accented with rhinestones

About Town, 1986, necklace $20, convertible c/p earrings $15 – tortoise, onyx and gold beads with gold earrings having interchangeable tortoise and onyx jackets; **Turtle Bay**, 1980, turtle slide necklace $25, tortoise bead necklace $15, c/p gold earrings $15, c/p tortoise earrings $15 – gold turtle on slide lariat or tortoise beads with gold bead spacers and earrings to match

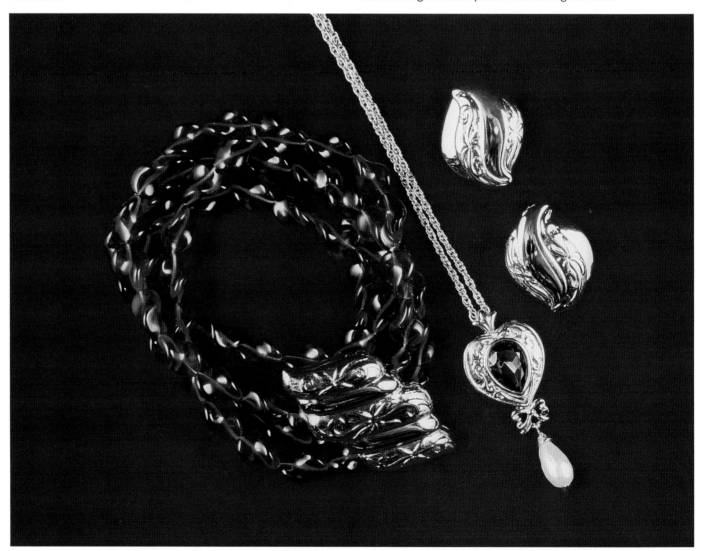

Renaissance Beauty, 1987, pendant necklace $15, bead necklace $20, clasp $15, c/p swirl earrings $15 – elegant amethyst collection with gold swirl accents. The bead necklace also came in sapphire

Royal Azura, 1981, choker necklace $35, bead necklace $25, pierced earrings $15 –
lapis beads with golden accents

Golden Bouquet, 1988, necklace $10, pierced earrings $10 – gleaming gold flower head with pearl accents;
Color Splash, 1986, necklace $15, c/p earrings $10 – look of enamel in red/black or blue/black with earrings in
all three colors

Classic Baroque, 1982, necklace $25, c/p earrings $10 – wonderful baroque pearls came in gray or cream; **Pearly Bug**, 1994, necklace $15, c/p earrings $15 – bee with large pearl body and gold filigree wings

Heather & Mist, 1984, amethyst pearl necklace $20, gray pearl necklace $20, c/p earrings $10 – pearls are shown twisted into a torsade and held by the Imari clasp. The earrings came with amethyst centers

Impressionistic Pastels, 1986, with **Genuine Cloisonne Pierced Earrings**, 1987, necklace $15, bracelet $10, earrings $25 – beautiful pastel colors in the necklace and bracelet with gold accents. The earrings have the same matching colors in the butterfly and flower.

Snow Sparkle, 1984, necklace $15, c/p earrings $15 – Austrian lead crystal flower set in silver; **Romantic Ribbons**, 1982, necklace $15, c/p earrings $15 – antique silver studded with marcasites; **Aqua Filigree**, 1984, pendant $15, c/p earrings $15 – aqua stone set in silver filigree prison

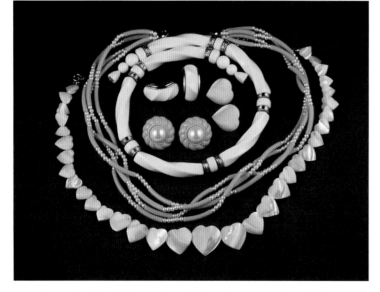

Classic Twist, 1988, necklace $15, c/p hoop earrings $15 – twisted plastic beads in white, red, or black with gold accents; **Elegant Twist**, 1989, necklace $15, c/p earrings $15 – necklace is four strands of twisted pearls combined with turquoise or onyx beads with matching earrings that can be worn without the twist jackets; **Genuine Mother of Pearl Heart**, 1987, choker necklace $30, c/p earrings $20 – a cascade of lovely, luminous hearts in genuine mother of pearl shell

Royal Facets, 1987, necklace $30, c/p earrings $20 – majestic royal blue or empress green beads with crystal-like links. Earrings are extremely rare.

Marrakesh Style, 1988, necklace $20, pierced earrings $15 – thin multi-colored plastic disks with large blue bead clasp and matching earrings

E.T. Pin, 1983, $15 – finely detailed antiqued gold tac pin; **ET Touch of Love Pin**, 1983, $15 – circle pin with rhinestone touch of love; **Dangling Telephone Earrings**, 1984, c/p, $15 – golden rotary telephone with dangling receiver; **Telephone Pin**, 1981, $15 – magnificent gold rotary phone with receiver stick pin

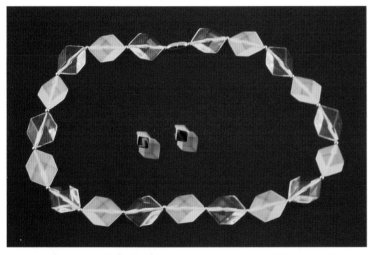

Crystal Impressions, 1985, choker necklace $20, c/p earrings $15 – clear and frosted crystal plastic in clear frost or lilac frost

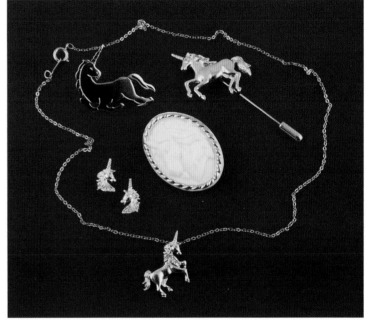

The gleaming gold unicorn collection consists of: **Unicorn Pin**, 1981, $10; **Unicorn Stick Pin**, 1989, $10; **Porcelain Unicorn Pin**, 1990, $20, **Unicorn Earrings**, 1985, released in 1987 as Magical Unicorn Earrings, pierced $10, **Pave Unicorn Pendant**, 1985, $20. The earrings and necklace have rhinestone accents

Spectator, 1986, choker necklace $20, c/p earrings, $15 – white alternates with red or black marquis-shaped plastic

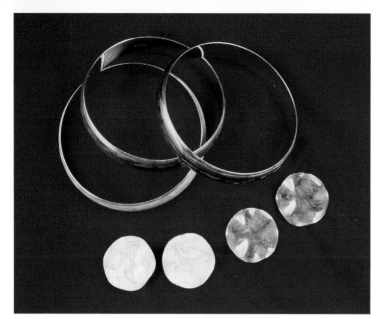

Pearlized, 1985, bracelet $15, c/p ruffle earrings $15 – lustrous pearly pastel tones in blue, pink, or white. In January 1986, Avon introduced the regal purple and emerald green colors.

Heart Charm, 1988, with **Pearly Dangle Bracelet**, 1993, necklace $15, pierced earrings $10, bracelet $15 – pearls captured in gold hearts; **Simply Hearts**, 1995, necklace $15, bracelet $10 – openwork golden hearts. There are no matching earrings

Royal, 1988, necklace $30, c/p earrings $25 – elegant dressy bead set with the look and feel of real stones. It came in lapis or malachite, and the earrings could be worn with either color. This set is extremely rare.

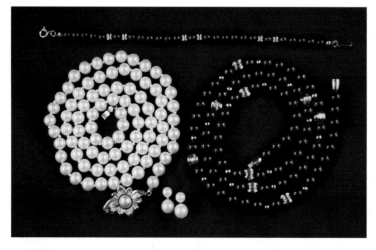

Porcelain Bouquet, 1989, pendant $15, c/p earrings $15 – wonderful porcelain flower motif; **Butterfly Accents**, 1988, long necklace $15, pierced earrings $15 – gold and pearl butterfly set also has a matching choker.

Pearlessence, 1980, necklace $50, c/p earrings $25 – necklace is 30-inches of hand-knotted pearls, and the earrings are two pearls in gold; **Lapis Blue Reflections**, 1985, 22-inch necklace $20, 28-inch necklace $25, bracelet $20 – beautiful lapis beads with gold accent bands. Matching ring in Ring Chapter.

Bold Heart Earrings with **Fashion Heart Choker**, 1986, and with **Draped Chains Necklace**, 1993, c/p earrings $15, choker necklace $30, chain necklace $20 – magnificently polished gold heart combinations. Both necklaces are extremely rare

Lady Bug, 1997, bracelet $10, pierced earrings $10 – nice detail of red epoxy ladybug set in silver; **Neon Brights**, 1986, bracelet $10, c/p earrings $10 – bright, shiny metal in yellow, pink, or teal

Rainbow Colors, 1988, necklace $10, bracelet $10, pierced earrings $10 – children's set of pearls with colorful bead accents having stud earrings with three pairs of interchangeable jackets; **Golden Hearts**, 1989, necklace $10, bracelet, $10 – delicate gold hearts on gold chain

Pretty Bow, 1990, necklace $15, c/p earrings $15 – pearl necklace with antique marcasite bow; **Subtle Shimmer**, 1980, necklace $15, c/p earrings $10 – tassel motif in shiny silver; **Scalloped Casual**, 1978, necklace $10, bracelet $10 – polished gold scallops make a terrific fashion statement. There are no matching earrings.

Draped Elegance, 1990, necklace $30, c/p earrings $25 –
gorgeous beads in lapis or coral with gold clasp and enamel accents

Fluttering Facets, 1990, pendant necklace $15, pierced earrings $15 – Austrian crystal butterfly in flight in clear or amethyst; **Precious Orchid**, 1992, necklace $15, pierced earrings $10 – rose coral enamel on gold; **Delicate Knot**, 1977, necklace $15, c/p earrings $10 – this set came in gold or silver; **Romantic Moments**, 1982, necklace $150, c/p earrings $15 – simulated pearl set in swirl of gold

Fashion Coin, 1990, bracelet $10, c/p earrings $10 – gold coin set; **Graceful Trellis**, 1989, bracelet $15, c/p earrings $15 – gold filigree set

Classic Drama, 1990, necklace $25, c/p earrings $15 – timeless look of marcasite and pearls; **Venetian Style**, 1993, necklace $25, clip earrings $20 – classic gold chevron with lapis, turquoise, and pearl accents with pearl or lapis earrings

East Side Style, 1990, necklace $25, c/p earrings $15 – stunning red and black marbleized plastic beads with pearls and gold accents

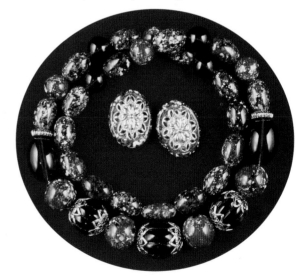

Winterberries, 1990, necklace $20, c/p earrings $15 – fuchsia, amethyst, and purple beads with golden accents

Romantic Renaissance, 1990, pin $15, c/p earrings $15 – antique silver with pearl accent; **Pastel Accent**, 1986, pin $20, c/p drop earrings $20 – pin has four teardrops of aquamarine, crystal, topaz, and rose quartz in gold. The earrings come in rose-quartz or aquamarine; **Pastel Lace**, 1995, pin $15, c/p earrings $15 – gold lace with porcelain rose motif; **Ship Ahoy**, 1992, pin $15, c/p earrings $15 – wonderful nautical motif set in gold

Moroccan, 1990, necklace $25, c/p earrings $15 – warm amber with antique gold or cool blue with antique silver

Frosted Petal, 1991, necklace $15, c/p earrings, $10 – pearls with center flower accented with rhinestones; **Delicate Hearts**, 1987, necklace $20, pierced earrings $15 – pearl hearts in gold chain

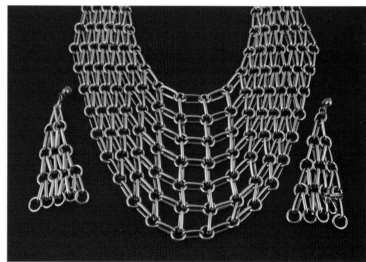

Dramatic Links, 1991, necklace $25, pierced earrings $20 – flexible gold links gently drape for the boldest fashion look ever

Port-of-Call, 1990, necklace $25, c/p button earrings $10 – white and matte gold beads in either a red or blue theme

Whispering Wings, 1991, pin $15, c/p earrings $15 – marcasite butterfly with pearlized white epoxy enamel wings; **Fall Grapes Pin** with **Grape Pierced Earrings**, 1993, pin $15, earrings $15 – majestic amethyst grapes with gold leaves and amethyst crystals; **Vintage**, 1989, pin $15, c/p earrings $15 – onyx and mother-of-pearl fan design in a silver marcasite setting

Golden Web, 1992, pin $15, pierced earrings $15 – large, lacy, gold openwork web with rich amethyst center; **Spring Butterfly**, 1997, pin $15, c/p earrings $15 – gold butterfly with pink glaze and crystal accents; **Full Bloom**, 1990, pin $25, c/p earrings $15 – gorgeous pansy flower in purple/yellow or blue/pink

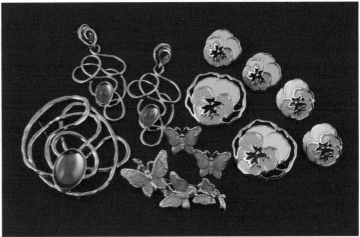

Floral Trellis, 1992, necklace $25, c/p earrings $20 – large gold floral pattern in texture and design; **American Treasures**, 1994, necklace $15, c/p earrings $15 – hammered matte gold finish with a heart and square motif

Bubbles, 1992, necklace $20, c/p earrings $15 – luxuriant large and small pearls in shell pink or cream; **Summer Frost**, 1985, necklace $20, c/p earrings $15 – frosted plastic with black or multi-colored bead accents

91

Fashion Hues, 1993, necklace $15, c/p earrings $10 – large pearl beads in muted tones of coral or cream

Golden Bloom, 1991, necklace $15, c/p earrings $10 – gold motif of graceful calla leaves with pearl accent;
Engraved, 1981, necklace $15, c/p earrings $10 – elegant etched flower motif came in gold or silver; **Gilded Mesh**, 1991, necklace $20, c/p earrings $15 – delicate open mesh motif in textured and shiny gold or silver

Pearlesque Elegance Pendant, 1994, $25 – pearly sphere set in gold on a pearl strand; **Delicate Pearly Hoop Earrings**; 1994, pierced $10 – multi-gold hoops with pearl accents; **Tailored Elegance Pendant**, 1992, $15 – large captured pearl in gold cage

Romantic Accent, 1991, necklace $20, c/p earrings $15 – Austrian crystals and pearls in marcasite setting; **Textured Heart Pendant** 1995 with **Rope Twist Earrings** 1986, pendant $25, c/p earrings $15 – amethyst beads with textured gold heart on gold chain with matching textured rope earrings; **Brick Chain**, 1996, chevron necklace $15, bracelet $15, c/p earrings $10 – versatile look of 14k gold in a brick chain design

Blue Seas, 1996, necklace $25, c/p button earrings $15, c/p dangle earrings $20 – magnificent azure blue beads with gleaming gold accents

Luscious Cluster, 1993, bracelet $15, c/p earrings $15 – stretch bracelet of white or multicolor pearls with matching earrings in gold hoop; **Classic Hoop Earrings**, 1992, with **Pearlesque Wrap Bracelet** and **Bold Pearlesque Earrings**, 1993, bracelet $15, earrings $10 – bold in size, big on style in pink or cream pearls

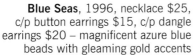

93

Moroccan Spice, 1997, beaded necklace $35, convertible c/p earrings $20 – magnificent beaded necklace in wonderful warm colors of amber and taffy with earrings that can be worn without the golden jacket; Club Capri, 1989, necklace $25, c/p earrings $15 – white plastic beads with fuchsia, teal, and yellow accent beads. The earrings have white domed centers and can be worn with or without the interchangeable fuchsia and teal disks

Festive Treasure, 1995, pin $15, c/p earrings $10 – colorful poinsettias with gold leaves; Blue Deco, 1987, pin $15, c/p earrings $15 – oval lapis pin with gold chevron and red teardrop. Earrings are gold chevron with lapis teardrop; Genuine Onyx, 1995, pin $25, pierced earrings $20 – onyx picture in gold filigree frame with pearl accent

Golden Tassel, 1988, lariat necklace $15, pierced earrings $15 – wonderful gold chain lariat with chain tassels; Blue Cat's Eye, 2004, pendant $20, pierced earrings $20 – blue moonstone cat's eye set in silver filigree frame; Shimmering Droplets, 2005, necklace $15, pierced earrings $10 – lightweight collection of silver leaves; Elegant Era, 1994, bracelet $15, c/p earrings $15 – amethyst stones in marcasite

Pink Tulip, 1996, pin $15, c/p earrings $15 – silvery marcasite with pink rhinestone tulips; Golden Crescent Stick Pin, 1990, with Gentle Drama Earrings, 1991, pin $15, c/p earrings $15 – although they have different names, Avon showed them as a set – opulent gold filigree design with black onyx accent; Sculptured Butterfly Pin, 1987, with Soft Sculptured Earrings, 1987, pin $15, pierced earrings $15 – sleek ribbing and dynamic design with air of importance in silver or gold. Matching necklace in gold is shown in the Necklace Chapter.

Woven Elegance, 1994, necklace $20, pierced convertible earrings $15 – mesh-textured gold. Wear the swirled button earrings alone or add the drop. Gilded Links Collection, 1992, necklace $15, bracelet $15, c/p earrings $15 – lightweight gold butterfly links

Color Disc, 1992, necklace $40, c/p earrings $30 – extremely rare set of colorful plastic disks looking like giant Life Savers in marbleized earthen colors; Neutral Hues, 1987 necklace $25, 1990 c/p earrings $15 – the look of stone disks in tones of tan, gray, and beige plastic. Avon completed this set three years apart

Garden of Eden, 1995, pin $25, clip earrings $20 – magnificent enamel butterflies and gold bees at rhinestone flower with teardrop pearl dangle. The pin is very rare.

Heirloom Riches, 1993, reversible pendant $35, ring $35 – pearl on one side and marcasite ray burst on the other with ring having both designs

Rose Passion, 1996, pin $20, pierced $15 – sculptured shiny gold rose with rhinestone accents; Artist Dimensions, 1991, pin $15, c/p earrings $15 –magnificent matte gold swirl

Loving Kitty Necklace with Cuddly Cat Earrings, 1993, necklace $15, pierced earrings $15 – gold kitty in heart frame; Sienna Heart Collection, 1996, necklace $25, pierced convertible earrings, $20 – rich tortoise heart on gold chain with earrings having removable heart flourishes

Classic Bead Hoop Earrings, 1997, pierced, $15 – gold bead in rings go well with **Golden Accent Necklace**, 1992, $15 – linked chains with gold bead accents; **Mesh and Bead Necklace**, 1983, $15 – twisted gold mesh intertwined with gold bead chain, **Golden Bead Necklace**, 1993, $15 – golden beads with golden chain accents; **Beaded Chain Necklace**, 1978, $15 – has five shiny gold beads on shiny gold chain

Turquoise Color Beaded, 2002, necklace $25, nugget stretch bracelet $15 – magnificent bold beads with silver bead accents. There are no earrings to this set

Cirelle, 1994, necklace $20, c/p earrings $15 – magnificent torsade of seed pearls in coral or cream with gold accents

Solar Magic Leaf, 1999, pin $15, c/p earrings $15 – the top layer of the leaf turns from gold to rust in sunlight; **Golden Ribbon**, 1996, pin $15, pierced earrings $15; **Victorian Rose Pin** with **Royal Crest Dangle Earrings**, 1992, pin $20, c/p earrings $15 – elaborate matte gold rose pin with three pearl teardrop accents. Earrings are a matte gold shield with three pearl teardrop dangles

Silvery Sands, 1990, bracelet $20, c/p earrings $15 – soft beige cabochon in silvery setting. Matching ring in the Ring Chapter; **Stonescape**, 1988, bracelet $25, pierced earrings $25 – bold simplicity of silver-plate with ombre jasper

Ornate Cross, 1994, pendant $15, pierced earrings $15 – gold cross with pearl accents; **Rialto**, 1991, necklace $20, c/p earrings $15 – sparkling rhinestones in amethyst or clear; **Delicate Sparkle**, 1987, $15, pierced earrings $15 – delicate gold butterfly design with pave rhinestones; **Heart Cross**, 1996, necklace $20, pierced earrings $15 – dainty cross framed in filigree heart

Bold Swirl, 1993, pin $15, clip earrings $15 – bold gold rope design with carnelian accents, very rare; **New Twist**, 1977, bracelet $15, c/p earrings $15 – copper, brass, and nickel silver wires twisted together, very rare; **Nestled Cloisonne**, 1995, bracelet $15, pierced earrings $15 – beads of genuine cloisonne combined with gold and freshwater pearls

Pearlesque Swirl, 1996, necklace $20, bracelet $15, pierced earrings $15 – 6 mm pearls with gold bow and rhinestone accents; bracelet is a double row of pearls with rhinestone rondell spacers

Teddy Bear Collection consisting of: **Cuddly Teddy Earrings**, 1991, pierced $10; **Precious Teddy Pin/Pendant**, 1992 - $15 – gold teddy bear on red satin cord; **Teddy Bear Pin**, 1989, $10 – cute little bear wrapped in red ribbon; **Front-Back Teddy Earrings**, 1998, pierced $10 – matches pin in texture and red ribbon

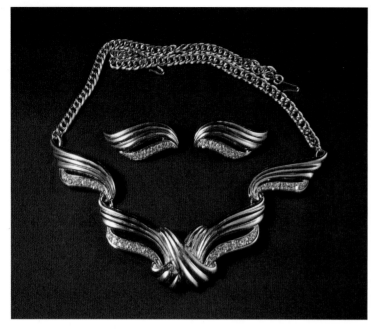

Undeniable, 1993, necklace $35, clip earrings $25 – a sweeping swirl design in gold with 2 rows of crystal stones linked to a smaller sweep of crystal stones on a wide, double-link chain. Inspired by the Billy Dee Williams Undeniable fragrance of 1991

Victorian, 1990, necklace $20, c/p earrings $15 – marquise-cut sapphire surrounded by seed pearls set in gold; **Juliette**, 1990, necklace $15, c/p earrings $15 – magnificent faceted garnet in lacy gold frame; **Evening Drama**, 1995, pendant $20, pierced earrings $15 – elegant gold ball of pave rhinestones; **Onyx Heart**, 1994, with **Genuine Onyx Ring**, 1993, necklace $20, c/p earrings $20, ring $25 – genuine onyx heart set in gold with crystal accents

Baroque Style, 1992, pin $20, c/p earrings $25 – lustrous large pearl in antique gold frame surrounded by lions and having onyx accents

Far Away, 1994, $60 – this is a complete vet of vnecklace, pierced earrings, and stickpin in blue lapis with gold accents used to promote the introduction of Avon's Far Away perfume. It was never offered for sale to the general public

Noah's Ark, 1997 pin $15, 2000 charm pin $15, 2000 bracelet $20 – antique gold boat with animals

Precious Luxury, 1996, necklace $35, c/p earrings $25 – magnificent double strand of pearls with a decorative rhinestone-burst clasp and matching earrings

Fashion Drop, 1993, bracelet $15, pierced earrings, $15 – luscious pearls with royal blue stones and gold accents.

Western Round-Up with **Western Style Earrings**, 1996 pendant $20, bracelet $15, 1995 pierced earrings, $15 – silver charm necklace of vest, hat, and boot. The bracelet is silver concho medallions, and the earrings are silver medallion or silver boot with colorful beads

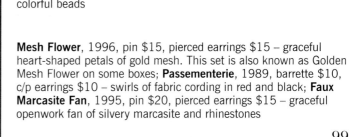

Mesh Flower, 1996, pin $15, pierced earrings $15 – graceful heart-shaped petals of gold mesh. This set is also known as Golden Mesh Flower on some boxes; **Passementerie**, 1989, barrette $10, c/p earrings $10 – swirls of fabric cording in red and black; **Faux Marcasite Fan**, 1995, pin $20, pierced earrings $15 – graceful openwork fan of silvery marcasite and rhinestones

Fashion Bead Necklace, 1993, with **Double Drop Earrings**, 1991, necklace $20, pierced earrings $15 – gray, cream and shiny gold pearls on shiny gold chain with shiny, double gold bead drop earrings

Café Society, 1994, necklace $30, c/p earrings $20 – magnificent bead set with rhinestones in black or white beads with gold accents

Sheer Style, 1990, necklace $30, c/p $15 – extremely rare triple strand of frosted plastic came in opaque pink or white

Elegant Acorn, 1994, pin $25, earrings, $15 - elegant acorn pin of gold and marcasite with the look of leaves blowing in the wind

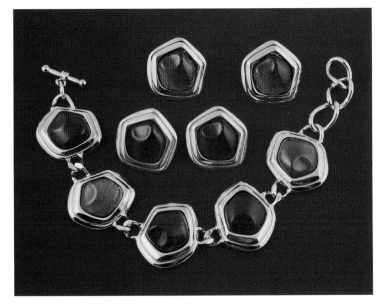

Grand Impressions, 1993, bracelet $25, c/p earrings $15 – unique gold link bracelet with earrings in amber or red

Convertible Charm Pendant and Earrings Gift Set, 1994, $25 – elephant, coin, and pearl drops in both necklace and earrings

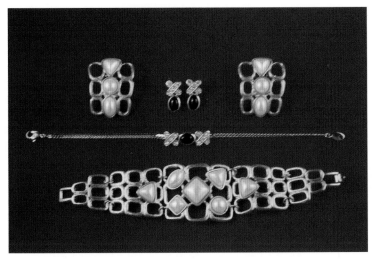

Genuine Onyx Kiss, 1995, bracelet $15, c/p earrings $15 – genuine onyx cabochon with crystal kiss accents; **Pearly Petal**, 1993, bracelet $15, c/p earrings $15 – openwork gold with multi-shaped pearls

Evangelista Pendant 1994 with **Etched Heart Earrings**; 1993, necklace $35, c/p earrings $15 – intricately crafted openwork marcasite heart with faceted aquamarine and rhinestone accents on a velvet black cord shown with dramatic puffed heart in silver or gold; **Sterling Silver Pansy**, 1987, necklace $35, pierced earrings $25 – elegant ice-gray pansy flower on black cord

Acorn Motif, 2000, pin $10, pierced earrings $10 – antique gold acorns; **Genuine Porcelain Rose**, 1994, pin $15, c/p earrings $15 – pink porcelain rose in brushed gold

Romantic Trellis Heart, 1994, pin $15, c/p earrings $15 – openwork gold heart studded with crystals; **Delicate Hues**, 1985, pierced earrings $10, stackable ring $15 – sparkling baguette stones in diamond, light sapphire, or amethyst. There was also a matching necklace with all three stones in one setting; **Victorian Spring**, 1988, pin $15, c/p earrings $15 – lustrous pink coral cabochon in a sea of seed pearls

Desert Sands, 1992, necklace $25, clip earrings $20 – brushed gold with cabochon stones in sand and brown tones. **Perusian**, 1992, necklace $25, c/p earrings $15 – epoxy enamel in white or lapis blue with gold accents

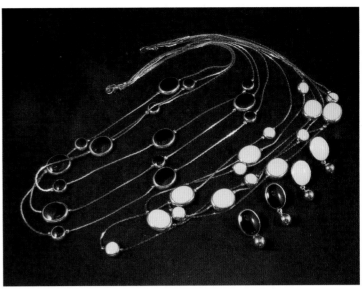

Golden Dangles, 2000, necklace $15, earrings $10 – hammered matte gold disks; **Beauty of the Nile**, 1995, necklace $25, pierced earrings $15 – polished gold bust of Cleopatra; **Starfish**, 1987, necklace $15, c/p earrings $15 – gold textured starfish

Tailored Classic, 1995, necklace $20, pierced earrings $15 – elegant 3-strand necklace with white or black glossy cabochons and earrings that dangle from a gold ball

Braided Pearly, 1996, necklace $15, bracelet $15, c/p earrings $15 – elegantly braided pearls in cream or pink

Rhinestone Accent Leaf, 2000, pin $10, c/p earrings $10 – antiqued brass finish with rhinestones; **Hearts Afire**, 1996, pin $15, c/p earrings $15 – gold with translucent red overlay, **Victoria Rose**, 1989, pin $20, c/p button earrings $15, c/p drop earrings $20 – genuine pink porcelain rose on a cream enamel background in a gold rose frame; **Tea Time Novelty**, 1997, pin $20, pierced earrings $15 – petite tea set with blue trim and porcelain rose accents on the earrings

Spectator Necklace with **Beaded Hoop Earrings**, 1996, necklace $20, pierced earrings $10 – triple twist strand mixed with black, white, and gold beads; **Gloriana**, 1974, necklace $15, clip earrings $15 – elegant pearls and rhinestones set in silver; **Cat's Eye**, 2005, drop necklace $15, stretch bracelet trio $15 – handcrafted glass cat's eye beads set in silver

Romantic Heart Necklace with **Heart Shaped Blue Earrings**, necklace, 1998, $20, c/p earrings, 1999, $20 – inspired by the Heart of the Ocean diamond necklace from the movie Titanic, set is a faceted blue crystal heart surrounded by clear crystals; **Sparkling Opalescent Drop**, 2005, necklace $25, pierced earrings $25 – extremely rare magnificent large faceted opal drop in shiny silver with sparkling opal accents

Key of Life, 1997, bangle bracelet $25, pierced earrings $20 – silver set with antiqued Greek design; **Turquoise Cuff** with **Turquoise Color Dangle Earrings**, 2005, bracelet $25, pierced earrings $15 – wonderful turquoise cabochons in burnished silver

Essential Treasures, 1994, necklace $25, c/p earrings $15 – nice heave piece of gold with jeweled stones; **Dramatic Brilliance Necklace with Mesmerize Pierced Earrings**, 1995 necklace $45, 1992 c/p earrings $20 – stunning large aquamarine stone in elaborate gold setting on velvet cord with earrings designed to match

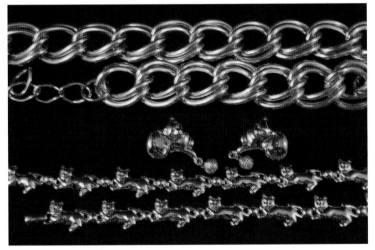

Bold Links, 1991, necklace $20, bracelet $15 – large gold interlocking links; **Purrfect Partners** with **Frolicking Feline Earrings**, 1992, necklace $20, bracelet $15, c/p earrings $15 – string of shiny golden cats. Earrings have silver ball

Sleek Texture, 1991, bracelet $20, c/p earrings $15 – bold, gold, and gorgeous with a nugget-like appearance; **Breathless**, 1987, bracelet $20, c/p earrings $15 – rich textured swirl design came in gold or silver

Precious Pretenders, 1991, pendant $20, pierced earrings $25 – diamond look-alikes in 14k gold; **Crystal Palace**, 1976, necklace $15, c/p earrings $15 – silver setting with large light blue sapphire and rhinestones accents has matching ring shown in Ring Chapter

Romantic Red Heart Pendant with Romantic Revival Pierced Earrings, 1995, pendant $25, earrings $15 – glossy openwork heart with antique gold and pearl accents. The earrings are glossy heart dangles set in gold with rhinestone accents and came in red or black; Lustrous Heart Necklace, 1991, with Lustrous Filigree Pierced Earrings, 1989, pendant $20, earrings $15 – pearlized plastic with gold and rhinestone accents

Sea Treasures, 1991, necklace $20, c/p earrings $15 – starfish inset with seed pearls; Desert Stones, 1975, necklace $20, c/p convertible earrings $15 – real agate and carnelian in gold with earrings that can be worn without drop; Captured Accents, 1987, necklace $15, pierced earrings $15 – coral or pearl beads captured in gold cage

Artful Expression, 1994, bracelet $20, pierced earrings $15 – wide gold cuff with rosy accents

Sterling Silver Opal, 1996, necklace $20, ring $25 – shimmering opal in filigree silver setting

American Glory, 1993, bangle bracelet $15, pierced earrings $10 – red, white, and blue enamel on gold metal

Heaven's Splendor, 1996, pin $15, pierced earrings $15 – gold filigree moon with star and rhinestone accents

106

Earthtone Fringe, 2003, necklace $15, pierced earrings $20 – copper tone beads with medallion in Aztec design; **American Spirit**, 1993, pin/pendant $20, c/p earrings $20 – antiqued silver with turquoise and coral cabochons in Native American design; **Violet Fashion**, 2003, pendant with rhinestone accent $20, pierced drop earrings $15 – lustrous beaded amethyst pearls with antique silver beads

Pearlesque Torsade Cameo Necklace and Cameo Button Earrings, 2002, torsade necklace $20, pierced earrings $15 – beaded torsade with cameo and gold accents

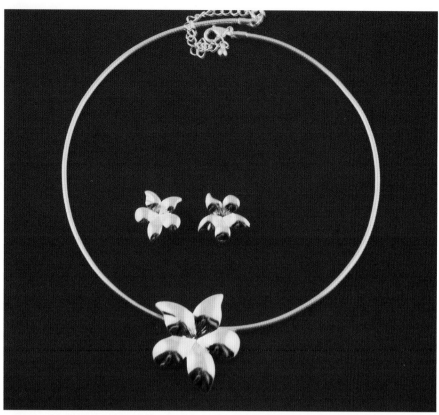

Polished Flower, 2005, omega necklace
$20, c/p button earrings $15 – polished
silver hibiscus blossoms

Tonal Burgundy, 2001, necklace $30,
c/p earrings $15 – multi-strand faceted
beads in ruby and garnet with ruby
rhinestones and enamel filigree earrings.

Goldtone Omega with Graduated Textured Design, 2001, necklace $20, earrings $15 – chic gold textured design goes well with everything

Genuine Tiger's Eye Accented, 2005, necklace $20, pierced chandelier earrings $15 – faceted tiger's eye drops in brass finish

Link Necklace with Oval Color, 2003, necklace $20, c/p earrings $15 – antique silver with blue marbleized stone; **Casual Heart Necklace**, 2004, with **Two-Tone Heart Earrings**, 2001, necklace $20, c/p earrings $15 – gold heart in antique silver frame on black cord

Textured Two-Tone Pave, 2004, necklace $20, earrings $20 – rhinestones set in gold with silver accents; **Sparkle Kiss**, 1992 necklace $15, 1988 pierced earrings $15 – this is a classic example of Avon taking several years to complete a set. There was a matching bracelet in 1988 and the 1988 matching ring is shown in the Ring Chapter. All pieces have a glamorous gold kiss studded with rhinestones, and the necklace and bracelet also included solid gold kisses on either side of the rhinestone kiss; **Cocktail**, 1989, necklace $15, c/p earrings $15 – dazzling waterfall of sparkling rhinestones. There is also a matching gold wire bangle bracelet; **Jewelesque Pastels**, 1991, necklace $15, c/p earrings $15 – gold open-work design entwines around amethyst, rose quartz, and crystal accents

Tonal Blue Floral, 2002, necklace $15, c/p drop earrings, $15 – burnished brass with pearlized and color accents

Sparkling Rose Color Drop, 2004, necklace $20, pierced earrings $15 – hand cut rose crystals with iridescent rose beads in silver; **Casbah Style**, 1993, necklace $40, pierced earrings $30 – magnificent spice-colored beads in gold setting, extremely rare; **Casual Necklace and Drop Earrings with Garnet Colored Accents**, 2003, necklace $15, c/p earrings, $15 – magnificent silver and garnet set with gold beading

Turquoise and Red Color, 2002, multi-strand floret pendant necklace $20, c/p floret drop earrings $15 – stunning multi-strand of turquoise and coral beads with removable pendant; **Parisian Impression**, 1987, chain necklace $20, pin $15, c/p earrings $15 – gold chain with deep gray pearls with gold bead accents having earrings and a pin with a center gray pearl surrounded with shiny and textured gold petals. This set also came with a 46-inch gray pearl or cream pearl necklace. The cream pearls are shown in the Necklace chapter; **Beaded Ropetwist**, 1989, necklace $15, pierced earrings, $10 – gold chain with garnet or black beads

Bold Color Nugget, 2001, necklace $20, pierced earrings $15 – large gem nuggets set in gold

Colors and Shapes, 2004, necklace $15, pierced earrings $15 – magnificent faceted aquamarine rectangle stone or topaz triangle stone set in sliver; **Color Pear with Luminous Accents**, 2005, necklace $15, pierced earrings $15 – bold pear-shaped amethyst stone in silver with rhinestone accents

Medallion on Velvet Cord Necklace with **Double Hoop Earrings with Beaded Accents**, 2006, necklace $15 – pierced earrings $15 – shiny gold set with faceted red crystal accents

Mediterranean Blue Multistrand, 2004, necklace $20, pierced earrings $15 – 4-strands of exotic ocean blue, clear, and gold beads with a magnificent gold center medallion pendant having an intricate cut-out design

112

Blue Cat's Eye and Silvertone Beaded, 2003, necklace $20, pierced earrings $15 – magnificent exotic lapis blue beads having dangling silver accents with the same exotic blue bead compliment – a truly dramatic ensemble.

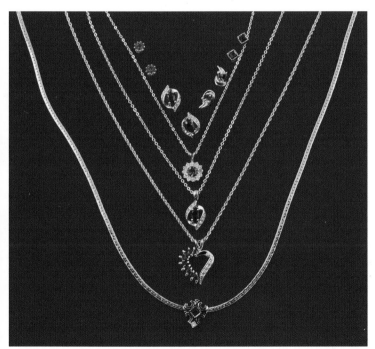

Simulated Birthstone Sparkle Gift Set, 1987, $15 – birthstone pendant surrounded by clear rhinestones with birthstone earrings; **Oval Birthstone Necklace and Earring Gift Set**, 2004, $15 – birthstones set in gold; **Goldtone Birthstone Heart Necklace and Earring Gift Set**, 2004, $15 – dramatic golden heart with birthstones; **Treasured Memories Gift Set**, 1991, $15 – ruby and sparkling crystal set in antique gold, not a birthstone series

Pink Rose Drop Gift Set, 2004, $20 – delicate necklace and earrings drop set with tiny pink rose accent; **Open Prize**, 2003, necklace $20, bracelet $10, pierced earrings $15 – look of real diamonds shimmer in shiny silver setting

Pearlesque Pastel Necklace and Earrings Gift Set, 2003, $20 – pastel pearls

Rhinestone Necklace and Earrings Gift Set, 2000, $40 – magnificent lace collar with sparkling rhinestone drops in shiny silver setting

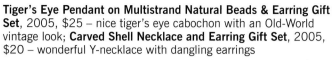

Tiger's Eye Pendant on Multistrand Natural Beads & Earring Gift Set, 2005, $25 – nice tiger's eye cabochon with an Old-World vintage look; Carved Shell Necklace and Earring Gift Set, 2005, $20 – wonderful Y-necklace with dangling earrings

Pearlesque Twist Gift Set, 1990, $25 – matching 8mm pearls braided into a necklace with matching stud earrings

Rhinestone Butterfly with Pearlesque Drop Gift Set, 2004, $20 – silver filigree butterfly pendant and earrings with pearl teardrop; Key of Life Gift Set with Rhinestone Accents, 2002, $20 – gold necklace and bracelet with rhinestone spacers and matching earrings; Bezel Set CZ Two Piece Gift Set, 2004, $15 – round rhinestone pendant and earrings in gold; Blooming Rose Gift Set, 2005, $15 – blue or pink rose pendant and earrings in silver

Pearlesque Teardrop Gift Set, 2000, $20 – lustrous teardrop pearl pendant with rhinestone accents having matching rhinestone earrings; **Pearlesque and Crystal Gift Set**, 2002, $20 – pearl and crystal pendant and earrings in silver; **Sparkling Crystal V-Shaped Necklace & Hoop Earrings Gift Set**, 2003, $15 – collar necklace studded in light rose or clear crystals with matching earrings

Summer Friends Gift Set, 2002, $15 – butterfly, ladybug, and dragonfly charm necklace on silver bead chain with matching ladybug earrings; **Rhinestone Ice Floral Vine Necklace & Earrings Gift Set**, 2002, $20 – collar necklace of sparkling rhinestones; **Silvertone Pearlesque and Rhinestone Bow Gift Set** aka Elegant Pearlesque and Rhinestone Bow Gift Set, 2001, $35 – magnificently elegant rhinestone bows necklace and earrings with pearl accents

Flower Collar Necklace and Earring Gift Set, 2005, $15 – red and pink rhinestone flowers in burnished brass; **Red Roses Necklace and Earring Gift Set**, 2002, $20 – bright red roses on burnished brass

Springtime Dangling Anklet and Ring Duo Gift Set, 2002, $10 – came in blue or pink crystal drops on antique silver bead chain

Golden Pearlesque Gift Set, 1996, $20 – magnificent large pearl pendant and earrings set in gleaming gold; **Rhinestone Cluster Necklace and Earring Gift Set**, 2003, $20 – sparkling rhinestones in traditional 3-prong design on gleaming gold; **Goldtone Heart and Pearlesque Drop Gift Set**, 2003, $35 – elegant necklace and earrings of tiny gleaming gold hearts with pearl dangles

Goldtone Cross and Crystal Necklace and Earring Gift Set, 2002, $20 – shiny gold crosses dangle from a gleaming gold chain

Turquoise Color Triple Strand Gift Set, 2005, $40 – magnificent turquoise strands with lever-back earrings; **Turquoise Color Cabochon Necklace and Earring Gift Set**, 2005, $25 – elegant Victorian design

Pearlesque Birthstone Gift Set, 1997, $15 – all birthstones available with pearls and sparkling crystals; **Reversible Faux Pearl Gift Set**, 1998, $20 – pearl clasp reverses to rhinestones and matching pearl earrings have rhinestone accents; **Tailored Elegance Gift Set**, 1995, $20 – double strand of pearls with either clear or amethyst rhinestone clasp and earrings.

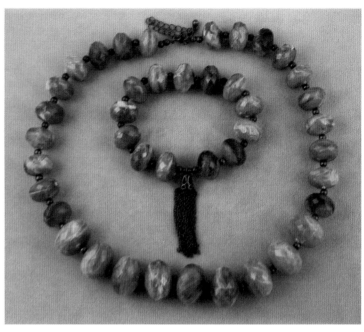

Turquoise Color Medallion Gift Set, 2005, $20 – pendant and earrings with a Native American look; **Turquoise Color Beaded Long Necklace & Earrings Gift Set**, 2005, $40 – long beaded strand of various turquoise colors

Chunky Beaded, 2006, necklace $20, stretch bracelet $15 – large, abstract beads with antique gold spacers came in topaz or amethyst, no matching earrings

Flower Blossom Gift Set, 1993, $20 – large gold filigree pin and earrings with pearl centers; **Colorful Daisy Pin and Earrings Gift Set**, 2005, $15 – bright shades of pink or yellow flower head; **Bold Starring**, 1997, pin $30, pierced earrings $25 – gold setting with pave rhinestone. This set was designed for the introduction of Avon's Starring perfume; **Heart Pin and Earrings Birthstone Gift Set**, 1996, $15 – nice openwork heart with birthstone accent and matching birthstone stud earrings; **Rosette Luster Gift Set**, 1991, $15 – lustrous pearl stick pin with gold leaves and matching leaf earrings

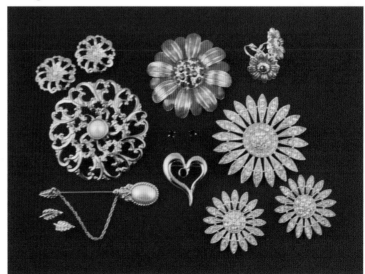

Topaz Color 'Y' Necklace Giftset, 2006, $20 – chandelier y-drape of brilliant topaz stones on burnished brass chain with matching stone earrings; **Decorative Seafoam Pendant Giftset**, 2006, $25 – elegant sea green stones with large sea green center drop and gold shield on silver chain with matching sea green earrings

Textured Collar Necklace and Earrings Gift Set, 2002, $20 – brown moonstone in antique gold setting or blue moonstone in antique silver setting with matching earrings; **Carnelian Color Charm Drop Gift Set**, 2003, $30 – gorgeous carnelian and antique silver charms on beaded necklace with matching earrings

Silvertone and Blue Fashion Y Gift Set, 2005, $15 – blue moonstone with silver accents necklace and earrings; **Scarlet Y Gift Set**, 2004, $15 – red bead Y necklace and earrings

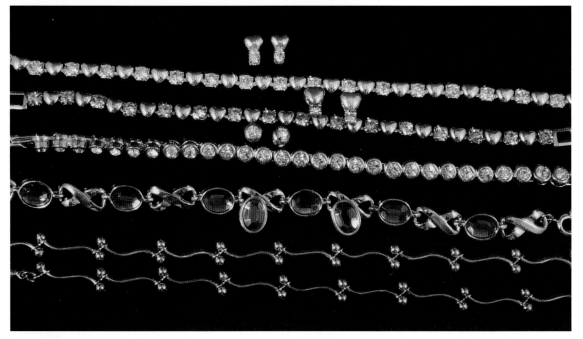

Rhinestone Heart Bracelet and Earring Gift Set, 2003, $15, clear or pink rhinestones alternate with silver heart, both shown; **Sparkling Crystal Tennis Bracelet and Earring Gift Set**, 2002, $15 – traditional tennis bracelet in gold; **Elegant Gift Set**, 1994, $15 – amethyst and gold bracelet having matching amethyst earrings; **Goldtone Vine Necklace & Bracelet Gift Set**, 2000, $15 – vine design in gleaming gold

Vintage Gift Set, 2004, $20 – traditional earthtone colors in vintage-look necklace and earrings;
Rhinestone Pearlesque Vine Necklace and Earring Gift Set, 2005, $20 – rhinestone Y necklace with pearl accents and matching earrings

Multi-Strand Turquoise Color Giftset, 2005, $30 – magnificent 3-strand turquoise beads accented with elaborately detailed antique silver bead spacers

Hibiscus Flower Gift Set, 2007, $20 each – colorful "y" necklace and leverback pierced earring set in ocean or sunset colors

Heirloom Medallion, 2007, necklace $15, pierced earrings $10 – topaz studded medallion in burnished bronze with matching hoop earrings; **Multicolor Shell Giftset**, 2007, $20 – delicate shells in rainbow colors on a multi-strand tan cord with long dangling pierced earrings on silver chain.

Lucky Clover Earrings, 1993, c/p, $10 – green enamel shamrocks; **Porcelain Shamrock Earrings**, 1996, c/p, $15 – white porcelain cabochon decorated with lucky shamrock; **Hats Off to Luck Pin**, 1994, $10 – lucky leprechaun hat in gold with transparent green shamrock overlay and rhinestone accent; **Leprechaun Pin**, 1996, $10 – golden leprechaun with green accents dancing an Irish jig

Pear Shaped Birthstone 3 Piece Set, 2004, $20 – silver necklace, bracelet, and pierced earrings with large pear-shaped birthstone. Shown is March; **Colorful Flower Necklace and Earring Giftset**, 2005, $15 – multi-color daisy flowers in silver with matching pierced earrings; **Silvertone and Blue Casual Giftset**, 2004, $20 – necklace and earrings in blue moonstones with antique silver accents

Refined Wreaths, 1992, pin $15, c/p earrings $15 – traditional gold wreath studded with gemstones; **Signature Style**, 1989, pin $15, c/p, $15 – gold or silver filigree crest; **Rhinestone Bunny** with **Precious Bunny Earrings**, 1993 pin $15, 1998 pierced earrings $15 – rhinestone studded bunny pin with gold bunny earrings holding crystal egg

White Christmas, 1987, pin $15, c/p earrings $15 – white poinsettias with gold accents. The pin doubles as a pendant; **Pearly Bunny**, 1994 pin $15, 1995 c/p earrings $10 – gold bunny pin studded with seed pearls having flop-ear bunny earrings with pearl body and gold head; **Jack O'Lantern**, 1990, pin $20, pierced earrings $15 – extremely rare shiny gold pumpkin with cut-out face

Festive Holiday, 2002, pin $10, pierced earrings $10 – gold bells with glitter and enamel accents; **Glistening Snowflake**, 1988, necklace $15, c/p earrings $15 – finely detailed snowflake with rhinestone accent

Mr. Snowman, necklace 1980 $15, pierced earrings 1992, $10 – snowman of frosted plastic with painted face and mittens with gold accents: **Angel Birthstovne**, 1995, necklace $10 – pierced earrings $10 – gold angel with birthstone

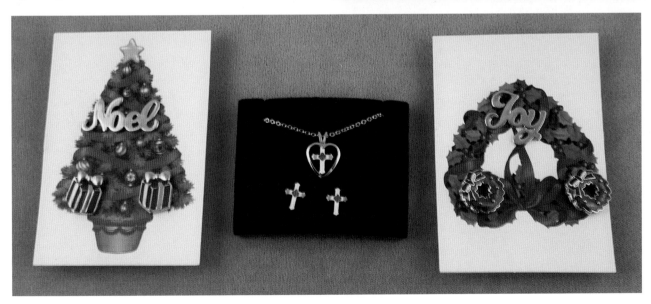

Noel Pin and Present Earring Bundle, 1999, $10 – colorful glazed gold with choice of c/p earrings; **Goldtone Heart with Cross Giftset**, 2000, $15 – colorfully glazed cross with pierced earrings; **Joy and Holly Earring Bundle**, 1999, $10 – colorful glazed gold with choice of c/p earrings

Snowflake, necklace (1982), $15, c/p earrings (1978), $15 – Avon made the earrings first in shiny silver or gold and then made the shiny silver pendant in 1982

Holiday Colors, 1996, pin $20, pierced earrings, $15 – gold cross shape with pearls and emeralds surrounding ruby center; **Rich Christmas**, 1993, pin $20, c/p earrings $15 – gold flower with pearl, ruby, and emerald accents

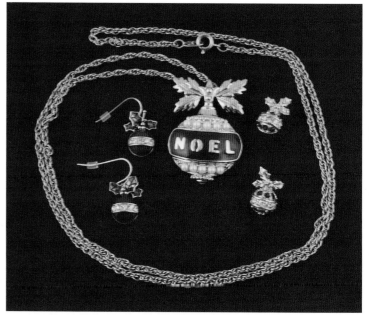

Ornament Earrings, 2006, $15; **Joyous Noel Necklace**, 1994, $15; **Sparkling Christmas Ornament Earrings**, 1993, pierced $15 – colorful Christmas ornament with crystal accents

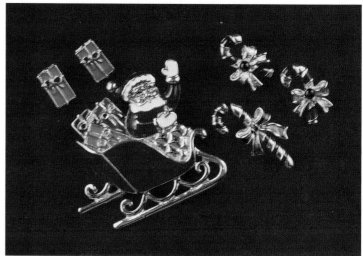

Sleigh Ride Surprise Pin and Pierced Earrings, 1996, $20 – colorful Santa in his sleigh and two of the packages detach to make earrings; **Candy Cane Pin** with **Holidays Pierced Earrings,** pin 1986 $15, pierced cane earrings 1996 $15 – these candy canes were made 10 years apart, but they go together beautifully as a set

Chapter Three
Necklaces

Avon made a variety of necklaces in a variety of materials. Most important for the pendants were the chains. The links came in a great variety of styles, including square, oval, flat, twisted, cable, and rope, and varied in shape from oval, round, square, and octagon. Some were sterling silver and karat gold, but the vast majority were non-tarnishing goldtone or silvertone, generic terms meaning jewelry with the look and feel of real gold or silver but which have no gold or silver content. A single-strand necklace, which fit snuggly around the throat, was called a choker. The single strand could be made of pearls, gems, beads, or even incorporate material such as rope or velvet to which Avon added elaborate pendants, many of them with the ability to be worn off-center. The dog collar choker could embrace the throat higher up than the simple choker and have row upon row of beads and stones cascading down to an elaborate center pendant that rested at the apex of the collarbone. Many of the clasps were the simple "spring ring," a tiny circle with a push-pin on a spring which opens and springs shut for closure, but Avon also used the "ball and chain" on many of the chokers for adjustment, the "rolled barrel" on the plastic pieces, and the newer version of the spring ring called a "lobster claw" on the gift sets. Plastic is a term applied to a group of synthetic chemical products which can be molded, carved, or pressed into many shapes and sizes, incorporating the looks of tortoise, turquoise, mother-of-pearl, marble, jet, coral, ivory, amber, agate, wood, and many other naturally occurring materials. Avon uses synthetic gems and pearls in most of the jewelry, and the term generally means a speeded-up way for man to duplicate the natural process, such as the cultured pearl, which is produced by man introducing an unnatural irritation within the oyster's shell.

Perfume Pendant, 1972, $30 – gold shell with pearl accent can be filled with perfume; **Tulip Perfume Pendant**, 1970, $30 - can be filled with perfume; **Golden Charmer Glace Necklace**, 1968, $30 – opens to accept a solid perfume compact; **Golden Moments Perfume Necklace**, 1971, $30 – antiqued brass pendant with the look of a Victorian timepiece can be filled with perfume

Multi-Strand Convertible Necklace/Bracelet, 1972, $25 – silver multi-chain set can be worn as one piece or separated into a necklace and bracelet

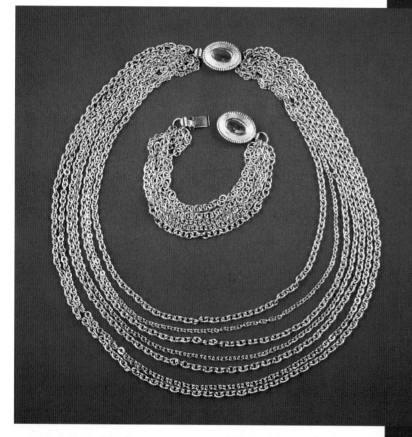

Convertible Creation Necklace/Bracelet/Belt, 1972, $35 – multi-chain with gold openwork balls and dangling chain accents

Abbey Pendant Necklace, 1975, $20 – large gold filigree cross with ruby accent; **Juliet Cross**, 1975, $20 – large gothic cross design in ivory or jade with gold accents; **Queen Anne's Lace Pendant Necklace**, 1974, $25 – large gold openwork pendant with large pink cabochon center and small pink and pearl accents; **Juliet Cross** in jade; **Autumn Glory Convertible Necklace**, 1973, $25 – large gold leaf with pearl acorns converts to a pin

Romanesque Necklace, 1972, $25 – silver filigree cross with stones of turquoise, lapis, jade, and carnelian surrounding a hematite center; **Ovalesque Pendant Necklace**, 1973, $25 – unique gold pendant with chain accents; **Ebony Teardrop Pendant Necklace**, 1974, $25 – jet black teardrop in silver; **Granada Pendant Necklace**, 1973, $25 – large ruby stone with double gold chain; **Ming Green Adjustable Necklace**, 1973, $35 – jade medallion slides on golden ball chain

Contempora Pendant Necklace, 1976, $35 – silver pendant with turquoise accents on brown cord; **Medallion Necklace**, 1974, $25 – large antique silver pendant with teardrop pearl accent; **Contempora Convertible Necklace/Pin**, 1972, $30 – white pendant with chain dangles can be worn as a pin

Purple Pendant Necklace, 1972, $30 – large amethyst stone surrounded by seed pearls on gold chain with tassel; **Town and Country Pendant Necklace**, 1974, $25 – tortoiseshell loops with gold loop; **Owl Pendant Necklace**, 1974, $25 – articulated gold owl

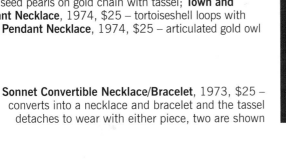

Sonnet Convertible Necklace/Bracelet, 1973, $25 – converts into a necklace and bracelet and the tassel detaches to wear with either piece, two are shown

Magnifying Glass Pendant, 1976, $35, traditional lorgnette magnifying glass; **Graceful Swan Magnifying Glass Pendant**, 1994, $35, gold pendant with swan motif; **Magnificent Magnifying Glass Pendant**, 1996, $35 – silver pendant with porcelain rose accent; **Angel Magnifying Glass Pendant**, 1997, $35, gold pendant with angel accent; **Apple Magnifying Glass Pendant**, 1992, $35, gold apple shape with gold leaves accent

Bicentennial Pendant, 1976, $45 – reversible large gold coin rimmed in gold rope frame in honor of America's birthday

Bengal Tiger Neckchain, 1979, $15 – ivory scrimshaw; **Anchor Pendant Neckchain**, 1978, $15 – reversible anchor is faceted on one side and smooth on the other; **Arrowhead Pendant Neckchain**, 1977, $15 – silver arrowhead with brass accents; **Adventure Pendant Neckchain**, 1979, $15 – large ivory tooth; **Wild Mustang Pendant Neckchain**, 1980, $15, silver galloping horse; **Infinity Symbol Neckchain**, 1978, $15 – pewter symbol with gold accents; **Roman Coin Pendant Neckchain**, 1980, $20 – reversible coin of antiqued gold faithfully reproduces a Roman Republic coin circa 211-209 BC; **Ankh Pendant Neckchain**, 1977, $15 – good luck pendant in silver with gold center; **American Buffalo Pendant Neckchain**, 1980, $15 – antique finish pewter; **Western Boot Pendant Neckchain**, 1979, $15 – highly detailed western boot with spur in gold or silver

Natural Wood Pendant Neckchain, 1979, $20 – real wood against a silver gleam; **Wild Country Pendant Neckchain**, 1978, $15 – pewter bull's head with ivory horns; **Eagle Pendant Neckchain**, 1978, $15 – gold or pewter dimensional eagle; **The Angler's Pendant**, 1982, $20 – 3-dimensional pewter fish design mounted on genuine wood; **Tomahawk Pendant Neckchain**, 1978, $15 – silver pendant with brass accent; **Genuine Tiger's Eye Arrowhead Pendant**, 1981, $25 – dimensional arrowhead; **Lucky Horn Neckchain**, 1981, $15, silver or gold

Winning Combination Pendant Neckchain, 1979, $15 – stationary combination lock; **Skateboard Pendant Neckchain**, 1979, $15 – colorful decal striped board with no-roll wheels; **Perfect Catch Pendant Neckchain**, 1981, $15 – pewter glove and brass ball; **Galactic Robot Pendant Neckchain**, 1979, $15 – silver robot with enamel accents; **Touchdown Pendant Neckchain**, 1981, $15 – brass-plated football; **Command Module 1 Pendant Neckchain**, 1980, $15 – silver rocket; **Fast Track Pendant Neckchain**, 1979, $15 – pewter running shoe

Tender Butterfly Ceramic Pendant, 1979, $25 – white ceramic pendant with butterfly hand-painted in Brazil; **Haiku Awakenings**, 2003, $20 – ceramic pendant on brown cord; **Tender Blossoms Ceramic Pendant**, 1977, $25 – white ceramic pendant with hibiscus flower hand-painted in Brazil

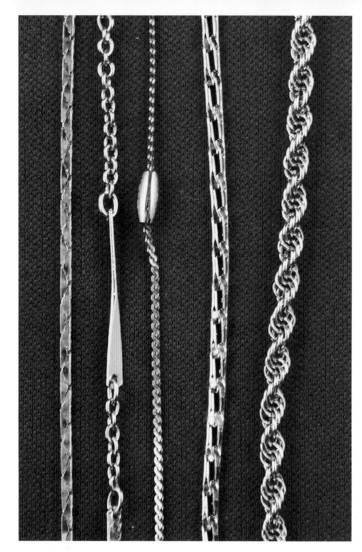

Ribbons and Roses, 1982, $10 – three grosgrain ribbons with three detailed plastic roses in mother of pearl, pink, and blue; **Script Initial Pendant**, 1992, $20 – big gleaming gold pendant in all letters of the alphabet except QUWXYZ, add your own chain

Sterling Silver Cobra Neckchain, 1982, $30 – highly polished cobra links; **Chainfall Necklace**, 1977, $10 – wonderful blend of chain and shiny bar came in gold or silver in 22-inches or 24-inches; **Silken Bead Necklace**, 1980, $10 – 5 oval beads on simple chain came in gold or silver and had a matching bracelet; **Esquire Sterling Silver Neckchain**, 1981, $30 – nice open-link chain; **Sterling Silver Ropechain**, 1984, $30 – traditional rope

Gilded Circles Pendant Necklace, 1977, $15 – interlocking circles of gold; **Versatile Links Convertible Necklace/Bracelet**, 1978, $20 – bracelet section detaches from necklace to be worn separately; **Lace Medallion Necklace**, 1975, $15 – shiny filigree medallions; **Goldtone Textured Double Rope Necklace**, 2001, $15 – shiny gold textured rope with knot stations

Birds of Nature, 1982, $35 – genuine porcelain set in gold, representing the Four Seasons, and inscribed on the back. Hummingbird – Summer Hummingbird; Robin – Welcoming of Spring; Pheasant – The Rich Splendor of Fall; Cardinal – Crimson Crest

Initial Charmholder Necklace, 1981, necklace $20, charm $5 each – every letter of the alphabet except QUWXYZ. Charms: Roller Skate, Running Shoe, Bicycle, #1, Star, Birthstone Heart, Bowling Pins, Clover, Tennis Racket, Boy Silhouette, Girl Silhouette

Floral Heritage Necklace, 1980, $30 – genuine porcelain pendant framed in gold and fashioned on a fine gold chain, extremely rare: From L-R, top to bottom: January carnation, February violet, March daffodil, April sweet pea, May lily of the valley, June rose, July larkspur, August gladiolus, September aster, October marigold, November chrysanthemum, December narcissus

Crystalique Necklace, 1976, $15 – simple silver chain lariat with sparkling crystal drops; **Genuine Lead Crystal Tree of Life Commemorative Pendant**, 1981, $40 – genuine lead crystal etched with a great tree; **Lead Crystal Bead Necklace**, 1977, $20 – lead crystal bead stations on silver chain; **Pearlesque Accent Necklace**, 1994, $30 – single strand of marcasite and pearls

Both sides of these reversible pendants are shown: **Reversible Cameo Pendant Necklace**, 1974, $35 – traditional cameo on brown background reverses to gold floral design; **Heirloom Riches Pendant**, 1993, $35 – pearl on one side and marcasite ray burst on the other; **Solid Perfume Locket**, 1966, $35 – solid perfume compact came in gold with topaz stone or silver with onyx stone; **Golden Moments Perfume Necklace**, 1971, $35 – antiqued brass with the look of a Victorian timepiece on one side and floral design on the other; **Black and White Reversible Pendant**, 1996, $25 – gold with black bead on one side and white bead on the other

Unforgettable Locket, 1981, $25 – silver keepsake locket to hold two tiny photos, shown is the Canadian version called Precious Memories; **Tender Touches Locket**, 1990, $25 – gold keepsake locket; **Sweet Violets Locket**, 1973, $25 – floral motif medallion surrounded by gold and seed pearls; **Floralpoint Locket Necklace**, 1977, $35 – large genuine machine-stitched petit point in gold frame; **Yesteryear Picture Locket**, 1973, $25 – gold filigree locket with lapis stone; **Victorian Locket Necklace**, 1975, $35 – large topaz stone in gold filigree; **Special Memories Locket**, 1993, $35 – gold locket with coral cabochon; **Treasured Moments Locket**, 1987, $35 – delicate filigree gold heart with pearl accent

Antique Style Initial Pendant, 1989, $15 – marcasite initial in antique silver; **Circle Necklace**, 2006, $15 – tiny circle studded with rhinestones on silver chain came in several colors; **Class of '78 Pendant**, 1977, $10 – silver school year drop on a silver chain; **Collector's Locket**, 1982, $25 – see-through locket with silk flower can be used to hold favorite sentiment; **Flip-Flop Necklace with Rhinestone Accents**, 2003, $10 – silver sandal in blue enamel also came in several other colors to compliment your summer wardrobe; **Heartfelt Sentiment Necklace**, 1989, $15 – in silver or gold and has the word Love inscribed on one side; **Sterling Silver Jade Elephant Necklace**, 2002, $30 – hand-carved genuine jade with sterling silver overlay; **Wishbone**, 1982, $15 – traditional wishbone design came in silver or gold

Darling Ducklings Necklace, 1979, $15 – gold mother duck and 3 babies all in a row; **Braided Sparkle Necklace**, 1990, $15 – rich gold choker with rhinestone accents; **Porcelain Rose Garden Necklace**, 1992, $20 – genuine porcelain rose with shiny glaze and antiqued gold setting; **Fashion Bow Necklace**, 1979, $10 – bow-tied golden beauty; **Shy Butterfly Necklace**, 1978, necklace $15 – blue and green enamel butterfly, matching ring in the Ring Chapter; **Heart Charmers Necklace**, 1986, $10 – cotton candy colored hearts on plastic bead necklace

Imari Simulated Pearls, 1985, $25 each – came in Sweet Cream, French Gray, Wild Rose, Soft Black, and Lustrous Peach. They are shown twisted together into a torsade and held with the **Imari Clasp**, 1985, $5

Romantic Blush Choker, 1983, $15 – pearl necklace with coral bead accent; Genunine Freshwater Pearl Necklace, 1996, $15 – twisted rope of pearls; Versatile Elegance Faux Pearl Necklace, 1989, $15 – classic pearl necklace came in gray (shown) or peach; Pearlustre Necklace, 1985, $25 – 8 mm pearls with gold clasp came in cream (shown) or gray and various lengths; Parisian Impressions Pearlesque Necklace, 1987, $25 – 40-inches of lustrous pearls can be worn a variety of ways, shown doubled in the photo

Petite Bow Necklace, 1981, $10 – pearl with gold bow; Treasured Friends Pendant, 1981, $15 each – gold whale, owl or rhino (not shown); Birthstone Bows Necklace, 1991, $10 – gold bow with birthstone accent; Put on the Dog Pendant Necklace, 1976, $20 – extremely rare hot dog in gold bun; From Teddy with Love Necklace, 1990, $15 – gold bear with red heart

Dancing Ballerina Pendant, 1977, $15 – gold dancer with moveable arms and legs; Swing Sweetly Pendant Necklace, 1978; $15 – little girl with bow in her hair sits in her favorite swing; Flopsy Pendant Necklace, 1976, $15 – gold bunny with moveable ears; Playful Angel Pendant, 1978, $10 – shiny gold angel with moveable wings and foot

Cameo Pin/Pendant, 1984, $20 – classic cameo of ivory and onyx with rhinestone accent; **Key to My Heart Pendant Necklace**, 1976, $25 – alabaster heart with gold key; **Romantic Elegance Necklace**, 1992, $20 – gold frames ivory enamel with pearl; **Bold Traditions Necklace**, 1993, $25 – intricate design with rhinestones, dangling pearl, and a large sapphire center

Nantucket Necklace, 1984, $15 – glamorous ribbed white beads with gold spacers on gold chain. This piece also has matching ribbed button c/p earrings; **Renaissance Beauty Necklace**, 1987, $20 – sapphire blue or amethyst beads; **Rope Twist Necklace**, 1972, $15 – twisted turquoise bead and gold chain torsade; **Shimmering Strands Necklace**, 1989, $25 – 3 strands of satin beads in metallic copper/brown or metallic blue/hematite

Personalized Calendar Pendant, 1983 - $15 – gold monthly calendar with a genuine birthstone to add for the day of birth; **Genuine Wrapped Quartz Necklace**, 1994, $20 – large lavender quartz wrapped in gold; **Silhouette Pendant Necklace**, 1975, $35 – elegant gold oval Greek cameo pendant with onyx frame; **Starblaze Pendant Necklace**, 1975, $25 – faceted plastic pendant on silver chain; **Goddess Diana Pendant Necklace**, 1973, $30 – Goddess Diana etched and frosted in a glass oval set in a silver braid border; **Queen's Ransom Pill Box/Charm Necklace**, 1974, $35 – gold pirate's treasure box with ivory, turquoise, emerald, and ruby stones; **Capture Your Heart Pendant**, 1993, $20 – gold open-work heart holds 3 pearls; **Crystal Apple Pendant Necklace**, 1978, $30 – genuine lead crystal apple with gold leaves; **Victorian Style Heart Necklace**, 1995, $20 – porcelain rose set in gold with pearls

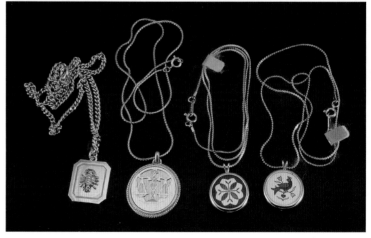

Zodiac Pendant, 1983, $15 – gold Zodiac motif on silver plaque; **Star Gazer Zodiac Pendant**, 1981, $15 – silver sign set in gold frame; **Country Signs Pendant** – Friendship, Bird of Happiness, 1982, $25 each – fine porcelain set in gold also came in Love & Romance pendant

Golden Swirl Necklace, 1991, $20 – classic swirl of shiny gold; **Finishing Touch**, 1979, $15 – alternating shiny and textured swirls came in gold or silver; **French Ropetwist Necklace**, 1985, $15; traditional rope; **Bold Connection Neck Chain**, 1986, $20 – large link rope; **Great Lengths Necklace**, 1976, $15-$25 – versatile chain came in 28, 32, and 36-inches, all 3 are shown

Hearts in Motion Necklace, 1984, $15 – unique necklace that can be worn closed as a pendant or open as a choker to reveal four hearts in a row

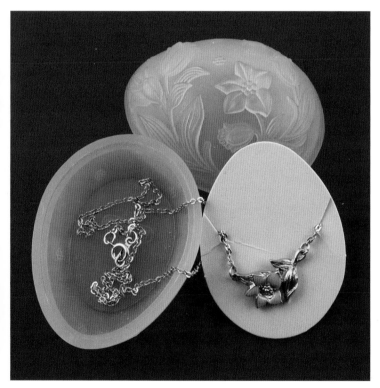

Lilac Treasures Box and Pendant, 1985, $15 – dainty orchid blossom on gold chain in plastic lilac egg box

Nugget Treasure Necklace, 1988, $20 – glass beads in agate colors; **Moroccan Necklace**, 1990, $35 – cool blue with antiqued silver accents or warm amber with antiqued gold accents; **Modern Art Necklace**, 1986, $25 – black or white abstract beads; **Indian Summer Naturals Necklace**, 1985, $30 – simulated old ivory, blue, and brown beads with gold.

Pleated Crescent Necklace, 1984, $15 – polished and textured gold; **Soft Sculpture Necklace**, 1987, $15 – soft sculptured center accent on flat chain in gold or silver; **Ghana Inspired Necklace**, 1993, $35 – elegant gold swirl medallions; **Alexandria Necklace**, 1985, $70 – richly embossed design with 18k gold electroplate finish

Variations Reversible Pendant Necklace, 1976, $25 – Avon's first sleek-looking, choker-length neck wire with reversible ivory and gold pendant; **Victorian Romance Porcelain Necklace**, 1993, $25 – genuine porcelain pendant on a pearl strand; **Sable Touch Bead Necklace**, 1981, $35 – rich black onyx beads; **Soft Sophisticate Necklace**, 1989, $20 – amethyst or clear plastic beads

Venetian Touch Necklace, 1986, $20 – gold chain with sapphires and pearls; **Faux Pearl Whisper Necklace**, 1986, $20 – cream or gray pearls set in gold; **Pearlized Cluster Necklace**, 1984, $20 – lustrous seed pearls on gold chain; **Easy Elegance Necklace**, 1991, $20 – large link gold chain with pearl or lapis beads

Royal Impression Pendant Necklace, 1980, $20 – satiny royal blue pendant framed in gold with delicate filigree and rhinestone accents; **Sweet Memories Pin/Pendant**, 1992, $15 – gold pin/pendant with epoxy enamel and rhinestones; **Easter Egg Pendant**, 1988, $20 – royal blue enamel with gold overlay; **Sea Turtle Pendant**, 1992, $35 – rich green-shell turtle on gold chain; **Plume Pendant**; 1996, $20 – silvery bird swings within a gilded cage; **Winter Wonderland Pendant**, 1982, $25 – a 3-dimensional effect using 3 different metallic shades, inscribed "Country Christmas 1982" on the back; **Cloisonné Pendant**, 1982, $25 – elegant genuine cloisonné framed in gold

Sparkling Initial Pendant, 1987, $15 – came in every letter except QUWXYZ; **Captured Heart Necklace**, 1980, $15 – two hearts linked together for a lariat look; **Birthstone Sparkle Pendant**, 1985, $15 – large birthstone surrounded by rhinestones; **Faux Amethyst Collection Necklace**, 1995, $25 – amethyst set against swirls of gold with pave rhinestones, matching ring in Ring Chapter; **Add-A-Birthstone Necklace**, 1984, $15 – gold chain came with one love knot birthstone charm. Extra birthstone charms sold separately at $5 each; **Baroque Accent Pendant**, 1991, $15 – pearl with rhinestone accent in a free-form gold setting; **Whispering Leaves Pendant Necklace**, 1979, $15 – gold pendant with tiny pearl accents; **Class of '79 Pendant**, 1978, $10 – school year pendant on gold chain; **Rose Gold Colored Heart Necklace**, 2000, $15 – rhinestone-studded heart; **Pearly Cherub Pendant**, 1997, $15 – matte gold cherub draping a large pearl representing Earth; **Sparkling Angel Pendant**, 1995, $15 – lightly antiqued gold with a faceted iridescent drop; **Sparkling Kitty Pendant**, 1994, $20 – gold kitty encrusted with rhinestones

Bottled Treasures Necklace, 1991, $45 – real glass bottle filled with tiny pearls and capped with a gold crown; **Timeless Sands Necklace**, 1991, $45 – real glass hourglass filled with fine sand. Both of these are extremely rare

These are all traditional religious designs on gold chains. **Star of David Necklace**, 1992, $15; **Genuine Porcelain Golden Cross Necklace**, 1995, $30 – white glazed porcelain cross trimmed in gold; **Cross Pendant**, 1986, $20 – garnet red or lapis blue with rhinestone accent; **Vintage Scroll Cross Necklace**, 2002, $20 – richly colored beads with antiqued gold; **Fashion Cross**, 1992, $25 – large gold cross with enamel and rhinestone accents; **Glistening Cross Pendant**, 1991, $20 – studded with rhinestones; **Goldtone Cross Necklace**, 1997, $20; **Goldtone Crucifix Necklace**, 2002, $35; **14 Karat Gold Cross Necklace**, 1999, $75 – 14k gold with real diamond accent

Moroccan Riches Pendant, 1993, $35 – large, fluted dimensional amber bead with rich gold accents and tassel; **Faceted Brilliance Necklace**, 1991, $35 – large, faceted, dimensional crystal pendant; **Elegant Apple Pendant**, 1995, $35 – dimensional red apple with gold leaves and crystal accents; **Jewelesque Splendor Pendant**, 1996, $30 – hand-glazed dimensional egg pendant with rhinestone and gold accents

Sterling Silver Turquoise Cross Necklace, 1997, $30 – genuine turquoise accent; **Elegant Faux Marcasite Pendant**, 1994, $35 – classic amethyst stone in elegant marcasite frame; **Sterling Silver Cross Necklace with Turquoise Accent**, 2003, $35 – nice cross pendant with turquoise accent; **Victorian Touch Pendant**, 1990, $20 – large amethyst stone in marcasite frame; **Soaring Dove Pendant**, 1978, $10 – shiny silver bird in flight; **Sterling Silver Pooh Pendant**, 1998, $15 – traditional Pooh on silver chain

Pearly Pastel Necklace, 1994, $15 – pastel pearls on opalescent beaded chain; Vibrant Hues Choker Necklace, 1986, $15 – dramatic coiled choker came in red or black; Fashion Duet Necklace, 1992, $15 – large gold matte bead choker; Fashion Hues Necklace, 1993, $15 – large baroque beads came in cream or pink; Rainbow Reflections Necklace, 1986, $25 – long strand of aurora borealis beads; Simulated Freshwater Pearl Rope Necklace, 1986, $15 – seashell pink pearls also came in cream or blue pearls

Birthstone Pearlesque Necklace in Shell Package, 2004, $20 – single pearl with birthstone accent for all twelve months

Mesmerize Perfume Pendant, 1992, $20 – flacon on blue cord promotional item for the release of Mesmerize perfume; Fragrance Scentsations Necklace, 1996, $20 – an Austrian crystal pendant accented with gold released with Imari perfume; Flacon Necklace, 1990, $20 – small bottle pendant to fill with your favorite perfume; Golden Glace Pendant, 1969, $35 – holds a solid perfume compact

Personally Yours Lariat, 1982, $15 – initial in oval circle with pearl accent; Butterfly Lariat Necklace, 1979, $15 – gold with silver pave wings, not a true lariat; Fashion Lariat Necklace, 1997, $15 – a Y-necklace with sparkling clear crystal stone accents; Pearly Y Necklace, 1997, $15 – lustrous pearls in gold chain

Antique Moments Pendant, 1992, $35 – lovely intalgio profile of lady in amethyst-colored glass pendant

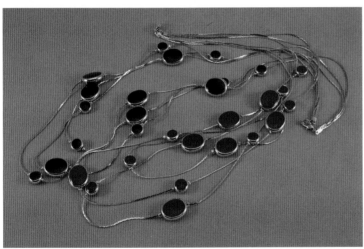

Color Classics Necklace, 1997, $25 – triple strand gold necklace with red, black, or blue ovals in various sizes

Goldtone Necklace Bundle, 1999, $15 – three gold chain necklaces in various styles and lengths; **Classic Colors Necklace**, 1986, $10 – a simple chain necklace in hot pink, white, or blue; **Tri-color Chain Necklace**, 1984, $20 – 3 open link chains in gold, rose gold, and white gold with 2-inch tassel; **Delicate Strand Necklace**, 1979, $15 – came in gold or silver; **Twisted Rope Chain Necklace**, 1989, $15 – classic gold rope; **Interweave Necklace**, 1978, $15 – two elegant swedged chains intertwined, one textured silver and one polished gold

Romantic Interlude Connection Pin/Pendant, 1990, $25 – large pearl cabochon in ornate golden frame with teardrop pearl dangle can be worn separately as a pin; **Initial Attraction Necklace**, 1978, $15 – small gold initial, no QUWXYZ; **Loving Heart Pendant**, 1990, $15 – puffed govld heart; **Lucky Clover Necklace**, 2003, $15 – sculptured gold clover choker; **Genuine 14K Double Heart Necklace**, 1983, $35 – heart within a heart; **Pretty Blossom Pendant**, 1990, $15 – blue enamel petals with crystal centers; **Loving Moments Necklace with Genuine Garnet**, 1995, $15 – gold "I Love Mom" sentiment necklace; **Elegant Reflections Pendant**, 1991, $15 – one side is a gold pendant with two pearl accents and the other is a circular mirror; **Elegant Evening Necklace Enhancer**, 1997, $10 – stunning blue faceted crystal trimmed in rhinestones

Prayer Locket Necklace, 2005, $20 – opens to reveal the Lord's Prayer; **Casual Silvertone Textured Necklace with Enhancer**, 2003, $20 – elaborate chain with onyx enhancer; **Silver Note Pendant Necklace**, 1975, $25 – ornate silver mock whistle pendant; **Sterling Silver Baby's Ring Pendant**, 1982, $50 – extremely rare baby ring pendant; **Pave Heart Pendant Necklace**, 1981, $15 – rhinestones in a silver heart setting; **Pave MOM Pendant**, 1984, $15 – three golden letters with the center of the O a glitter of pave diamonds; **Sterling Silver and Jade Pendant**, 1980, $35 – semi-precious jade heart with sterling silver accent; **Glowing Bells Pendant Necklace**, 1980, $15 – shiny gold bells with ruby rhinestone clapper

Ribbed Cross Pendant, 1993, $40 – 14k gold-filled

Pearlesque Rosary, 2001, $30 – extremely rare pearl rosary in satin pouch

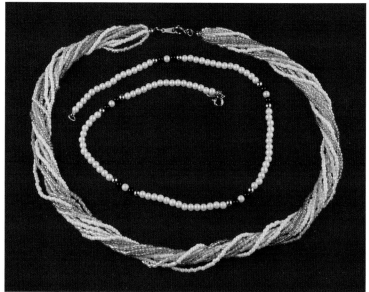

Coloressence Necklace, 1980, $20 – pearls and gold beads with onyx, lapis, or carnelian accent beads; **Genuine Glass Bead Necklace**, 1991, $25 – ten strands of glittering glass beads in blue or pink tones

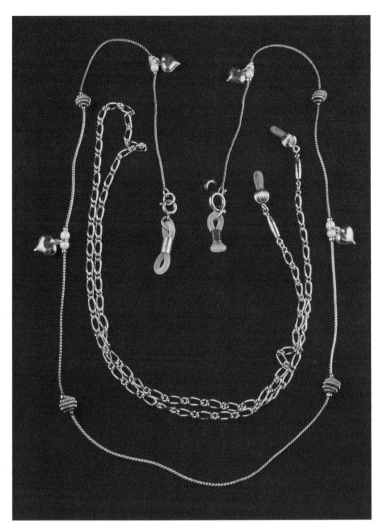

Baby Bootie Birthstone Necklace, 2002, $20 – one gold charm and gold chain provided; extra charms and gold spacer beads sold separately; **New Dimensions**, 1976, necklace $15 – sculptured beauty in gold and silver with matching ring in the Ring Chapter; **Florette Lariat Necklace**, 1979, $15 – gold chain with jade beads

Optical Necklace, 1995, $15 – gold hearts with pear accents can be worn as a necklace or an eyeglasses holder, also came in coral/turquoise beads; **Convertible Eyeglass Holder Necklace**, 1985, $15 – versatile gold chain keeps glasses elegantly at hand, then converts to a tailored necklace

Genuine Lead Crystal Pendant, 1981, $30 – frosted, fan-shaped lead crystal imported from Bavaria; **Star Signs Pendant Neckchain**, 1980, $15 – all signs of the Zodiac in gold; **Bold Fashion Pendant/ Pin**, 1993, $25 – large Maltese cross with amber and pearl points surrounding a ruby; **Color Burst Necklace**, 1997, $25 – large gold cross pendant studded with ruby, emerald, sapphire, and clear rhinestones; **Genuine Onyx Lucky Horn Necklace**, 1989, $25 – fabulous onyx horn on gold chain

Fashion Caramel Pin/Pendant, 1997, $25 – dramatic pendant in warm caramel hues detaches to become a pin; **Opalescent Necklace**, 2004, $25 – burnished brass with oval cabochon and glass accents; **Coral Colour Rose Pendant Beaded Necklace**, 2003, $20 – carved plastic rose with faceted bead chain

Twist of Color Bead Necklace, 1985, $15 – plastic bead necklace could be purchased in shades of coral, ivory, carnelian, turquoise, green onyx, red, or blue to be used separately or several twisted together into a torsade as shown

Big Bauble Necklace, 2005, $15 – long necklace with big beads in purple or green

Nostalgic Reflections Necklace, 1988, $20 – delicate filigree alternates with crystal beads to create a rope with subtle shimmer in silver or gold; **Glimmering Slide Necklace**, 1980, $25 – gold or silver double slide, rare; **Lily Lariat Necklace**, 1978, $15 – silver Y-necklace of lilies with gold stamens; **Sea Gull Slide Necklace**, 1984, $25 – shiny silver bird on lariat; **Mother of Pearl Butterfly Necklace**, 2005, $20 – two-tone shell butterfly on double strand silver chain

Expandable Locket, 1997, $25 – gold locket which opens on both sides; **Three Heart Necklace**, 1995, $25 – movable gold hearts; **Black & Golden Links Necklace**, 1986, $15 – jet black entwined with gold; **Spectator Link Necklace**, 1993, $20 – neat gold links with white, red, or black plastic links

Baroque Pearlesque Necklace with Removable Enhancer, 2000, $45 – elegant 3-strand pearls with removable rhinestone and pearl dangle enhancer

Pear Brilliantelle Pendant, 1983, $70 – pear-shaped, 1-carat, man-made diamond set in sterling silver; **Solitaire CZ Necklace**, 2003, $25 – 2-carat diamond weight cubic zirconia; **Sterling Silver Teddy Bear Necklace**, 1999, $15 – cut-out teddy bear in sterling silver; **Pearlustre Pendant**, 1985, $25 – single pearl on golden chain, extremely rare; **Love Doves Necklace**, 1985, $15, delicate choker; **Romantic Ensemble Necklace**, 1985, $15 – lustrous pearl in ribbon weave marcasite

Cashmere Necklace, 1987, $30 – gorgeous 4-strand necklace of sleek gold tubes and choice of all cream pearls or a mixture of grey, cream, and champagne pearls; **Pearly Impressions Necklace**, 1992, $20 – gold filigree links with 8mm pearls; **Parisian Butterfly Necklace**, 1995, $30 – triple strand of pearls joined by a gold butterfly clasp; **Classic Pearlesque Necklace**, 2001, $20 – lustrous single strand of pearls

Soft Leaf Choker, 1983, $15 – shimmering multi-leaf chain in gold or silver; **Delicately Yours Necklace**, 1976, $15 – pearls in gold; **Personal Style Necklace**, 1981; $20 – layered look with three garnets and gold beads glistening on two delicate gold chains; **Pearlesque & Goldtone Multirow Necklace**, 2004, $15 – flat gold and pearl disks on illusion chain

141

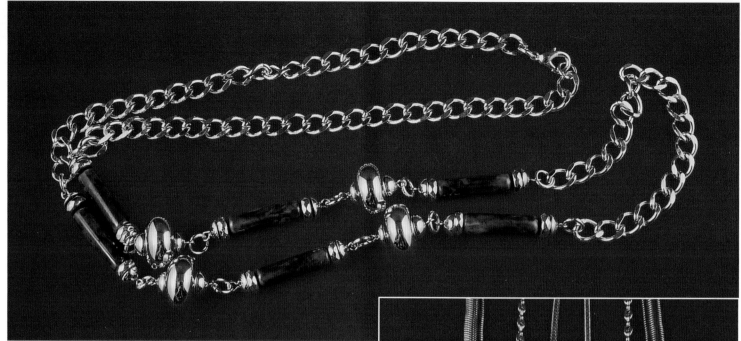

Sienna Sunset, 1995, $30 – extremely rare nice long necklace of shiny gold links with blue or brown tubular beads and large shiny gold bead accents

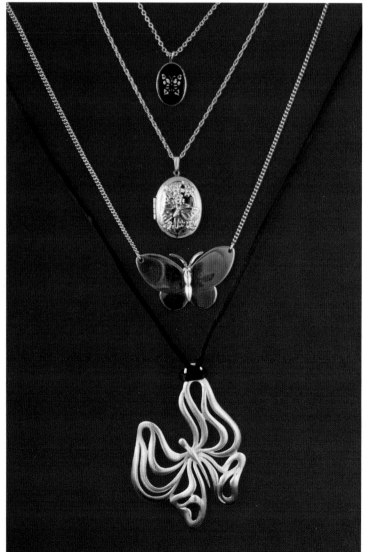

Tailored Chevron, 1985, $10 – nice chevron chain came in either silver or gold; **Florentine Chain**, 1984, $10 – dramatic decorative gold chain; **Fashion Statement Necklace**, 1989, $15 – bold flexible golden chain; **Bold Links Choker**, 1985, $15 – a smooth curve of gold or gunmetal in a link design

Shimmering Butterfly Pendant, 1982, $25 – black opal look with iridescent butterfly motif in gold setting; **Butterfly Fragrance Locket**, 1983, $25 – gold locket with fragrance tablets; **Butterfly Pendant Necklace**, 1977, $15 – polished silver and gold; **Breezy Butterfly Necklace**, 1993, $25 – abstract butterfly in silver or gold on black silk cord

Victorian Heart Necklace, 1989, $20 – rose quartz heart in seed pearl frame on a pearl strand; **Ivory Color Carved Heart Necklace**, 2003, $15 – rhinestone accented ivory pendant on beaded strand of turquoise nuggets; **Glistening Heart Pendant**, 1993, $25 – bold carved plastic heart on black cord; **Unlock My Heart Necklace**, 1993, $25 – gold heart and key on black cord

Porcelain Wild Flower Pin/Pendant, 1993, $25 – large porcelain blossom of carmine pink with a gold center on a pink cord to wear as a pin or a necklace; **Lotus Blossom Pendant**, 1991, $35 – reversible genuine porcelain pendant with a blue floral motif side and a glazed white motif side on a midnight blue cord; **Crystal Aura Pendant**, 2006, $10 – large emerald-cut crystal pendant can be worn on the black cord or the included silver chain. This was a free gift with the purchase of Crystal Aura perfume.

Goldtone Wise Owl, 2007, $25 – large articulated gold owl pendant on 42-inch shiny gold link chain

143

Chapter Four
Bracelets

Bracelets have been popular for centuries. What started as jointed, wide-cuff designs quickly evolved to un-jointed bangle types. The bangles were originally called a "bangle ring," since it was a narrow band in the shape of a large wedding ring for the wrist, and they were so popular that artisans soon made them in a variety of colors and widths, molding and carving them from various materials. Bakelike was an early resin process that went out of fashion in the 1950's. Just as Bakelite replaced the highly flammable celluloid of an earlier generation, Lucite and other forms of hard plastic replaced Bakelite. Lucite is a petrochemical product which can be transparent, translucent, or opaque and once formed, it cannot be bent out of shape. Avon used the metal cuff and the plastic bangle, as well as linked chains and fitted band, and many of Avon's bracelet designs were studded with gemstones and pearls, or included charms for added appeal. Charms were once considered "love tokens," and they came in all shapes, including religious symbols, hearts, animals, clocks, signets, beads, and lockets, to name a few. Most of Avon's bracelets are hallmarked on the clasp or have a hangtag, but nearly all the plastic bangles are not stamped.

Classic Twist Bangle Bracelet, 1979, $10 – twisted gold or silver metal bangle; **Whispers of Spring Bracelet**, 1992, $15 – nuggets with the look of semi-precious stones, has matching earrings; **Special Moments Charm Bracelet**; 1986, $15 – wide double links came in silver or gold; **Textured Link Bracelet**, 1981, $10 – large double links in shiny gold; **Pearlesque Single Row Bracelet**, 1997, $15 – large 8mm pearls

Luminesque Bangle Bracelet, 1977, $10 – Misty Red, Foggy White, Hazy Green or Smoky Black plastic bangles

Genuine Sterling Silver Heart Toggle Bracelet, 1995, $10 – nice link chain with heart toggle closure; **Buckle Chain Bracelet**, 1974, $10 – sliver flat-looped links with belt buckle closure; **Special Dad ID Bracelet**, 1987, $15 – silver link bracelet which can be engraved

Copper Cuff Bracelet, 1979, $15 – Avon's first piece of real copper jewelry for men; **"2 for" Color Bangles**, 1998, $10 – one each of sky blue and sea green plastic; **Fashion Wardrobe Bracelet**, 1981, $15 – came in caramel or burgundy plastic with gold accents and hinge; **Interlock Wristband**, 1978, $15 – silver hinged cuff with interlocking closure

Clint Wrist Chain, 1976, $15 – Avon's first piece of body jewelry for men has heavy silver links with a hook catch; **Jet Stream Wristchain**, 1978, $15 – heavy gleaming silver; **Trazarra Wristchain**, 1978, $15 – gold chain with rust brown enamel inserts designed to promote Avon's Trazarra After Shave; **Tortelle Bracelet**, 1975, $15 – tortoise shell beads in gold knot design; **Bold Stroke Wristchain**, 1979, $15 – gold or silver polished links; **Modern Silhouette Bracelet**, 1980, $15 – double row of textured and polished links in silver or gold; **Heart to Heart Bracelet**, 1991, $10 – gold or silver linked hearts; **Classic Herringbone Bracelet**, 1994, $10 – wide gold traditional herringbone design

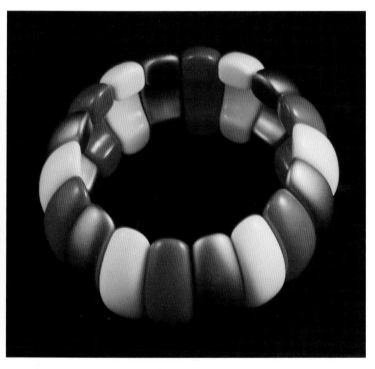

Summer Naturals Bracelet, 1992, $15 – wide red, gold, and white stretch plastic bracelet. This bracelet has been the topic of controversy in some books, probably because it is not marked

You Charm Me Bracelet, 1992, $15 – a variety of hearts in gold; **Fragrance Replica Charm Bracelet**, 1997, $15 – tiny charms of Avon perfume fragrance bottles; **Birthstone Bear Charm Bracelet**, 1992, $10 – gold bear with birthstone heart on gold link chain with two dangling gold heart charms; **Mickey & Friends Charm Bracelet**, 1990, $15 – gleaming gold charms of Mickey Mouse and his pals; **Snow White Bracelet**, 1994, $15 – gold bracelet with the Seven Dwarfs charms having their names on the back

Tailored Bracelet, 1995, $10 – stretch bangle of gold gooseneck chain; **Classic Style Bangle**, 1991, $10 – distinctively designed gleaming gold bangle; **Edwardian Lace Bracelet**, 1980, $15 – open filigree gold cuff with opal

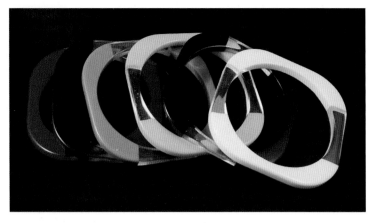

Summer Rainbow Bangle, 1978, $10 – square plastic bangle with two clear sections in red, black, green, yellow, blue, or white

Yesterday's Memories Locket Bracelet, 1979, $15 – silver locket bangle with Old World scrollwork on face; **Burst of Spring Bracelet**, 1978, $15 – butterfly-shaped porcelain with floral decal; **Catch A Birthstone Bracelet**, 1979, $10 – delicate gold bangle with Austrian glass birthstone for each month; Bottom: **Avant Bracelet**, 1976, $15 – shiny silver chevron cuff; **Counterparts Interlocking Bracelet**, 1977, $15 – gold and silver locking bracelet can be separated and worn as two bracelets

Have It All Charm Bracelet, 1991, $20 – daydream fairytale with bar of gold, engagement ring, Rolls Royce, castle, and cruise ship

Slender Link Bracelet, 1979, $10 – gold or silver with center flat section; **Silken Bead Bracelet**, 1980, $10, gold or silver beads on a chain has matching necklace; **Heart Accent Bracelet**, 1988, $10 – gold heart with rhinestone accent; **Triple Strand Bracelet**, 1992, $10 – each strand a different size link; **Delicate Facets Bracelet**, 1988, $10 – faceted crystals on a gold chain

Birthstone Tennis Bracelet, 2003, $15 – elegant tennis bracelet for each month

Marlboro Wristcuff, 1980, $15 – gold metal cuff with two wire wraps in silver; **Fashion Crossroads Cuff Bracelet**, 1979, $10 – a triple ropetwist design over a band of ribbed wire makes a textured X in the center; **Treasured Jade Bracelet**, 1978, $15 – genuine jade bar in gold goes well with other Avon jade pieces; **Gilded Knot Bracelet**, 1977, $15 – gold metal cuff with lover's knot design

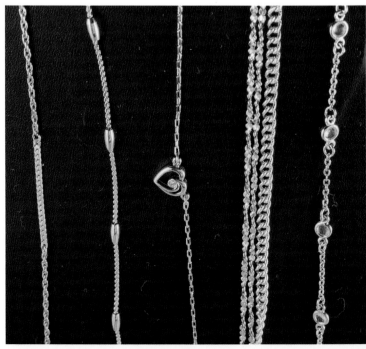

Lady Luck Bracelet, 1983, $10 – gold or silver horseshoe; **Butterfly Bracelet**, 1986, $10 – extremely rare gold filigree butterfly; **Sterling Silver Cheerful Charm Anklet**, 2003, $10 – antique finish silver charms on adjustable chain; **Luxuriance Bracelet**, 1980, $10 – gold curve on a gold chain; **Polished Silhouette Bracelet**, 1982, $15 – extremely rare intricate design gold chain; **Hearts Entwined Bracelet**, 1981, $10 – two moveable interlocking hearts; **Gilded Bar Bracelet**, 1977, $10 – simple gold bar

Classic Twist Bangle Bracelet, 1979, $10 – gold or silver metal bangle; **Rope Twist Bracelet**, 1987, $10 – double twist bangle in gold or silver; **Star Sign Bracelet**, 1979, $15 – came in all signs of the Zodiac; **Color Stripe Cuff Bracelet**, 1980, $15 – black enamel stripe on gold

Buckle Bracelet, 1972, $15 – extremely rare gold bangle in buckle design

Modern Links Bracelet, 1994, $15 – classic gold or silver links; **Genuine Freshwater Pearl Bracelet**, 2004, $15 – simple pearl chain; **Heirloom Classic Bracelet**, 1992, $15 – marcasite with rhinestones; **Captured Treasure Bracelet**, 1995, $15 – genuine onyx or adventurine in gold; **Classic Style Wristchain**, 1979, $15 – gold or silver chain, both shown

Tennis Bracelet, 1993, $15 – gold bracelet of ruby, diamond, or sapphire stones, the white stone bracelet is from 1992 and has circular stones and also came in red; **Touch of Color Bracelet**, 1980, $15 – gold filigree chain holds jade or ivory beads; **Delicate Anklette**, 1979, $10 – gold or silver chain with swedged sections; **Oval Accent Ankle Bracelet**, $10 – gold or silver oval

Color Crazy Bracelet, 1989, $10 – plastic bangle in teal, green, ivory, red, or purple

147

Regent Street Wristband, 1977, $20 – gleaming bangle of stainless steel with copper insert and snap lock

Bold Flowers Bracelet, 1993, $15 – silver with aqua stones or gold with rose stones; **Genuine Rose Quartz Bracelet**, 1993, $15 – rose quartz cabochon in gold lace; **Faux Marcasite Link to Link Bracelet**, 1994, $15 – silver with marcasites and rhinestones; **Lustrous Links Bracelet**, 1994, $15 – double row of pearl cabochons set in gold

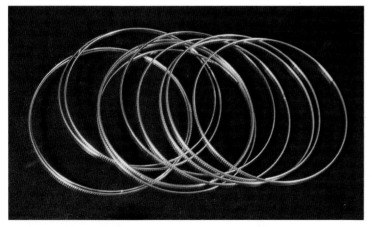

Tri-tone Textured Bangle Bracelets, 1999, $20 – nice collection of multi-width bangles of gold, rose gold, and silver

Dramatic Textures Cuff, 1994, $15 – gold ribbed cuff; **Sculptured Drama Bangle**, 1987, $15 – large sculptured plastic bangle came in sleek red or black; **Heart Locket Bracelet**, 1993, $15 – large heart cuff bracelet opens to receive your favorite memento

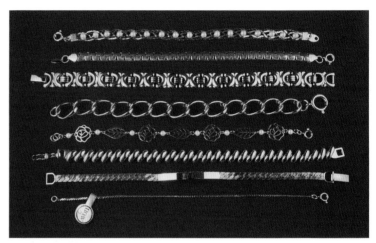

Pearlesque Treasurers Bracelet, 1995, $15 – beautifully ornate gold twist with pearls; **Polished Style Bracelet**, 1993, $10 – classic gold link; **Polished Link Bracelet**, 1989, $15 – butterfly link design; **Bold Cable Bracelet**, 1990, $10 – open link gold chain; **Romantic Expressions Bracelet**, 1987, $15 – gold filigree of rosebuds and leaves with pearl accents; **San Marco Bracelet**, 1990, $15 – Avon's look of real gold came in yellow or white gold; **Polished Bar Wrist Chain**, 1977, $10 – gold chain with center bar; **Shimmering Touch Bracelet**, 1978, $10 – came in polished gold or silver

Add-A-Charm Cuff Bracelet, 2004, $15 – sea life or travel charms with four spacers on easy-to-wear bangle; **Sea Life Charm Bracelet**, 2005, $15 – nice silver bracelet with all sorts of sea life charms

Colors of Feelings, 2003, $15 – stretch bracelets of colorful beads and findings in Peaceful Blue, Creative Amber, or Happy Red

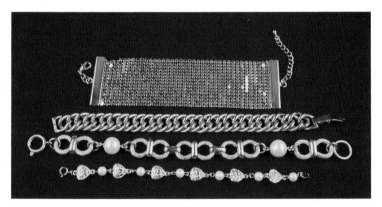

Goldtone Mesh Bracelet, 2000, $15 – wide reversible disks. **Bold Connection Bracelet**, 1988, $15 - large double open link; **Classic Style Bracelet**, 1993, $10 – gold links with pearl accents; **Pearly Heart Bracelet**, 1994, $15 – embossed gold hearts alternate with pearls

Ten Commandments Bracelet, 1998, $15 – gold plaque link-bracelet inscribed with one Commandment on each plaque

Snowman Stretch Bracelet, 2004, $10 – Christmas bracelet of colorfully decorated enamel snowmen with silver bead links

2-Pack Colorful Stretch Bracelets, 2007, $15 – stretch tubular plastic with silver stations in grape and mauve

Winter Wonderland Charm Bracelet, 2002, $10 – silver bead stretch bracelet with winter charms

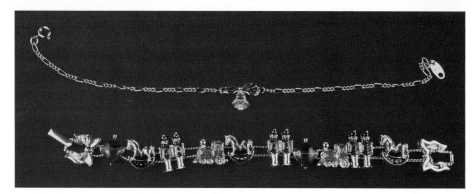

Holly Day Ankle Bracelet, 1992, $15 – holly and bell on a sparkling gold chain; **Holiday Toys Slide Bracelet**, 2000, $15 – all sorts of colorful glazed toys on a slide bracelet

Charms, $5 each: Back: **Be Mine Valentine**, 1987 – silver or gold charm large enough to be worn as a pendant; **Genuine Sterling Silver Cross**, 1994, $10 – embossed silver design large enough to be worn as a pendant; **Times of Your Life**, 1991 – gold baby carriage or elephant, there was also a gold diploma; Bottom, gold charms from 1981: **Roller Skate, Running Shoe, Bicycle, #1, Star, Heart, Bowling Pins, Clover, Tennis Racket, Girl Silhouette, Boy Silhouette**

Clockwise: **Keepsake Rose Convertible Pendant/Keychain**, 1986, $15 – gold rose key ring converts to pendant with included gold chain; **Dangling Heart Key Ring**, 1986, $10 – golden heart dangles from gold key ring; **Pharaoh Key Chain**, 1996, $15 – antique gold King Tut; **Lucky Heart Key Ring**, 1988, $15 – gold die has indented heart-shaped dots and a glittering ruby stone set in the #1 dot; **Etchings in Brass Keychain**, 1993, $50 – extremely rare key chain designed in solid brass; **Initial Key Ring**, 1982, $10 – shaped like an old-fashioned skeleton key ring with initial as the bit; **Family Favorites Key Chain**, 1994, $15 – pewter cat or gold dog; **Interlocking Initial Key Ring**, 1985, $10 – traditional circle key ring with initial attachment; **Initial Key Ring**, 1987, $10 – half-circle with initial attachment; **Double Take Key Ring**, 1986, $20 – shown is Indy 500 racing car and the pickup truck, but this also came in a Ford Mustang in embossed metal with front and back design; **Key Connection Key Chain**, 1980, $20 – extremely rare silver house and gold car can be taken apart and used individually

Pearlustre Barrette, 1988, $10 – pearls and gold beads; **Island Beauty Hair Comb**, 1988, $10 – two fabric blossoms in white or pink

Blue Enamel Button Covers, 1972, $10 – blue covers identical to the gold covers; **Button Style Button Covers**, 1972, $10 – small gold covers in sets of four; **Western Saddle Belt Buckle**, 1980, $15 – pewter belt buckle; **Golden Pinwheel Button Covers**, 1985, $15, larger, decorative gold pinwheels came in sets of two; **US Flag Money Clip**, 1981, $15 – gold flag; **Collar Accent Clips**, 1993, $10 – extremely rare silver collar tips for western wear dress shirts

Chapter Five
Pins

It's been theorized by some jewelry historians that the very first piece of jewelry adornment was a brooch, since collars and cuffs were detachable, requiring something to hold them in place, and a nice-sized jeweled pin was considered the perfect choice. True or not, the popularity of the pin and brooch continues today. They range in size from a simple tack pin, having a tiny stud on the back to pierce the garment, which is then held in place with a simple clamping nut, to the exceptionally large and grandiose bar pins. Traditionally, pins are considered small and utilitarian, whereas brooches are large pieces of adornment laden with gemstones. Avon made both styles, as well as the chatelaine, a fancy term for a pin "holding" another pin with a connecting chain.

State of States Pin, 1982, $10 each – small gold tac pins available in all 50 states and Washington DC

Moonlight Couple aka Loving Owls Pin, 1980, $10 – two gold owls sitting on a tree branch - these pins are identical in every respect, but Moonlight Couple is the only one shown in the brochures

Flower Basket Pin Perfume Glacé, 1971, $15; **Golden Leaf Pin Perfume Glacé**, 1969, $15; **Solid Perfume Jewel Locket Pin**, 1965, $25 – extremely rare and could also be purchased as a necklace with an 18-inch chain; **Cameo Pin Perfume Glacé**, 1970, $20; **Jeweled Owl Pin Perfume Glacé**, 1969, $15; **Daisy Pin Perfume Glacé**, 1970, $15

Bold Stallion Tie Tack, 1979, $10 – came in gold or silver; **Classic Accent Tie Tack**, 1971, $10 – ebony cabochon framed in gold; **Lion's Head Tac Pin**, 1988, $10 – came in gold or silver; **Midas Mouse**, 1974, $15 – textured gold mouse with crystal eyes and tail; **Cute Cuckoo**, 1981, $15 – antiqued gold with dangling weights; **Man in the Moon**, 1978, $15 – gold moon with rhinestone eye and dangling silver stars

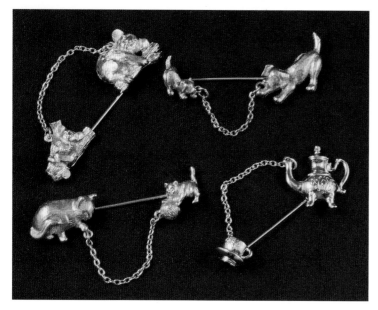

Mother's Love (Koala, Dog, Cat), 1983, $15 each – 2-part gold pins; **Colonial Tea Pin**, aka Colonial Teapot Pin, 1981, $15 – 2-part shiny silver teapot with cup and saucer

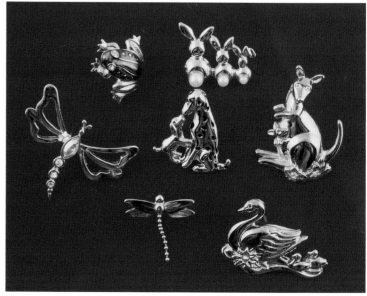

Nature's Garden Tac Pin (Dragonfly, Frog), 1993, $15 each – colorful tac pins for lapel or collar; **Three Bunnies**, 1995, $15 – gold with pearl bodies; **Precious Love** (Kangaroo, Swan), 1993, $15 each – gold mother with baby; **Perfect Love**, 1996, $10 – charming silver dog with gold puppy or silver cat with gold kitten; **Dragonfly**, 1984, $10 – gold body of beads that actually move with pearlized wings in blue/green or all white

My Favorite Hobby (Tennis, Golf, Gardening, Bowling), 1996, $15 each – large matte gold pins representing favorite sports with tennis and golf having pearl accents; **Fruity Trio Stick Pin** (Cherries, Apple, Pineapple), $10 each – cheerful, openwork, shiny gold stickpin

Frog Tac Pin, 1985, $15 – gold frog with emerald back, **Graceful Swan**, 1985, $10 – textured gold wings on pearl white plastic; **Partridge in a Pear Tree**, 1979, $15 – silver bird can be worn alone or with the gold tree jacket; **Frivolous Frog**, 1975, $15 – gold frog with emerald eyes, **Gilded Bird**, 1976, $15 – gold bird in flight; **Pretty Parrot**, 1980, $15 – gold bird on swing; **Class of 80**, 1979, $5 – polished and textured gold – there was also a Class of 78, 79, 81, 82 with **Class of 83**, 1982, $5, the last in the series

Dream Car Tac Pin, 1985, $50 each – these finely detailed dimensional model cars are extremely rare and highly collectible. There are five of them in the series, all of them in gold. Back: 1955 MGA 1600, 1929 Model A Ford, Front: 1984 Cadillac El Dorado, 1955 Chevy Bel Aire Convertible, 1963 Corvette Stingray

Lucky Friends (Elephant, Turtle, Owl), 1984, $10 each – finely detailed green jade elephant, tortoise shell turtle, ivory owl; Precious Pet (Cat, Frog, Lovebirds, Bunny), 1989, $15 each – cute marcasite animal pins with various gemstone eyes; Fluttering Butterfly, 1983, $10 – gold body with translucent wings in frosted apricot, blue, or white

Jeweltone Peacock, 2004, $50 – magnificent large peacock studded with colorful crystals and jewels; Spring Bouquet, 1984, $15 – porcelain disk with floral design; Porcelain Siamese Cat, 1982, $20 – beautifully hand-painted cat cast in porcelain

Golden Eyeglass Holder Pin, 1994, $10 – gold frames accented with rhinestones designed to hold eyeglasses when not in use; Cat Eyeglass Holder Pin, 1996, $10 – gold cat with rhinestone eyes holds eyeglasses; Fashion Facets, 1985, $15 – magnificent diamond and sapphires creation or diamond and amethyst; Impressionist's Flower Pin, 1992, $15 – graceful vase of colorful flowers in epoxy enamel; Pansy, 1981, $15 – glazed yellow porcelain flower

Wise Guy, 1975, $15 – gold owl on tree branch with movable eyes and dangling chain tail feathers; Fashion Keynote Stickpin, 1978, $10 – gold or silver skeleton key; Gilded Apple, 1974, $10 – magnificent brushed gold apple; Staffordshire Gardens Bar Pin, 1979, $10 – antiqued gold leaf design with rhinestone; Fashion Tactics, 1989, $10 – genuine pewter "In Love" heart. There was also "Rock & Roll" guitar, "Party Line" telephone, or "Jet Set" airplane; Ladybug, 1972, $15 – translucent white body with crystal accents

#1 Giftable Tac Pins (Manicurist, Hairdresser, Teacher, Nurse), 1997, $15 each – gold with rhinestone accents; You're My Favorite Hobby Scatter Pin (You're Sew Special, You Strike My Fancy), 1993, $15 each

Rose Corsage, 1998, $10 – delicate fabric rose with pearl trim on gold doily; **Thomas Kinkade Home for the Holidays**, 2002, $30 – has battery and switch to turn light off and on; **Country Days**, 1988, $10 – genuine straw hat with blue-checked or red-checked bow trim; **Flower Pot**, 1993, $10 – fabric flowers in gold metal pot

Birthday Bouquet, 1987, $10 – white porcelain heart with flower decals, one for each month; **Hearts and Flowers**, 1998, $15 – genuine porcelain in a variety of pastel colors; **Snowflower**, 1972, $20 – white enamel petals on gold stem; **Dew Touch Maple Leaf**, 1985, $15 each – detailed maple leaf in marbleized plastic amber or jade with a twinkling rhinestone dew drop accent; **Filigree Fantasy**, 1995, $25 – luxuriant topaz center stone in filigree frame with sparkling crystals and pearls can also be worn as a pendant; **Graceful Tulip**; 1980, $15 – carved ivory tulip in golden stem

Tea Time Tac Pin, 1997, $15 – shiny gold tea pot with crystal drop, extremely rare

Seasonal Bouquets Pin (Winter Lily of the Valley, Autumn Aster), 1991, $20 each – large gold flower pin. There is also a Spring Violet and a Summer Rose, and all pins are extremely rare; **Love and Kisses Chatelain Pin**, 1989, $20 – heart on one side, hugs and kisses on other side; **Cameo Stickpin**, 1978, $15 – traditional cameo in gold frame; **Luminous Wings**, 1975, $10 – beautiful butterfly with coral-colored and yellow translucent wings; **Cameo Silhouette**, 1982, $15 – bouquet of flowers against translucent coral-colored background; **Moonwind Pin/Scarf Holder**, 1972, $10 – introduced with the Moonwind perfume; **Sentiment Pin**, 1986, $10 – elegant gold heart dangling from bow with either I Love You Grandmother or I Love You Mother inscribed on the back; **Rhinestone Initial Pin**, 2005; $15 – large silver initial pin studded with rhinestones

Melody in Flight, 1995, $15 – dramatic butterfly with opaque wings, pink crystal body, and seed pearls; **Owlette**, 1972, $15 – filigree owl with ruby eyes; **Gilded Rose**, 1972, $15 – gold beauty with glowing pink sapphire rosebud, **Cat N' Fishbowl**, 1994, $15 – gold whimsical cat after the fish in the bowl

Tropics (Fish, Parrot) 1991, $10 each – tropically styled, brightly painted plastic fish or parrot; **Love Bug**, 2005, $15 – gold ladybug with red enamel body, black enamel head, and crystal eyes; **Birthstone Butterfly**, 2004, $10 – silver butterfly with birthstone-colored wings and dangling crystal accent; **Tropical Brights**, 1997, $10 – translucent plastic fish or pineapple washed with gold and sparkled with color

Rose Pin, 2001, $10 – red rose on gold stem; **Fancy Hat**, 2004, $15 – Avon's contribution to the Red Hat Society is a fancy red enamel hat with a purple hat band sporting a colorful crystal-studded flower; **Dangling Heart**, 1991, $15 – gold filigree frames a red dangling heart; **Fanciful Fashion Pins** (Shoes, Bag), 2002, $10 each – textured gold pin with enamel

Romantic Style Pin, 1995, $20 – magnificent dress pin with pearl and amethyst accents

Abstract Star, 1997, $20 – gold freeform design; **Special Touch Initial**, 1986, $10, gleaming gold initial; **Graceful Bow**, 1989, $15 – glossy white or red fancy bow also had matching c/p earrings; **Charming Claddagh**, 1994, $15 – traditional design with lustrous pearl heart; **Initial Rope Pin**, 1996, $10, gold rope initial; **Cherished Moments Locket**, 1996, $15 – gold locket with pearl accent

American Harvest, 1990, $15 – gold pea pod with 3 pearl peas; **Nest Egg Pin**, 1975, $10 – golden chick in silver shell; **You're A Sheriff**, 1983 - $10 – nice western star badge comes with insert to add name to badge; **Winds of Charm**, 1994, $15 – hot air balloon in pink overlay; **Heart**, 2004, $10 – fuchsia heart shot with gold arrow; **Tortoise Style Tac Pins** (Turtle, Snail), 1997, $15 each – amber cabochon in gold; **Musical Instrument**, 1996, $20 – amber piano, very rare; **Love Match**, 1976, $15 – gold tennis racket with pearl tennis ball

Spirited Steps, 1980, $15 – extremely rare two shoe prints in silver or gold; **Flower Basket**, 1982, $10 – antiqued silver floral arrangement; **Millennium Clock**, 1999, $15 – silver inauguration clock heralding in the New Millennium, not a true clock; **Crowning Touch**, 1991, $10 – black felt trimmed with gilded thread, pearls, and gems

Nature's Flight, 1992, $20 – large bumblebee with pearl body; **Poodle**, 1972, $15 – textured gold dog; **Pekinese**, 1972, $15 – gold filigree dog with emerald eyes; **Spectacular Mouse**, 1973, $15 – textured gold mouse with topaz eyes and eyeglasses that move up and down; **Flower Power Turtle**, 1994, $15 – blue and green rhinestones adorn flower-strewn gold turtle shell; **Frisky Kitty**, 1974, $15 – gold kitty with sapphire eyes playing with dangling bell

Clockwise: **Bouquet of Love**, 1992, $10 – delicate pink rosebuds; **Embellished Two-Tone Flower**, 2001, $20, gold metal with clear and colored crystal accents; **Delicate Spring Corsage**, 1985, $10 – pink silk tulips; **Special Bouquet Corsage**, 1980, $10 – gold bow with fabric flowers; **Sachet Fan**, 1982, $5 – fabric fan with scent of lavender

Add-A-Star Birthstone Pin, 1982, $10 – gold pin with two stars that hold birthstone star charms, $5 each charm

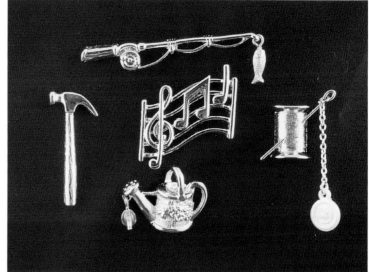

Favorite Pastimes Pin, 1983, $15 each – gold **Hammer** with silver head; gold **Fishing Pole** rod with silver reel; gold treble **Musical Staff** with removable silver notes; gold **Needle & Thread** spool with silver needle and gold chain to simulate the thread; gold **Watering Can** with a crystal water drop

Convertible Fruit Pin, 1981, $15 – gold stem holds red apple, yellow pear, and purple grapes; **Tropical Tac Pins**, 2005, $15 – a trio of colorful enamel pins of blue whale, pink flamingo, and green palm tree (not sold separately); **Garden Party Convertible Hat Pin**, 1981, $15 – plastic hats in blue, pink, and purple with gold bow

Clockwise: **Love Struck**, 1983, $10 – gleaming openwork gold heart and arrow; **Signs of the Future**; 1990, $10 – all signs of the Zodiac; **Fall Friends**, 1994, $20 – gold squirrel on branch with pearl acorn; **Mother's Nest**, 1991, $20 – mother bird waiting for 3 pearl eggs to hatch; **Touch of Whimsy**, 1991, $15 – cat in window; **Precious Sentiments**, 1989, $15 each – gold elephant with red enamel accents, gold turtle with green enamel accents. There is also a gold owl with a topaz enamel belly in the series, all with crystal eyes; **Fall Impressions**, 1996, $15 – gold acorn with crystal accents; **Sparkling Heart**, 1990, $10 – faceted blue heart set in gold

Basket of Love (Bunnies, Kittens), 1990, $15 each – antique gold; **Starshine Stickpin**, 1979, $10 – gold and silver stickpin in the shape of a 5-point star; **Peace Pin**, aka Peace on Earth Pin, 1993, $15 – gold on iridescent blue enamel; **Garden of Love**, 1994, $15 – gold wheel barrel full of red apples; **Bumble Bee**, 1975, $15 – finely detailed textured golden bee

Fluttering Hummingbird, 1992, $20 – marcasite bird with red crystal eyes drinking at flower; **Beautiful Butterfly**, 1996, $20 – silvery marcasite with pearl and crystal accents; **Personal Treasurers**, 1991, $10 – marcasite initials in antique silver, **Regal Cat**, 1993, $20 – exquisitely detailed marcasite cat with green eyes

Butterfly, 1972, $15 – brushed silver with gold accents and sapphire eyes; **Holiday Glamour**, 1991, $20 – aka Hollywood Glamour, big gold ribbon with crystal accents; **Beautiful Butterfly**, 1994, $20 – exquisite filigree butterfly with pearls, blue rhinestones and amethyst squares

Elegant Sea Life (Starfish, Sea Horse, Octopus), 1995, $15 each – gold with crystal and pearl accents; **My Favorite Pet Pin** (Dachshund, Poodle, Cocker Spaniel, Sheep Dog), 1984, $15 each – extremely rare brushed gold dog pin also came in Lovable Mutt, Scottie, Beagle, Golden Retriever, and German Shepherd

Tropical Bird, 1994, $25 – gold bird with blue and plum inlays; **Salamander**, 1991, $25 – black lizard with crystal body; **Beautiful Bee**, 1997, $20 – charming gold bee with glossy blue and green body and ruby eyes; **Enchanted Bird**, 1997, $45 – impressive swirl-style gold bird accented with crystals and green glaze

Clockwise: **Pride and Joy**, 1990, $10 – beautiful golden frame to hold your favorite photo; **Ring Shaped Pin**, 1998, $10 – dramatic big-as-a-rock engagement ring in textured gold; **Squiggle Pin**, 1997, $15 – gleaming gold squiggle with pearl accent; **Mother's Day Pin**, 1996, $15 – antique gold with black silhouette of mother and child; **Touch of Tassel Pin**, 1991, $20 – elaborate gold bow with silk tassel came in black or burgundy; **Heirloom Style Bicycle**, 1995, $20 – gold with front wheel that spins; **Painter's Palette Pin**, 1994, $10 – an artistic accent of openwork gold with four vibrant-colored rhinestones; **Victorian Regard**, 1984, $15 – circular charm suspended from a bow with diamond, emerald, amethyst, and ruby on one side and the word DEAR on the reverse – charm can be worn on a chain; **Victorian Elegance Pin**, 1991, $15 – gold portrait of woman with gemstone accents

Novelty Flower Pin Berry Accents, 2001, $10 – fabric pin with iridescent accents in blue or red berry; **Spectator Flower**, 2004, $10 – white flower with black trim in classic spectator styling; **Perfect Loveliness Corsage**, 1984, $10 – blooming fabric rose

Bold Fashion Heart, 1997, $15 – elegant shiny gold heart with crystals and pearl accent; **Graceful Leaf**, 1981, $15 – a dramatic, beautifully detailed autumn leaf in gold; **Triple Heart**, 1996, $15 – gleaming hearts with crystal accents and arrow through centers; **Fashion Bow**, 1986, $20 – brushed gold with sparkling rhinestones

Sweet Memories, 1990, $15 – large filigree heart with favorite memories in silver or gold; **Rising Star**, 1990, $10 – silver shooting star tac pin; **Flower Bouquet Vase**, 2001, $15 – ocean blue vase filled with silver flowers

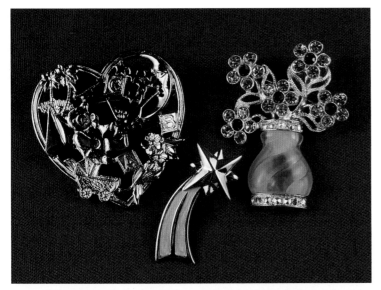

Wise Eyes, 1992, $15 – large gold openwork owl; **Kangaroo**, 1975, $15 – gold with topaz eyes has a baby that moves up and down in the pouch when mother's tail is moved; **Filigree**, 1997, $15 – large gold filigree butterfly

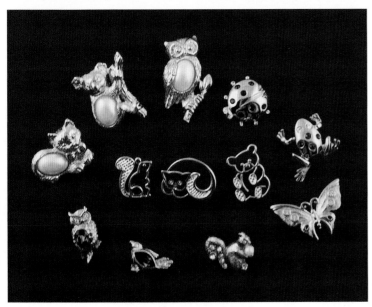

Fashion Blue Flower Pin, 1998, $25 – large faceted crystal dress pin; **Bold Spring Color Fashion Pin**, 2003, $20 – large dress pin with multi-color faceted stones

Clockwise: **Friendly Critters** (Cat, Koala, Owl), 1995, $15 each – gold pins with pearl cabochon bodies; **Garden Friends** [Ladybug, Frog, Butterfly (1996)], 1995, $15 each – gold with crystal eyes and colored crystals on body. There was also a gold pansy in 1996 with crystal dew drops; **Wilderness Scatter Pin** (Squirrel, Bluebird, Owl), 1993, $15 each – gold pins with crystal eyes and colorful jewels as body – squirrel holds pearl acorn in mouth; **Animal Pins** (Squirrel, Cat, Teddy Bear), 1980, $15 – open gold pin with silver pave accent

Sweet Rose, 2005, $15 – large yellow rose with marcasite stem and leaves; **Flower Pin**, 2005, $15 – large flower head of red facet stones in gold trim or black facet stones in silver trim

159

Prayer Sentiment, 1997, $10 – praying hands tac pin based on the famous Albrecht Deurer drawing of 1508

St. Patrick's Angel, 1997, $10 – gold sculptured angel holding a green glazed shamrock; **St. Patrick's Day Angel**, 1999, $10 – the first pin of 1997 was so popular that Avon brought it back in green crystal with clear crystal wings

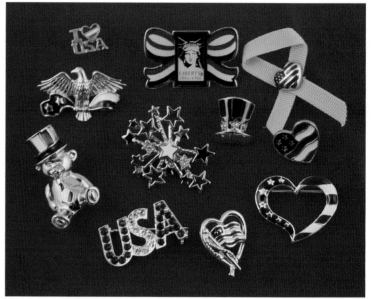

Clockwise: **I Love USA Tac Pin**, 1981, $10; **Statue of Liberty Pin**, 1986, $10; **The Yellow Ribbon Pin**, 2003, $10; **The Heart of America Pin**, 1990, $10 – has matching pierced earring shown in the Earrings Chapter. This set is so popular that Avon continues to release it. Some boxes for the pin do not have the word "The" in the name; **American Pride**; 2004, $10 – large open heart striped like the American flag; **Forever America Tac Pin**, 1994, $10 – flag in heart; **USA Pin**, 2005, $10 – large letters studded with colored rhinestones; **Stars & Stripes Bear Tac Pin**, 1996, $10 – 3-dimensional bear with hat; **American Eagle Tac Pin**, 1996, $10 – gold eagle holding flag in claws; **American Stars**, 1996, $10 – fireworks display of patriotic stars; **Independence Day Tac Pin**, 1997, $10 – patriotic hat

Captivating Cupids Pin, 1995 - $10 – gold cupid with glossy red heart connected by removable chain; **New Year's Eve Tac Pin**, 1996, $10 – rhinestone studded hat and cane; **Crown of Hearts Tac Pin**, 1994, $10 – glossy red heart with gold trim; **New Year's Eve Tac Pin**, 1994, $10 – rhinestone and shiny gold for the New Year 1996, also came in a champagne glass

Clockwise: **Scarecrow Pin** (Boy, Girl) 1990, $20 each – extremely rare gold scarecrow with enamel accents; **Gleeful Ghost Pin**, 1991, $20, extremely rare gold ghost with rhinestone eyes and Boo accent; **Halloween Tac Pins** (Spider, Ghost, Bat) 1995, $15 each – extremely rare shiny silver pins with pearl and/or crystal accents; **Bewitching Cat Pin**, 1989, $25 – extremely rare gold cat riding on broom

All That Glitters Sequin Pin (Poinsettia, Bow Tie), 1988, $10 each – large cloth pins covered in sequins; **Fall Cornucopia Pin**, 1992, $10 – charming wicker basket filled with silk flowers

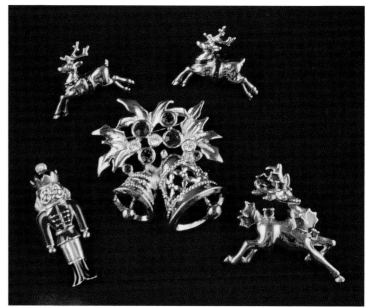

Festive Reindeer, 1987, $10 – gold or silver reindeer with red collar; **Toy Soldier**, 1996, $10 – festive nutcracker with red epoxy; **Joyous Bell**, 1994, $15 – beautiful gold bells and mistletoe with red and green accents; **Holiday Reindeer**, 1993, $15 – gold reindeer with green holly collar and red and green crystal accents in antlers

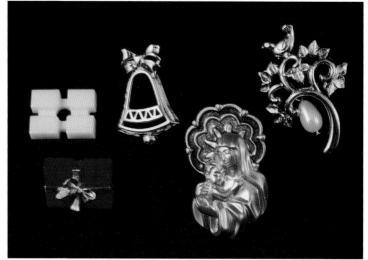

Surprise Package Convertible Pin, 1979, $15 – tie tac style of interchangeable white and red boxes tied with gold bow; **Festive Bell Pin**, 1981, $10 – silver openwork bell; **Madonna and Child**, 1993, $10, gold with green enamel backdrop; **The First Day of Christmas**, 1990, $15 – gold partridge in a pear tree motif with pearl pear

161

Holiday Ornament Tree Pin, 2000, $15 – enamel tree with colorful bead accent dangles; **Angel Tree Pin**, 1999, $15 – angel tree of crystal bodies, pearl heads, and gold wings; **Festive Lights Pin**, 1980 - $10 – tiny gold tree with rhinestone top; **Victorian Tree Pin**, 1993, $20 – marcasite tree with ruby ornament accents; **Christmas Tree Pin**, 1992, $20 – gold tree with aurora borealis rhinestone ornaments

Angels of Harmony Pin, 2002, $15 – silver angels with gold wings and halos; **Holiday Wreath Pin**, 1984, $10 – red plaid fabric wreath; **Rose Wreath Pin**, 2003, $15 – porcelain red rose wreath with big gold bow; **Festive Wreath Pin**, 1994, $15 – antique gold wreath with jewels

Clockwise: **Holiday Cat in Boot Pin**, 1995, $10 – gold cat with green crystal eyes in golden Santa boot; **Santa Tac Pin**, 2004, $10 – silver with enamel accents; **Santa's Sleigh Pin**, 1991, $15 – gold sleigh filled with goodies; **Sleigh Chatelaine Pin**, 1983, $15 – extremely rare gold Santa with his favorite reindeer; **Cat in a Present Pin**, 1999, $10 – adorable kitty playfully perches inside a decorative gift box; **Holiday Candy Cane Pin**, 1997, $10 – large candy cane with enamel leaves and rhinestone accents; **Porcelain**

Winter Scene Pin, 1991, $25 – very rare charming Victorian snow scene with 24k gold-trimmed porcelain; **Holiday Charm Pin**, 1995, $10 – Santa, Christmas tree, and gift dangle from gold safety pin; **Whimsical Winter Pin** (Penguin, Snowman, Cat) 2006, $10 each – colorful enameling and dangling accents; **Jingle Bells Pin**, 1995, $10 – gold pin with holly and dangling bell accents; **Holy Family Tac Pin**, 1994, $10 – gold cut-out of Joseph, Mary, and infant Jesus under blue enamel sky

Chapter Six
Rings

According to legend, Prometheus is the father of jewelry. Hercules cut Prometheus loose from the chains that bound him to Mount Caucasus, and Prometheus then made a ring out of one of the links by carving a groove in the link to set a portion of the rock into the link, thus fashioning the first ring using the first gem with the first method of stone setting called a bezel-set. Many Avon rings are designs with real or faux gems, making them versatile for dinner or daily wear, while others are so elaborately crafted they can substitute for expensive wedding and anniversary rings. Rings utilize all kinds of stones. The precious stones are diamond, ruby, sapphire, and emerald, which can be cut and faceted into any shape and size. A colorless-quartz is the crystal, not to be confused with man-made glass, which can also be cut and faceted to dazzling brilliance and is also called a crystal. Abalone, coral, and mother-of-pearl come from the ocean, while hematite, turquoise, lapis, quartz, and agates are dug from the earth. Rhinestones are faceted glass, which is set with a foil backing to give it brilliance. Marcasite is white iron pyrite, a form of fool's gold, which can be cut and faceted and set in silver. Most Avon rings are stamped inside the band, but some are not marked.

Cameo Silhouette, 1983, $25 – unusual round cameo of white doves on a sky blue background in a silver setting; **Cameo**, 1978, $25 – traditional oval cameo of a white lady on brown background set in delicate gold filigree; **Sentimental Cameo**, 1994, $25 – traditional oval cameo of a white lady on pink background set in an elaborately ornate gold frame

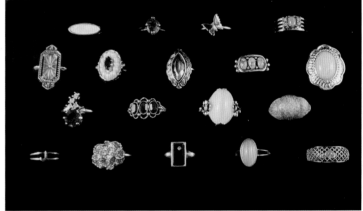

Mother-of-Pearl, 1978, $25 – mother-of-pearl oval set horizontally in gold; **Smoky Topaz-Quartz**, 1983, $60 – genuine smoky topaz quartz in 18k gold; **Shy Butterfly**, 1978, $20 – gold with enamel insets; **Sea Treasure**, 1981, $20 – bands of gold with coral center stone and rhinestone accents; **Frostlights**, 1977, $20 – frosted glass with rhinestone; **Opulent**, 1981, $35 – garnet and seed pearls set in gold; **Shadow Play**, 1977, $20 – marquis cut hematite that sparkles smoky gray; **Desert Azure**, 1976, $25 – three turquoise cabochons in a silver setting; **Silvery Sands**, 1990, $25 – sand-colored cabochon set in ornate silver; **Indiglow**, 1975, $30 – brilliant rhinestones set off a sparkling large sapphire stone in a silver setting; **Purple Brilliance**, 1975, $30 – amethyst stones surrounded by silver beads in silver setting; **Victorian Splendor**, 1982, $30 – large blue moonstone set in silver; **Tailored Classics**, 1976, $20 – timeless look in woven strands of gold; **Initial Ring**, 1980, $20 – gold initial; **Flowerblaze**, 1976, $25 – large carnation flower head with tiny rhinestone dew drop; **Delmonico**, 1976, $20 – simulated onyx with a single rhinestone set in gold; **Porcelain Pastel**, 1981, $30 – rose quartz in gold setting; **Lattice Lace**, 1978, $25 – lattice-style gold ring with center rhinestone accent

Ring of Pearls Perfume Glacé, 1970, $20; **Bird of Paradise Perfume Glacé**, 1971, $20 – plastic turquoise carved in the shape of a bird of paradise; **Cameo Perfume Glacé**, 1970, $20 – large brown stone with carved plastic cameo; **Patterns Fashion Perfume Glacé**, 1970, $20 – large hematite ring

Versailles, 1976, $25 – emerald green stone with pearl accents; Viennese, 1976, $25 – lapis and pearls in antiqued gold; **Venetian Lace**, 1977, $25 – gorgeous amethyst stone set in gold filigree

Emeraldesque, 1986, $35 – faceted emerald stone with four rhinestone accents; **Evening Classic**, 1975, $30 – three emerald baguettes and 6 rhinestones set in silver; **Emeraldesque**, 1994, $25 – faceted emerald with two rhinestone accents

Ribbon, 1974, $20 – silver entwined ribbons; **French Twist**, 1973, $20 – classic tailored twist; **Orchard Blossoms**, 1975, $20 – delicate bouquet of flowers

Purring Kitty, 1991, $35 – extremely rare perky little pussy cat all ready to pounce

Mountain Flower, 1980, $15 – silver band with openwork floral pattern; **Tailored Buckle**, 1976, $15 – polished and textured buckle; **Spellbound**, 1976, $20 – rhinestone studded crescent meshes with gold crescent to symbolize the bonds of love

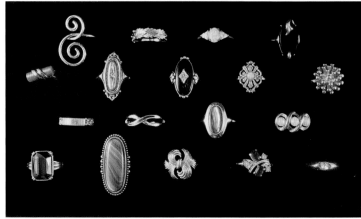

Spun Swirls, 1977, $20 – bright silver spirals; **Laurel Leaf**, 1979, $25 – silver band ring of leaves; **Sterling Silver Opalesque & CZ Accents**, 2003, $25 – brilliant opal with two cubic zirconia accents; **Nightflower**, 1978, $25 – large black onyx set in gold; **Captured Jade**, 1978, $25 – cylinder of jade in gold setting; **Kensington**, 1976, $20 – antique gold design with center rhinestone; **Victorian**, 1983, $30 – simulated onyx with center rhinestone; **Renaissance**, 1982, $25 – lacy open-work gold ring with center opal; **Sunflare**, 1975, $30 – extremely rare and highly unusual ring resembling a bursting sun; **Friendship**, 1979, $15 – open filigree in either gold or silver; **Swirl of Color**, 1979, $25 – lapis loops in silver; **Abalone**, 1977, $25 – abalone shell in silver, no two are alike; **Triple Twist**, 1973, $20 – three pearls in gold twists; **Shimmering Sands**, 1978, $25 – agate striated in sand shades; **Shimmering Smoke**, 1982, $35 – stunning hematite set in gold; **Whirlwind**, 1975, $20 – free form gold swirl design; **Royal Radience**, 1975, $25 – rhinestones and fuchsia stones in gold setting; **Polished Sparkle**, 1986, $25 – gold band with marquis cut rhinestone

Genuine Opal and Brilliantelle, 1981, $70 – opal with crystal accents in sterling silver; **Genuine Tiger's Eye**, 1982, $90 – genuine tiger's eye set in 18k heavy gold

164

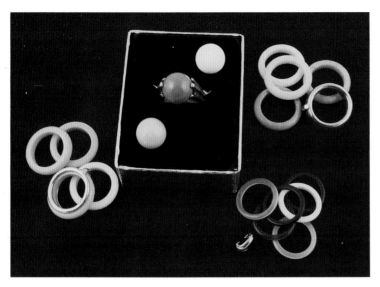

Color Go Round Convertible Ring, 1979, $15 – pastel colors of yellow, white, peach, and aqua; **Color Fling Ring**, 1972, $20 – snap on beads of white, turquoise, and coral; **Color Go Round Convertible Ring**, 1977, $15 – marbleized colors of cream, tan, white, green, and coral; **Color Convertible Ring**, 1981, $15 – extremely rare red, white, blue, pearl pink, pearl lavender, and pearl white rings with gold connector to hold three rings together simultaneously

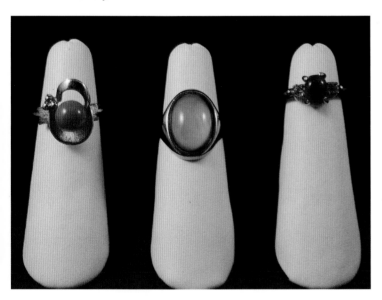

Spindrift, 1975, $25 – large coral stone in sweeping gold leaves; **Mood Ring**, 1987, $35 – very rare in gold setting changes colors with body temperature; **Oriental Jade**, 1974, $20 – jade and rhinestones set in gold

Precious Braid Ring, 1978, $45 – very rare ring of 14k gold and sterling silver in a twisted braid

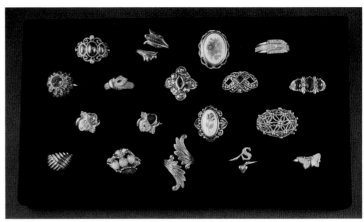

Midnight Splendor, 1972, $25 – hematite and rhinestones in silver setting; **Sterling Silver Lily Ring**, 1977, $35; **French Flowers Locket**, 1975, $20 – opens to hold favorite memento; **Buckle**, 1973, $20, nice buckle of rhinestones on textured gold; **Sunflower**, 1974, $25 – faceted topaz stone in tiers of gold leaves; **Textured Ribbon**, 1975, $15 – gold ribbon tied in knot with a textured surface; **Faux Marcasite Filigree**, 1994, $25 – ruby stone in diamond-shaped marcasite setting; **Woven with Faux Marcasites**, 1994, $25 – colorful crystals in marcasite setting; **Amber Lights**, 1979, $30 – topaz stones with crystal accents; **Two Hearts**, 1994, $30 – two sparkling hearts, one rose and one clear in genuine Austrian crystal; **Two Hearts**, 1992, $30 – Avon's first Two Hearts ring in red and clear Austrian crystals; **Floral Porcelain**, 1993, $30 – genuine porcelain cabochon set in antiqued gold; **Spun Blossoms**, 1979, $30 – gold wire with all the beauty of spun gold; **Ribbed Dome**, 1981, $25 – fluted accent crafted in bright polished gold, **Opalescent**, 1975, $25 – shimmering opals in gold setting; **Sterling Silver Wing Ring**, 2003, $25 – adjustable by-pass ring with antique finish; **Sterling Silver Pave Initial Ring**, 2002, $25 – bypass initial ring with pave crystals; **Butterfly Enamel**, 1986, $15 – gold butterfly with pearly white wings and rhinestone accent

Rosegay, 1974, $25 – pink and pearl flowers in antique silver setting; **Moon Magic**, 1974, $25 – large pale blue stone surrounded by blue sapphires; **Rosamonde**, 1975, $20 – rose in silver filigree

Evening Creation Duet, 1971, $40 – two large pearls surrounded with gold leaves; **Evening Creation Cluster**, 1971, $45 – small pearls set on silver rhinestone leaves; **Chesterfield**, 1980, $25 – oval ring set with marcasites and tiny rhinestones in silver

Burnished Roses, 1975, $25 – two gold finishes create a beautiful burnished effect; **Arabesque Cluster**, 1972, $35 – coral pearls and rhinestone accents; **Bamboo Magic**, 1972, $15 – gold twig design

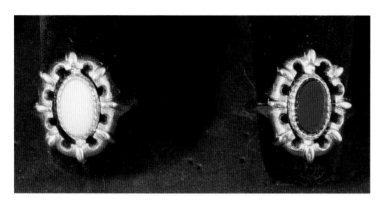

Lights and Shadows, 1975, $20 – lacy gold frame with center that reverses from onyx side to pearl side

Serena Rose, 1973, $30 – carved imitation rose ivory set in gold; **Pale Fire**, 1974, $35 – pink coral with rhinestones; **Creation-In-Blue**, 1972, $45 – large blue sapphire surrounded with clear crystals later released as Regal Style ring in 1987

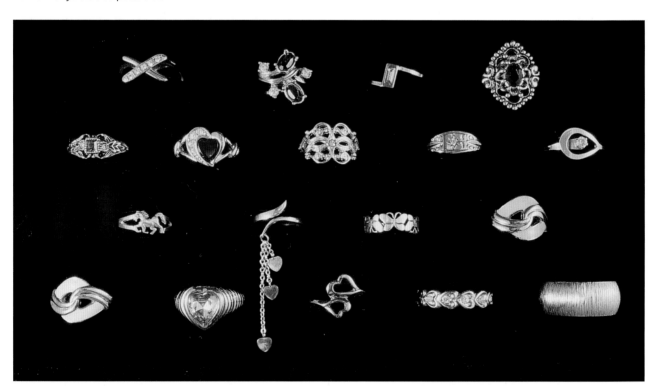

Sparkle Kiss, 1988, $40 –gleaming gold studded with rhinestones; **Dazzling Facets**, 1991, $35 – sapphires and rhinestones set in gold; **Delicate Hues Stackable Ring**, 1985, $15 – baguette of amethyst, diamond, or sapphire stones set in gold; **Family Heirloom**, 1991, $30 – large green center stone surrounded by intricate gold flower petals; **Treasured Memories**, 1992, $30 – luxuriant sapphire stone in antiqued gold setting with crystal accents; **Genuine Onyx Heart**, 1993, $25 – pinky ring of genuine onyx in a heart shape with a rhinestone crescent set in gold; **Glistening Touch Filigree**, 1979, $20 – gold design reflects fine 19th Century English filigree with rhinestone center; **Glimmering Star**, 1980, $15 – nice gold ring with center star effect; **Catch A**

Star, 1977, $15 – brilliant rhinestone in a delicate gold setting; **Sterling Silver Anywhere Horse Ring**, 2003, $20 – pinky ring of galloping horse; **Sterling Silver Pinkeez Ring**, 2002, $20 – pinky ring has 3 dangling hearts; **Sterling Silver Butterfly Cuff**, 1999, $20 – band ring with butterfly cut-out; **Key Biscayne**, 1989, $30 – intricate gold swirl ring with turquoise or ivory insets; **Bold Sparkle Heart**, 1987, $40 – large sapphire heart in heavy ribbed gold band; **Touching Hearts**, 1984, $20 – two open hearts meet at a center angle in child or adult sizes; **Heart to Heart Band**, 1992, $25 – gold heart band with rhinestone centers; **Florentine Band Ring**, 1992, $20 – nice wide band in a brush gold Florentine finish

Baroness, 1973, $25 – emerald cabochon flower center surrounded by gold leaves; **Black Cabochon**, 1973, $25 – black center cabochon surrounded by seed pearls set in gold; **Sweetheart**, 1973, $20 – very rare ring of turquoise and pearl beads set in gold

Evening Splendor, 1973, $30 – pearls and rhinestones in silver; **Royal Occasion**, 1973, $25 – marquise cut amber stones separated with clear rhinestones; **Serena**, 1972, $30 – large angelskin coral surrounded by seed pearls

Birthstone Accent, 1979, $10 – gold birthstone stack ring, several are shown

Queensbury, 1974, $25 – deep amethyst center stone with seed pearl accent; **Moonlustre**, 1973, $20 – large center pearl surrounded by pink seed pearls; **Starsong**, 1974, $25 – rhinestone center surrounded by sapphires

Left to right, top to bottom: **Sterling Silver Semi-Precious Bead Accent**, 2000, $20 – pink marble bead accent; **Sterling Silver Genuine Pearl & Blue Topaz**, 2000, $25 – has matching earrings in Earrings Chapter; **Genuine Sterling Silver Wrapped CZ**, 1994, $25 – has matching earrings in Earrings Chapter; **Sterling Silver Dolphin**, 2005, $25 – nice bypass ring; **Sterling Silver Pear Shaped CZ**, 2002, $25; **Star Scene**, 2005, $55 – gigantic diamond-like stone; **Brilliant Marquis**, 1986, $35 – large dinner ring; **Sterling Silver Heart Shaped Green Onyx Claddagh**, 2005, $45 – brilliant green onyx stone in heart shape; **Aztec Style Pinky**, 1993, $35 – nice turquoise stone set in antique silver; **Sierra**, 1973, $25 – heavy silver ring with turquoise and silver beads and a twisted rope accent; **Boy's Simulated Onyx**, 1984, $20 – black stone in gold setting; **Mirabella**, 1974, $30 – unique silver filigree ring having a hematite center and turquoise points; **Friendship**, 1984 – shiny silver hands holding heart; **Best Friends**, 1989, $10 – two hands clasped in friendship; **Rosebud**, 1975, $20 – tiny pearl in gold flower; **Delicate Cameo**, 1985, $20 – traditional cameo for pinky; **Pretty Penny**, 1979, $20 – copper penny in gold setting

Leaf Lights, 1974, $20 – peridot and jonquil colored stones in leaf shape; **Lustre**, 1972, $20 – pearls with tiny turquoise pearl accents; **Roseglow**, 1973, $25 – faceted ruby surrounded by pearls

Fireflower, 1972, $25 – opal and rhinestones in gold; **Fan Fare**, 1975, $30 – large center pearl set off by rhinestones in a fan shape; **Opaline**, 1987, $35 – a trio of opals set off by rhinestones

Earthstone, 1979, $25 – carnelian in gold; **Crystal Fashion**, 1997, $40 – faceted rose heart stone in 22k gold; **Smoky Lustre**, 1978, $30 – large topaz stone in gold

Flowerburst, 1974, $25 – pearl set in gold petals; **Eclipse**, 1975, $20 – dark and light pearls in silver; **Sun Brilliants**, 1974, $30 – gold leaves and peridot stones surround a larger center peridot stone

Convertible Ring Collection, 1997, $60 – gold band with 7 colorful insets

Reversible Crystal, 1999, $30 – reverses from green emerald on one side to clear crystal on the other

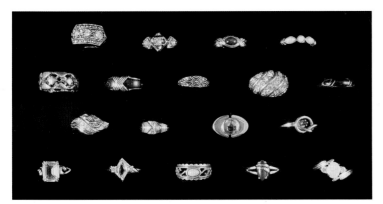

Out of the Past, 1991, $30 – wide band ring of marcasite; Romantic Impressions, 1991, $25 – antique look in silver with crystals; Blue Iris, 1990, $20 – large sapphire stone in heavy gold setting; Turquoise Impressions, 1983, $20 – mother-of-pearl and turquoise set in gold; Gilded Trellis, 1981, $30 – shiny gold band with intricate geometric openwork design; Lapis Blue Reflections, 1985, $20 – lapis band with gold kiss accent; Antiqued Pinky, 1983, $15 – silver pinky with marcasite; Hollywood Style, 1992, $35 – large rhinestone studded ring in a swirl pattern; Midnight Drama, 1980, $15 – black onyx with gold accents; Starswept, 1975, $25 – a swirl of rhinestones in a sweeping gold setting; Chevron Sparkle Pinky, 1985, $20 – rhinestones in a chevron pattern set in gold; New Dimensions, 1976, $20 – sculptured beauty in gold and silver; Love-Me-Knot, 1978, $25 – gleaming gold twist with purple-fired amethyst set in the center; Blue Ice, 1981, $25 – large square aquamarine in silver setting; Crystal Palace, 1976, $25, light blue sapphire with rhinestones in silver setting; Sterling Silver and Genuine Turquoise Ring, 1995, $25; Sterling Silver Genuine Lavender Jade, 2000, $25; Sterling Silver Opalesque with CZ Accents, 2004, $25 – brilliant opal with two cubic zirconia accents

Cultured Pearl, 1977, $45 – genuine cultured pearl in delicate nest of heavy gold; Cultured Pearl, 1979, $45 – 5mm cultured pearl in heavy gold; Cultured Pearl and Sterling Silver, 1980, $60 – lustrous cultured pearl set in precious sterling silver

Plaza IV, 1975, $25 – amethyst in gold with four sparkling rhinestones; Fashion Waves, 1978, $30 – five bands of silver and gold designed to wear in different combinations; Park East, 1976, $25 – emerald in silver with four sparkling rhinestones

Sutton Square, 1977, $25 – sparkling baguettes set horizontally in gold; Glimmer Point, 1978, $15 – dainty glimmering rhinestone set in gold; Captured Rhinestone, 1979, $20, polished gold wide band holding one single rhinestone

Secret Key Sterling Silver, 1976, $30 – bypass skeleton key design; Heart-to-Heart, 1976, $20 – sculptured heart design; Treasured Heart Sterling Silver Spoon, 1975, $30 – bypass spoon ring

Sterling Silver Three Band, 1997, $40 – three band rings with different designs; Aqua Stackable, 2001, $20 – silver rings with blue accents; China Fantasy Band, 1982, $15 – plastic band rings in cinnabar, jade, and ivory

Sterling Silver CZ, 1996, $45 – dramatic 3-carat diamond look-alike set in sterling silver; Brilliantelle Solitaire, 1979, $60 – large diamond look-alike set in sterling silver; Men's Brilliantelle Ensemble, 1983, $90 – large diamond look-alike set in 18k heavy gold

Genuine Cubic Zirconia Sparkle, 1995, $30 – gold band with genuine cubic zirconia center stone; Simulated Pink Diamond, 1984, $35 – pink diamond oval accented with rhinestones; Diamond Style CZ Pear, 1998, $80 – large pink diamond in 18k gold; Sterling Silver Cross Ring with Scroll Design, 2003, $20; Sterling Silver Elephant, 2004, $25; Sterling Silver Victorian Filigree CZ Band, 2000, $20 – nice band ring of crystals; Bold Treasurers, 1994, $30 – large emerald surrounded by rhinestones; Safari, 1990, $25 – leopard spot design in black or white on gold; Royal Radience, 1990, $30 – marcasite and amethyst in the regal style of a precious heirloom; Pleated Ruffle, 1990, $25 – graceful fan fold with five rhinestones; Trio Ring Band, 1994, $20 – this ring was sold as a set of three rings before it was sold separately; it is a wide gold band with an intricate design; Classic Dome, 1989, $25 – fluted gold dome; Faux Amethyst, 1998, $30 – large amethyst with rhinestone accents set in gold; Elegant Sweep, 1989, $25 – sweep of gold with twisted rope accents; Burgundy Wine, 1979, $35 – huge amethyst stone set in gold; Casual Classics, 1989, $25 – stamped fluted ring set with oval aquamarine or amethyst stone; Romantic Cloisonne, 1989, $35 – genuine cloisonne set in gold; Blue Ice, 1990, $30 – heart-shaped aquamarine stone with rhinestone accents set in gold

Leafglow, 1979, $20 – a tiny rhinestone dew drop on a green enamel leaf; Pink Champagne, 1976, $25 – pink sapphires and rhinestones set in gold shape; Smokeblaze, 1978, $25 – topaz stone in gold filigree

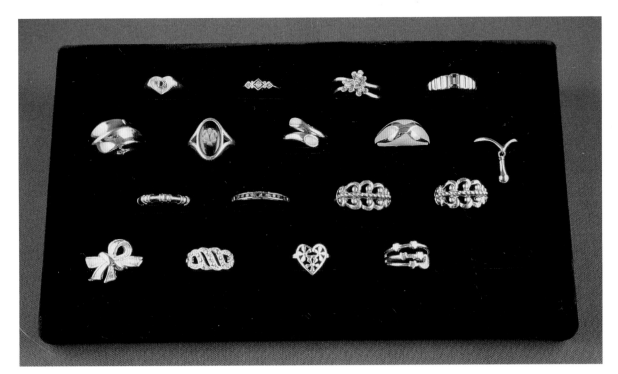

Left to right, top to bottom: **Scarlet Accent**, 1982, $10 – gold heart with red stone center; **Romantic**, 1981, $15 – gold sparkler with crystal accents; **Flower Brights**; 1980, $20 – nice double band gold ring with rhinestone flower heads; **Golden Baguette**, 1985, $20 – gold ring with clear stones flanking amethyst center stone also came with clear center stone; **Sleek Sculpture**, 1987, $15 – wide band ring in shiny gold swirl design; **Midnight Rose**, 1981, $25 – gold with onyx center and carved coral rose accent; **Opalesque**, 1980, $20 – two fiery opals in gold bypass design; **Fashion Pastel**, 1987, $10 – gold ring with ivory, turquoise, or coral enamel accent; **Raindrop Dangle**, 1979, $20 – rare shiny gold ring with gold raindrop, **Royal Circle**, 1979, $10 – gold band with blue or green enamel accents; **Timeless Band**, 1984, $15 – gold circle ring studded with red, green, or amethyst stones, **French Filigree**, 1977, $20 – filigree band ring in gold or silver, **Beau Knot**, 1975, $10 – rare silver ring in simple knot design; **Monaco**, 1980, $15 – extremely rare shiny marcasite-style; **Love Blossoms**, 1980, $10 – shiny silver filigree heart; **Galaxy**, 1980, $20 – silver stars and crescent moon delicately arranged to adorn triple band

Blue Opalesque, 1991, $25 – large opal in silver band

Eternity Stackable Ring Set, 1997, $45 – two gold bands designed to be worn together, one studded with rubies and the other studded with rubies and clear crystals in an alternating pattern

Ring Trio, 1994, $45 – extremely rare set of three rings, one being a trio of Austrian crystals flanked by glossy white swirls in gold, one being a gold band with antique-etched flowers which was later sold by itself, and one being a pear-shaped aquamarine set in gleaming gold

Goldtone Precious Colored Interchangeable Ring Set, 2004, $100 – rhinestone studded ring jacket designed to hold an interchangeable gold band of rings studded with rubies, emeralds, and sapphires

w

Solar Magic Adjustable Flower, 1999, $20 – goes from lavender to blue in sunlight

Fleur de Lys Scarf Ring, 1989, $10 – gold or silver

Silk Weave, 1980, $10 – flexible gold band with crossed gold accent design

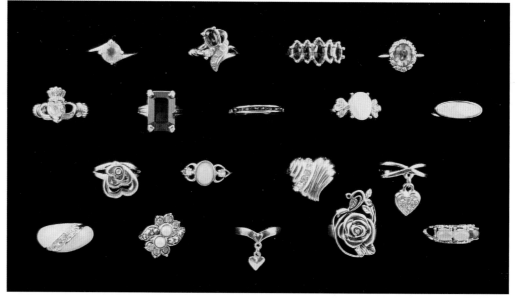

Simulated Canary Diamond, 1982 $25 – extremely rare yellow diamond; **Faux Amethyst Collection**, 1995, $25 – amethyst stone with rhinestone accents; **Marquis Sparkle**, 1994, $25 – amethyst stones in anniversary design; **Rosey Facets**, 1991, $20 – faceted rose stone in gold frame; **Claddagh**, 1992, $20 – traditional design with faceted crystal heart; **Glamorous Touch**, 1991, $20 – large square emerald cut ruby; **Eternal**, 1995, $15 – gold wedding band filled with emeralds, sapphires, or rubies; **Genuine Mother-of-Pearl**, 1991, $20 – large mother-of-pearl center flanked by rhinestones on either side; **Mother-of-Pearl**, 1978, $15 – oval mother-of-pearl in gold setting; **Hearts in Motion**, 1995, $15 – twirling hearts set in gold; **Fiery Opalesque**, 1989, $15 – fire opal with rhinestone accents; **Scalloped Heart**, 1994, $15 – nice ribbed heart with rhinestone accents; **Dangling Heart**, 1993, $15 – gold rhinestone studded heart charm; **Tailored Elegance**, 1991, $15 – enamel with rhinestone accent; **Heirloom Riches**, 1993, $30 – extremely rare marcasite and pearl design; **Genuine Sterling Silver Dangle Heart**, 1995, $20 – simple chevron design with heart charm; **Sterling Silver Rose on the Vine**, 2004, $30 – large carved rose design; **Sterling Silver Multi-Color Jade**, 2001, $45 – band with yellow, green, and rose jade

Chapter Seven
Earrings

Earrings are the foundation stock of a jewelry wardrobe. The designs must be versatile and practical, for daytime or formal wear, and they must flatter the wearer's ear, face, hair, and personality. They date back thousands of centuries. The earliest ones were lightweight, hollow-gold wire hooks designed to pierce the ear lobes, but as artisans used more interesting heavy stones and materials, they needed different methods of attaching them. The post, screw-back and clip came into being in the 1930's, and they stayed in fashion until the 1970's, when dangling pierced earrings became the fad. Avon uses the wire fishhook, the post, leverback, and the clip designs, and they incorporate a wide variety of sizes and styles, from a simple stud centered entirely within the circumference of the ear lobe to dangles measuring 4-inches or longer. Most of the stones and pearls are glass and synthetic, but Avon uses karat gold and sterling silver in their hypoallergenic ear wires and posts. Avon generally made earrings in both clip and pierced versions, but some came in only one style.

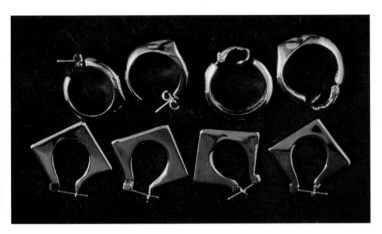

Pacesetter, 1977, pierced, $15 – shiny gold or silver diamond-shaped treasures; **Sleek & Sassy**, 1978, c/p, $15 – shiny gold or silver sculptured hoops

Safari Style, 1989, c/p, $15 – gold square with leopard or silver square with zebra; **Filigree Hoop**, 1988, pierced $15 – extremely rare shiny gold or silver-plate filigree hoops; **Celebration Star**, 1986, pierced, $10 – large gold or silver dimensional star;

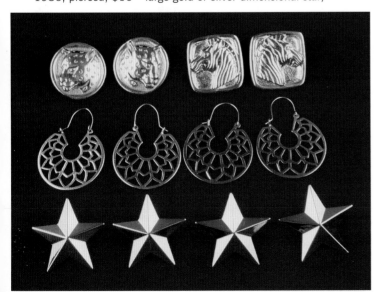

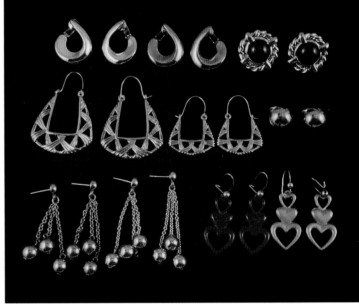

Back: **Polished Profile**, 1980, c/p, $15 – designed to imitate the curve of the ear in gold or silver; **Cable Style**, 1998, c/p, $15 – gold with twisted silver and lapis center; Center: **Basket Weave Hoop**, 1991, pierced, $15 (large), $10 (small) – gold baskets on wire loop; **Gilded Compliment**, 1980, c/p, $15 – gold button dome earrings; Front: **Silvery Cluster Dangle**, 1990, pierced, $15 – three silver balls on silver chains; **Golden Cluster Dangle**, 1990, pierced, $15 – identical to Silvery Cluster Dangle in gold; **Heart-to-Heart**, 1988, pierced, $15 – pink, lilac, or cherry heart dangle

Grand Style, 1989, pierced, $20 – three free-form concentric designs in silver or gold

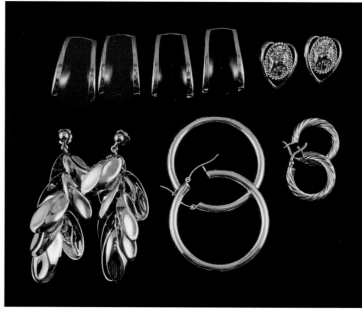

Back: **Bold Color Hoop**, 1996, c/p, $15 – bold enamel hoops in red or black; **Horoscope**, 1991, pierced, $10 – all zodiac signs in gold; Front: **Tropical Leaves**, 1992, pierced, $15 – silver or gold dangling leaves; **Sterling Silver Snap Top Hoop**, 1996, pierced, $30 (large), $20 (small) – shiny polished silver in the large earrings and shiny rope twist in the small pair

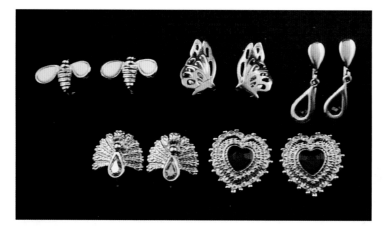

Fashion Bee, 1979, c/p, $10 – textured and polished gold bee has wings with mother-of-pearl inserts; **Filigree Butterfly**, 1983, c/p, $15 – openwork lacy butterfly; **Birthstone Teardrop**, 1977, c/p $10 – sparkling Austrian glass crystal set in gold; **Pretty Peacock**, 1991, c/p, $15 – gold feathers with blue Austrian crystal teardrop body; **Harmonious Heart**, 1995, c/p, $10 – faceted red hearts rest amidst gold filigree hearts

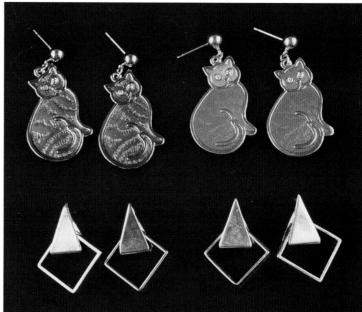

Pretty Kitty, 1990, pierced $15 – silver with blue overlay or gold with amber overlay – Avon did not make them left and right the way they did other figural earrings; **Fashion Touch**, 1978, c/p, $15 – swinging square hanging from a pyramid came in gold or silver

Ship Ahoy, 1989, pierced, $15 – red, white, or blue enamel sail on gold; **Color Hearts**, 1987, pierced, $15 – big heart dangle in teal, red, or lapis; **Just For Spring**, 1994, pierced, $10 – gold ladybug with red overlay or marcasite hummingbird with amethyst eyes

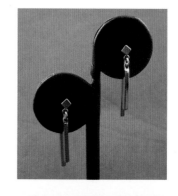

Gentle Breeze, 1979, $20 – extremely rare dual dangle with front gold and back silver

174

Frosted Grapes, 1989, c/p, $15 – came in white or lavender frost pearls; Frosted Grapes, 1991, c/p, $15 – came in peach or cream pearls

Back: **Modern Drama**, 1986, c/p $10 – classic gold wave design with colored enamel; **Paradise Colors**, 1987, c/p, $15 – same earring as Summer Pastels of 1990 only these have enamel leaves in shades of blue or orange; **Fireworks**, 1988, c/p, $10 – spiffy white sparkler of red, blue, and gold fireworks; Middle: **White Lights**, 1987, c/p, $10 – white rounds with rhinestone accents; **Porcelain Art**, 1990, c/p, $15 – large blue or pink porcelain art; **Safari**, 1990, c/p $15 – shiny gold button-style with black enamel leopard print has matching ring in Ring Chapter; Front: **Magnetic Collage**, 1987, c/p, $15 – blue metal disk with magnetic elements that can be moved around or removed at whim; **In Full Bloom**, 1992, c/p, $10 – oval rose and lavender flower motif; **Springtime Delight**, 1996, pierced $10 – antique silver with glossy cherry or watermelon and marcasite accents

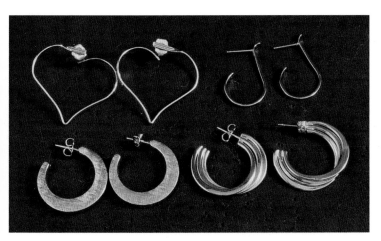

Back: **Spring Bouquet**, 1997, pierced, $15 – faceted stones linked in gold in pink, blue, or clear; **Two-Tone Magnetic Convertible**, 1999, c/p, $15 – oval shaped button with interchangeable inserts of gold or silver; **Roundabout Hoops**, 1979, c/p, $15 – large hoops in shiny gold or silver; Center: **Shades of Fashion Reversible**, 1978, c/p, $15 – enamel colors in gold reverse from navy to cream; **Roundabout Hoops**, 1979, c/p, $15 – large hoops in gold or silver; Front: **Silver Tone X Cuff** aka Silvertone X Hoop, 2000, c/p, $15 – silver shrimp hoop with golden X cross; **Shades of Fashion Reversible**, 1978, c/p, $15; enamel colors in gold reverse from brown to beige

Touchpoints, 1977, pierced, $15 – delicate hearts in silver or gold; **Modern Scroll**, 1978, pierced, $30 – delicate hoops in sterling silver or 14k gold-filled; Front: **Crescent**, 1976, c/p, $15 – thick half-moon hoops in silver or gold; **Crescents III**, 1980, pierced, $15 – three linked hoops in silver or gold

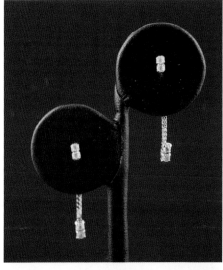

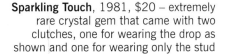

Sparkling Touch, 1981, $20 – extremely rare crystal gem that came with two clutches, one for wearing the drop as shown and one for wearing only the stud

175

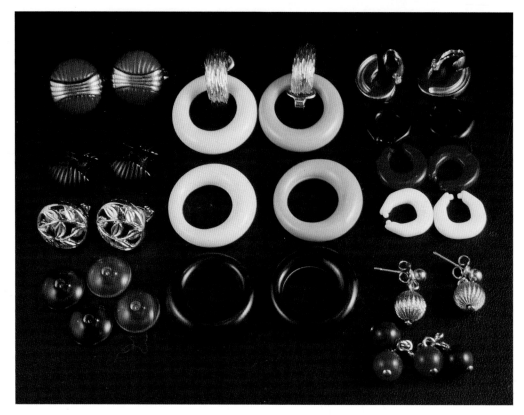

Back: **Color Change Convertible**, 1981, c/p, $20 – jade and onyx with gold stripe accent; **Color Convertibles**, 1975, clip, $20 – plastic hoops in cream, black, and blue slip over textured gold hoop disks; **Fashion IV Convertible**, 1981, c/p, $20 – gold hoops with slide-on disks in black, white, and red: Front: **Convertible Floral**, 1981, c/p, $20 – gold filigree motif with slide-in disks of blue and pink; **Fashion Drop Convertible**, 1980, pierced, $20 – gold stud with dangles of gold, lapis, and carnelian

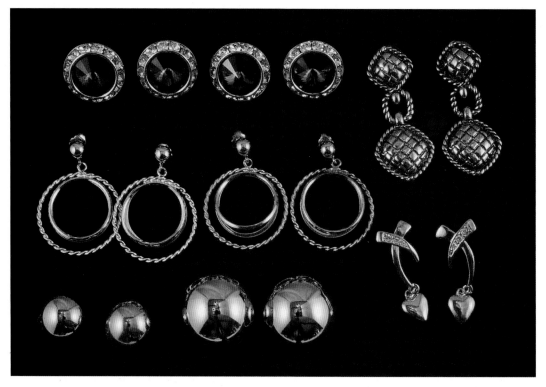

Back: **Glitzy Clip**, 1999, clip, $20 – large amethyst, emerald, or Siam red gemstone surrounded by shiny crystals in gold setting; **Quilted Heirloom**, 1993, c/p, $15 – gold diamonds in traditional quilt pattern; Center: **In a Whirl**, 1976, c/p, $15 – extremely rare two polished hoops with one rope twist hoop in gold or silver; **Heart & Kisses**, 1994, pierced, $15 – gold hearts dangle from kisses; Front: **Polished Dome**, 1990, c/p, $15 – gleaming gold in 3 sizes. Shown are small and medium

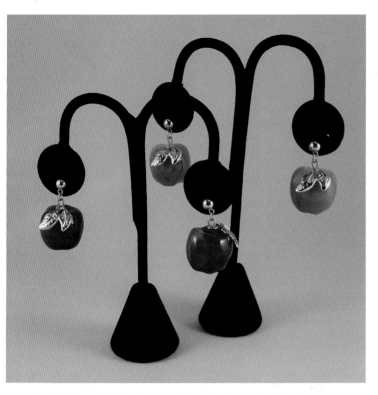

Apple A Day, 1993, pierced, $15 – 3-dimensional red or green apple with gold accents

Back: **Le Frog**, 1981, pierced, $20 – tiny frogs delicately sculpted in three dimensions and finished in brightly polished gold; **Delicate Question**, 1980, pierced, $20 – gold question mark with ball dangle; **Heart Sparks**, 1985, pierced, $10 – gold hearts with rhinestone accents; Center: **Brilliant Simulated Birthstone**, 1989, pierced, $10 – birthstone set in gold pinwheel jackets; **Star Struck**, 1985, pierced, $15 – gold with faceted points; Front: **Heirloom Rose**, 1993, pierced $15 – antique gold rose; **Regal Crown**, 1989, c/p, $10 – detailed gold crowns; **Spring Tulip**, 1990, c/p $10 – graceful tulip in gold or silver

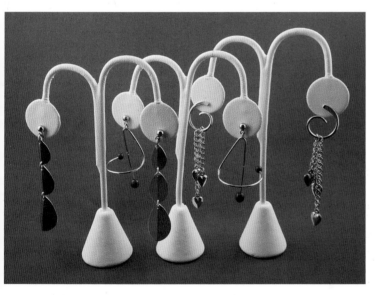

Savvy Style, 1989, c/p, $15 – silver or gold 3-tier dangle; **Spiral Motion**, 1991, pierced, $10 – gold spiral with lapis accent beads; **Unchain My Heart**, 1991, pierced, $10 – gold heart dangles can be removed from jackets

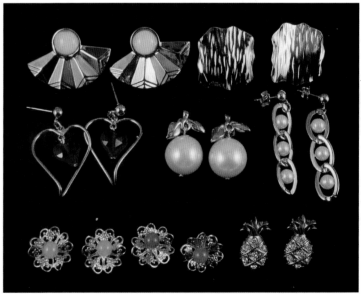

Back: **Pleated Fan**, 1987, c/p, $15 – gold fan with white moonstone or sapphire center; **Polished Leaf**, 1987, c/p, $15 – silver or gold sculpted leaf; Center: **Two of Hearts**, 1994, c/p, $15 – gold openwork heart with a dainty red suspended heart; **Pearly Elegance**, 1993, pierced, $10 – 15mm pearl suspended from gold leaves; **Pearly Drop**, 1993, c/p, $10 – pearls captured by gold links; Front: **Semi-Precious Filigree Flower**, 1995, pierced, $15 – genuine rose quartz or adventurine beads with removable gold filigree jackets; **Pineapple Sparkle**, 1993, pierced, $15 – gold pineapples studded with rhinestones

Back: **Blossom & Pearlesque**, 1995, clip, $15 – exquisite gold flourishes with center pearls; **Bold Starfish Weave**, 1992, clip, $15 – dramatic gold openwork starfish; Front: **Contemporary Dangle**, 1990, c/p, $15 – bold abstract shape in black or red with gold top; **Dramatic Lion**, 1989, c/p, $15 – large gold lion with full mane

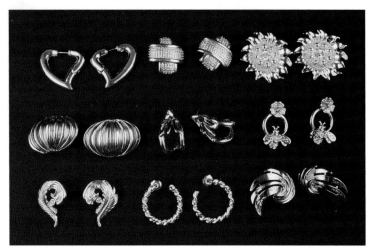

Back: **Golden Heart Hoop**, 1998, pierced, $15 – gold hearts are hinged to hug the ear; **Golden X**, 1998, c/p, $15 – beaded gold in a crisscross design; **Sunny Flower**, 1991, pierced $15 – gold flower head with crystal accent; Center: **Classic Dome**, 1989, c/p, $15 – shiny gold fluted hoop, matching ring in Ring Chapter; **Initial Hoop**, 1993, pierced, $15 – polished gold script initial; **Bee Brilliant**, 1994, c/p $10 – gold bee with crystal wings in flower hoop; Front: **Precious Plume**, 1990, pierced, $15 – gold feather with rhinestone accent; **Braided Hoop**, 1984, c/p $15 – traditional gold hoop in braided design; **Golden Sweep**, 1991, c/p, $15 – graceful shiny gold sweep

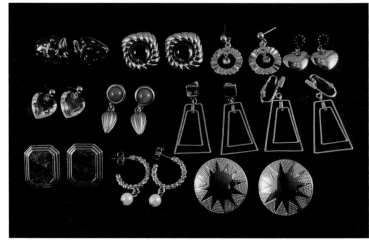

Back: **Very-Berry**, 1990, c/p, $15 – red enamel with green enamel accents; **Spotlight**, 1986, c/p, $15 – brilliant blue or dazzling pink cabochon stone in gold rope frame; **Birthstone Dingle Dangle**, 1995, pierced, $15 – birthstones within fluted gold hoops; Center: **Romantic Facets**, 1985, pierced, $15 – dangling hearts in aqua, clear, or rose; **Delicate Drop**, 1992, c/p, $10 – gold dangle with jade cabochon; **Sweet Whispers**, 1977, c/p, $20 – extremely rare square dangles in silver or gold; Front: **Park Avenue**, 1985, c/p, $15 – marbleized blue or green in golden frame; **Classic Earring Gift**, 1993, pierced, $15 – golden hoop with pearl dangle; **Sunburst**, 1987, c/p, $15 – silver or gold sunburst motif

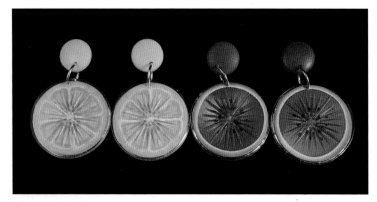

Tooty Fruity, 1993, pierced $10 – large size dangles in lemon or watermelon

Confetti, 1984, pierced, $15 – aluminum ribbons in gold, turquoise, red, or violet; **Delicate Drop Convertible**, 1982, pierced, $10 – silver wire came with amber, rose quartz, and turquoise drop; **Kaleidoscope**, 1992, c/p, $15 – wonderful teardrop motif in shades of pink, red/white/blue, shades of blue, or shades of beige

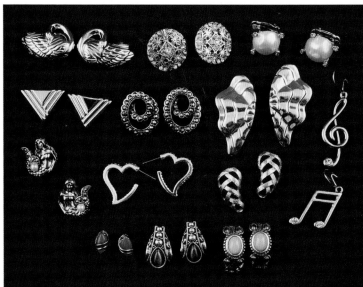

Back: **Graceful Swan**, 1989, c/p, $15 – silver or gold swan; **Medallion**, 2005, pierced $15 – shiny silver circle with sparkling accents; **Baroque Pearlesque Button**, 2000, c/p, $15 – pearl with rhinestones in silver setting; Center: **Chevron**, 1985, pierced $10 – shiny silver triangles; **Heirloom Accent**, 1993, c/p, $10 – marcasite circles; **Enchanted Wings**, 1986, c/p $10 – graceful butterfly wing motif in silver or gold; **Musical Note**, 1989, pierced, $20 – extremely rare bar note and treble clef with rhinestones in silver or gold; Center: **Mystical Mermaid**, 1996, pierced $10 – enchanting Lorelei in marcasite and pearl; **Heart Hoop**, 2003, pierced $15 – silver with rhinestone accents; **Spunweave**, 1980, c/p, $15 – silver or gold half hoops with openwork pattern; Front: **Sterling Silver and Lavender Color Jade**, 2001, pierced $15 – silver wrapped jade; **Silvertone Textured Color**, 2004, pierced $15 – nice beaded half-hoop with amethyst stone accent; **Sterling Silver Bold Turquoise**, 2002, pierced $15 – antique silver half-hoop with center turquoise cabochon accent

Back: **Traditional Teardrop**, 1993, c/p, $15 – pearl or amethyst stone in teardrop marcasite; Center: **Floral Hoop**, 1982, c/p, $10 – carved leaf design in amethyst or jade; **Soft Petal Rose**, 1993, c/p, $10 – gold rose motif; Front: **Floral Hoop**, 1982, c/p, $10; **Soft Geometrics**, 1994, c/p, $15 – gold octagons with pastel inlays

Back: **Pink Lace**, 1996, pierced, $15 – pink rhinestone with gold bow; **Colorful Pansy**, 1995, pierced, $15 – colorful pansies framed in gold with rhinestone center in green or pink tones; Center: **Pink Rosette**, 1998, $10 – nice metallic rose studs; **Pearlessence**, 1986, pierced, $10 – double pearl drop; Front: **Ladybug, Ladybug**, 1980, pierced, $10 – red and black enamel; **Venetian Pastel**, 1986, pierced, $10 – small mosaic design in blue/white or purple/white

Pearly Spray, 1993, clip $10 – pearls looped together to make flower; **Captured Rainbow**, 1989, c/p, $10 – look of rich mother-of-pearl chips gleam and glitter in white frame or choose black confetti in black frame; **Twisted Hoop**, 1972, clip $10 – traditional gold rope twist design

Back: **Modern Contrast**, 1993, pierced, $15 – unique combination of gold and silver in a fan design; **Pearly Cluster Dangle**, 1991, pierced, $15 – three pearls on gold chains; **Fiery Irisee Dangle**, 1986, pierced, $15 – smooth gold ball holds a faceted crystal drop that flashes with iridescent fire; Front: **Heart Charms**, 1989, pierced, $15 – gold hoop with removable heart, crystal, and pearl charms; **Nostalgic Reflections**, 1988, c/p, $15 – lacy gold or silver openwork design with crystal accent; **Golden Billow**, 1990, c/p, $15 – classic gold openwork design

Floral Loop, 1991, pierced $15 – gold matte flowers; **Melody Dangle**, 1991, pierced $15 – shiny gold swirl with crystal accents; **Spiro Gyro**; 1993, pierced $15 – shiny gold spiral conceals a lustrous pearl

179

Floral Hoop Convertible, 1988, pierced $15 – three great color looks from one versatile pair of earrings having ivory flower studs and marbleized coral and turquoise loops; **Convertible Flower**, 1983, pierced $10 – ivory and coral flowers; **Frosted Floral Convertible**, 1980, pierced, $15 – white and amethyst flowers with center rhinestone

Filigree Dangle, 1991, pierced $15 – large shiny gold fans

Color Collections, 1988, pierced, $15 – gold openwork spiral with interchangeable colored disks in black, malachite green, and carnelian; **Charm Convertible**, 1991, pierced, $15 – holiday accents of bell, crystal, and star; **Beguiling**, 1990, pierced, $15 – large gold textured swirl originally released as the Breathless Collection in 1988 with a matching bracelet

Faux Tortoise & Silver Tone aka Tortoise Color and Silvertone, 1999, c/p, $15 – large tortoise doorknocker with silver accent; **Linear Chain**, 2006, $15 – large faceted green drop on burnished brass chain; **Tortoise Style**, 1997, pierced, $15 – elongated tortoise hoops with gold accents

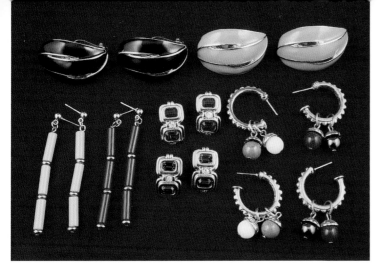

Back: **Sophisticated Stripe**, 1994, clip, $15 – bold gold with black enamel or aqua enamel; Front: **Color Play**, 1986, pierced, $15 – slender dangle in red, turquoise, or black; **Glamorous Touch**, 1990, c/p, $15 – faceted emerald or ruby stone framed in gold with rhinestone accent has matching ring in Ring Chapter; **Precious Choices Hoop**, 1995, pierced, $20 – interchangeable white quartz/turquoise beads or red quartz/hematite beads in traditional rope hoops

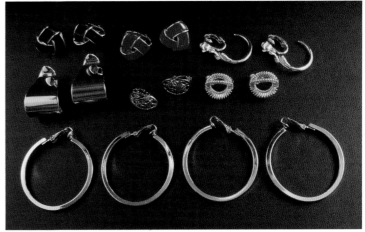

Tailored Button, 1995, c/p, $10 – classic twist in black or red; **Rose Hoop**, 1982, c/p, $15 – gold or silver hoop with rose accent; Middle: **Polished Ribbons**, 1977, c/p, $15 – wide gold or silver hoop; **Engraved**, 1981, c/p, $10 – openwork flower in gold or silver; **Bright Dimensions**, 1979, c/p, $10 – gold or silver rope twist design; **Great Hoops**, 1977, c/p, $20 – large gypsy hoops in gold or silver

Metallic Color Drop, 1989, pierced, $15 – purple, green, or red balls; **Braided Fashion Drop**, 1990, c/p, $15 – purple or pearl drops from braided gold shield; **Marble Mosaic**, 1993, c/p, $15 – gold chain with multi-colored balls

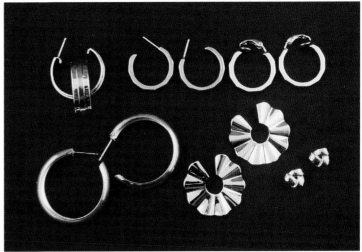

Back: **Sleekline Hoop**, 1978, c/p, $15 – shiny silver hoops with gold center stripe; **Stylepoint Hoop**, 1978, c/p, $15 – multi-faceted gleamer in gold or silver; Front: **Sterling Silver Wedding Band Hoop**, 1987, pierced, $35 – generous loops sweep almost full circle; **Sculptured Swirl**, 1991, pierced, $10 – two intertwined hoops, one textured and one shiny gold; **Tailored Knot**: 1989, c/p, $15 – a gold fashion classic

Back: **Shimmering Drape**, 1994, pierced, $10 – light weight aluminum chains in fuchsia, gold, or blue; **Fashion Lustre**, 1991, $15 – pearl brightened by rhinestone and gold accents; Front: **Playful Parrot**, 1996, pierced $10 – gold bird with blue and green glaze; **Lucky Elephant**, 1989, pierced, $15 – blue or white enamel on gold; **Heart Stripes**, 1987, pierced $10 – colorful two-heart dangle in blue with silver stripes or red with gold stripes; **Lucky Shamrock**, 1998, pierced $10 – gold clover with green glaze; **Drop Anchor**, 1993, c/p, $15 – dainty red or blue anchor swings within gold braided hoop

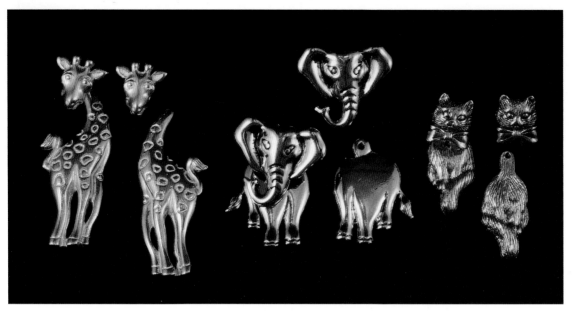

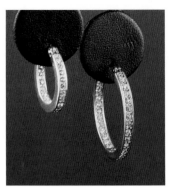

Jungle Animal, 1993, pierced, $15 – gold giraffe or silver elephant designed for the head in front and the body behind the ear; **Novelty Cat**, aka **Front to Back Cat**, 1994, pierced, $15 – tails waggle behind ears with kitty heads in front

Back: **Pretty Plume**, 1990, c/p, $10 – pearlized plastic with colorful bird; **Cheery Cherry**, 1992, c/p, $15 – red enamel cherries with gold accent; **China Sea**, 1993, c/p, $15 – jade circle suspended from gold filigree; Center: **Mirrored Magic**, 1988, c/p, $15 – real mirror silk-screened with abstract design in yellow or blue; Front: **Pebble Accent**, 1992, pierced, $15 – gold hoops with stones of amethyst, jade, and cinnabar; **Pearlized Cloud**, 1988, pierced, $15 – pearlized plastic featuring two cumulus clouds joined by gold jump rings in blue or white

Butterfly Dazzling Dangle, 1993, c/p, $10 – plastic butterflies in three shades of pink; **Aqua Beaded Hoop**, 2001, pierced, $15 – silver with turquoise dangles; **Lavender Floral**, 2001, pierced, $10 – rhinestones in burnished brass

Bamboo Snap Top Hoops, 1998, pierced, $15 – lightweight gold hoops; **Casual Hoop**, 1993, c/p, $15 – gold loops with delicate seed pearls

Fan Dangle, 1990, $15 – silver or gold fan design; **Gala Nights**, 1991, c/p, $20 – large marquis crystals in an elegant cluster of diamond-like brilliance; **Soft Sculptured**, 1987, c/p, $15 – silver or gold butterfly wing design; **Silver-Plated Basketweave**, 1986, $15 – traditional basket weave design; **Silver-Plated Polished Perfection**, 1986, c/p, $15 – gleaming silver free-form design

Filigree Fun, 1995, $15 – traditional gypsy-style with movable drops; **Golden Maze**, 1993, c/p $15 – large gold dangle with Greek maze design

Starburst, 1978, c/p $15 – rhinestone studded dazzler in silver or gold; **Shrimp Tailored**, 1981, c/p, $15 – updated classic hoop in sleek half circle of graceful gold; **Glazed Strawberries**, 1979, c/p, $10 – bright red berry with gold and green accents; **Sparkling Reflection**, 1980, c/p, $15 – gold oval earrings with starburst effect and center rhinestone

Frosted Classic, 1993, clip, $15 – large rose quartz or frosted white; **Color Doorknocker**, 1997, clip, $15 – elegant hoops in white, black, or red; **Fabric Blossom**, 1989, c/p, $10 – flower petals with pearl-tipped stamens in white or peach

Flipover Color Hoop, 1999, pierced, $15 – dramatic hoops flip from red to blue or black to white; **Beautiful Basics**, 1993, pierced, $30 – large white, medium red, and small blue hoops; **Two-tone Bold**, 1999, clip, $15 – bold interlocking square of gold and silver

Loop De Loop, 1993, c/p, $10 – lightweight aluminum rings came in blue, purple, or gold; **Star Sparkle**, 1993, pierced, $10 – looped aluminum wire buttons in royal blue, fuchsia, or gold

Oasis, 1992, pierced, $15 – gold shield with turquoise bead accents and golden drops; **Endless Circles**, 1991, c/p, $10 – gold or silver cascading circles; **Modern Filigree**, 1992, c/p, $15 – classic red or blue in fanciful jacket of gold filigree

Golden Dangle, 1997, pierced, $15 each – there are two styles and both are shown. The left is artistic cascades of gold wires and the right is elegant dangling gold spirals

Rhinestone Heart in Keepsake Box, 2005, pierced, $15 – slide-open rhinestone heart in gold or silver

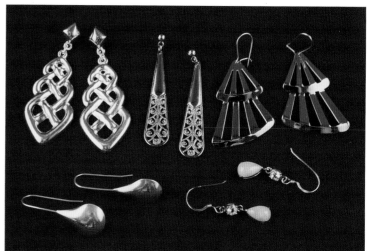

Polished Weave, 1987, pierced $15 – long silver dangle in braid design; **Lace Drop**, 1989, pierced $10 – silver or gold filigree lace; **Fashion Fan**, 1989, pierced, $15 – gleaming silver or gold fan dangle; Front: **Genuine Sterling Silver Teardrop**, 1995, pierced, $20 – flowing teardrop design; **Sterling Silver Genuine Jade and Genuine Blue Topaz**, 2001, pierced $25 – fishhook drop of genuine stones

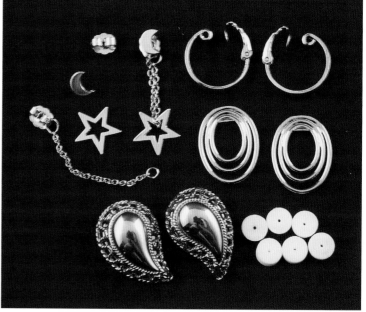

Starswept Convertible, 1980, pierced, $15 – moon, chain, and star dangle can be worn several ways; **Triple Hoop Convertible**, 1982, c/p, $15 – polished gold can be worn without the hoop dangles; **Paisley Fragranced**, 1982, pierced, $15 – gold with fragranced tablets

Rhinestone Slide Illusion, 2002, $15 – clear or blue rhinestones on slide wires designed to slip over the ear lobe; Goldtone Round CZ Leverback, 2000, pierced $20 – 2 carats total weight of shiny crystals

Bountiful Harvest, 1994, c/p, $25 – clusters of genuine stone beads with gold leaf accents

Playful Pastel, 1993, $10 – long matte pink or aqua; Caribbean Rain, 1994, c/p $15 – turquoise beads and inlay set in gold; Lilac and Lavender, 1994, $15 – frosted lavender blossoms with gold and amethyst

Back: Polished Blossoms, 1987, pierced, $15 – gold or silver flower with pink cabochon center; Tailored Scallops, 1991, c/p, $10 – gold or silver sea shell; Front: Regal Style, 1990, c/p, $15 – dramatic gold crest; Glitter Swirl, 1987, c/p, $15 – gold or silver with pave accents

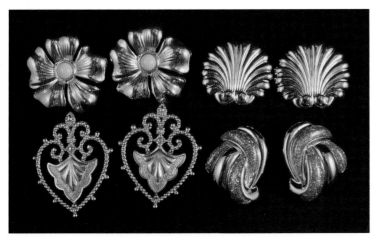

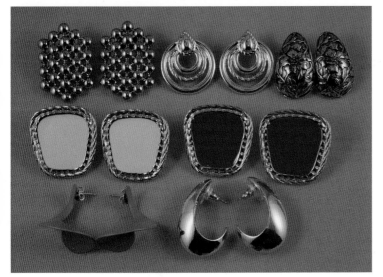

Back: Bold Dimensions, 1990, c/p, $15 – gleaming metal beads in abstract design; Stylish Hoop, 1988, c/p, $15 – polished triple-play of rope-textured hoops held with a teardrop in gold or silver; Floral Garden, 1988, c/p, $15 – antiqued silver or gold hoops of flowers; Center: Summer Style, 1993, c/p, $15 – red or white enamel in gold rope frame; Front: Whirlwind, 1989, pierced, $15 – metal swirls in summer pastels of mint, white, or peach; Sculptural Hoop, 1997, pierced, $15 – stylish gold half-hoops

Metallic Melody, 1993, c/p, $10 – two hammered gold disks; Glamorous Links, 1997, c/p, $15 – gold rings dangle from gold ball; Textured Loop, 1993, pierced, $10 – long gold or silver triangle design

Faceted Crystal, 1993, c/p, $15 – a quartet of real crystals; **Velvet Impressions Pierced Earrings**, 1991, $10 – dressy silk drops suspended from a gold medallion; **Pearly Shower**, 1991, c/p, $15 – 3 strands of pearls in gold

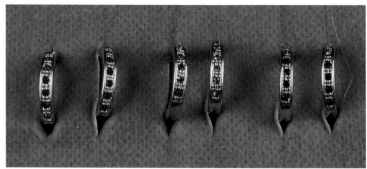

Goldtone Precious Colored Hoop Earrings Set, 2004, $20 – ruby, emerald, and sapphire hoops

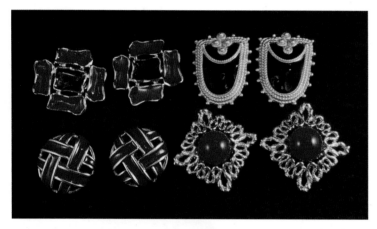

Back: **Color Splash**, 1991, clip, $15 – pink and blue epoxy enamel; **Bold Shield**, 1991, clip, $15 – black with matte gold border; Front: **Bold Basketweave**, 1997, clip, $15 – gold with glossy color overlays in red or green; **Bold Burst**, 1992, clip, $15 – openwork gold frames a black or red cabochon

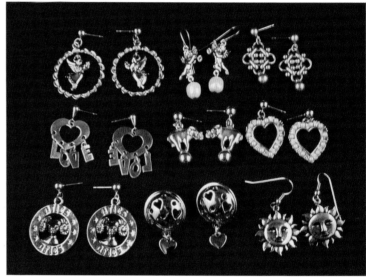

Back: **Soaring Angel**, 1993, pierced $10 – tiny gold angel swings in gold hoop; **Frolicking Cherub**, 1995, pierced $15 – gold cherub with dangling pearl; **Burnished Dangle Drop**, 2000, c/p $15 – gold beads in chain frame; Center: **Love**, 1994, c/p $10 – gold L O V E suspended from an open heart; **Good Fortune Elephant**, 1996, pierced $15 – playful gold pachyderm on gold ball has a matching bracelet; **Special Heart**, 1994, pierced $15 – classy little pearl-studded hearts; Front: **Sign of the Zodiac**, 1993, pierced, $15 – gold circle with center zodiac emblem; **Open Your Heart Earrings**; 1992, pierced $15 – shiny gold cutout sphere with heart dangle; Fun Sun

Back: **Genuine Sterling Silver Wing**, 1994, pierced, $15 – classic wing design; **Sterling Silver Triple Wire Hoop** aka Genuine Sterling Silver Triple Wire Hoop, 1995, pierced, $15 – wire circles linked together; Front: **Spoken Love**, 1996, pierced $10 – gold drops engraved with LOVE; **Firebird**, 1986, pierced, $15 – semi-hoops in pink, violet, blue or yellow, green, blue; **Sleekly Simple**, 1990, pierced, $10 – gold or silver hammered-look dangles

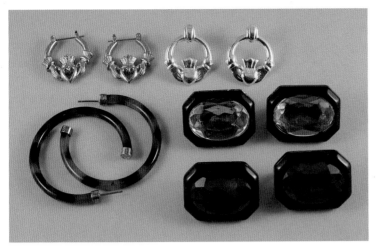

Back: **Claddagh Hoops**, 1991, pierced, $20, gold traditional Irish design; **Sterling Silver Claddagh Hoop**, 1994, pierced, $25, silver traditional Irish design; Front: **Faux Tortoise**, 1998, pierced, $10 – tortoise hoop with silver cap; **Sparkle Magic**, 1989, c/p, $10 – faceted red or clear stone in an emerald-cut black frame

Back: **Burnished Goldtone Flower Button**, 2002, c/p, $15 – pastel rhinestones; **Emerald Cut Button**, 1999, c/p, $15 – sapphire or amethyst stone surrounded by crystals; **Square Color**, 1999, c/p, $15 – gold square with interchangeable white and black inserts, Center: **Birthstone Bee**, 1998, pierced, $10 – gold bee with birthstone body, clear rhinestone wings and pearl head; **You Are My Sunshine**, 1994, pierced, $10 – gold sun face with rhinestone rays; **Pearlesque Cluster**, 1997, pierced $15 – pink or cream pearls in gold jackets, often confused with Pearlesque Cluster of 1990, which is a Christmas earring; **Precious Brilliance Fashion**, 1996, c/p, $15 – button earrings of brilliant rhinestones on black enamel; Front: **Goldtone Satin Polish Hoop**, 1999, c/p, $15 – omega style gold hoops; **Pearlesque Drama**, 1998, c/p, $15 – large 16mm baroque pearl set in textured gold jackets; **Twist Hoop**, 1996, pierced, $15 – traditional gold rope hoop earrings

Graceful Leaves Hoop, 1988, pierced, $10 – two leaves touch and create a fashionable hoop in gold or silver; **Oval Hoop Wire**, 1989, pierced, $15 – gigantic gold or silver oval hoops; **Dangling Treasures**, 1991, c/p, $15 – crystal drop in gold with pearl

Back: **Oriental Jade**, 1977, c/p $15 – genuine jade in gold; **Sterling Silver Radiant CZ**, 2002, $25 – clear cubic zirconia 6.75 carat weight total; **Sterling Silver Faceted Blue Stone Earrings with Vine Motif**, 2002, $20 – blue crystals with silver accents; Center: **Cubic Zirconia**, 1996, $15 – stud equivalent to half a carat set in gold in clear or lavender stones; **Center Rhinestone Knot**, 1999, $10 – textured and polished gold with center rhinestone; **Rose Blossom**, 1985, $10 – fabric blossom in purple or rose; Front: **Goldtone CZ Flower**, 2001, $15 – large flower earrings; **Personal Creations**, 1983, $10 – 14k gold-filled heart with carnelian ball

Interchangeable Earrings Set, 2003, $15 – rhinestones in silver can be worn several different ways; **Earrings Duos**, 1995, $15 – porcelain heart and lavender roses; **Color Accent Earring Collection**, 1993, $25 – extremely rare set of large yellow metal hoops, medium blue metal hoops, and red plastic buttons

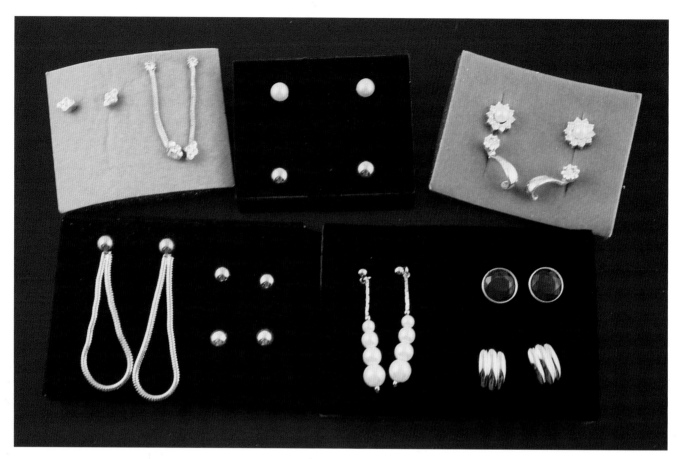

Goldtone Earrings Set with Diamond Shaped Accents, 2003, $15; Duo Stud Earrings Gift Set, 1998, $10 – 6mm pearl and gold studs; Shimmering Interchangeable Earring Set, 2002, $15 – rhinestone set that can be worn six different ways; Tri-tone Snake Chain Convertible Earring Set, 1999, $15; Classic Trio Earring Set, 1995, $15

Summer Shower, 1995, c/p, $15 – gold shells and seed pearls; Beaded Beauty, 1994, c/p, $15 – ringlets of gold with pearls or gold beads; Two-Tone Heart Cluster, 1999, pierced, $15 – puffed hearts in gold and silver; Seaside Shower, 1994, pierced, $15 – gold sea life motifs with pearls

Summer Pastels, 1990, c/p, $15 – identical to Paradise Colors only in pearlized blues or pinks with pearlized white accents; Day and Night Convertible, 1987, pierced, $15 – lapis circles and gold hearts with fluted gold studs; Soft Sweep, 1981, c/p, $15 – gold sculptures; Golden Rings, 1994, pierced, $15 – three gold rings; Beaded Button, 2000, c/p, $10 – red or green beads in burnished metal; Classic Finish Sterling Silver Earrings, 1981, pierced $20 – extremely rare textured silver hoop

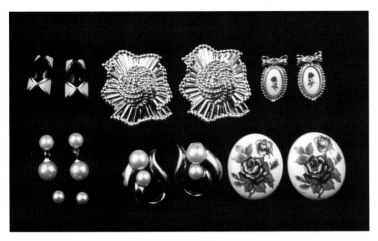

Back: **New Spectator "J" Hoop**, 2002, pierced, $10 – classic spectator styling in black or red; **Fashion Fan**, 1991, c/p, $10 – gold shields with fan design; **Vintage Rose**, 1996, pierced, $10 – porcelain cabochon with single rose; Front: **Pearlesque Earring Duo**, 2001, pierced, $15 – one pair is a combination of cream pearl with pink pearl drop and the second pair is 5mm studs; **Modern Classic**, 1992, c/p, $15 – go-with-everything gold swirls with pearl accents; **Birthday Bouquet**, 1990, pierced, $10 – porcelain ovals with flower of the month

Dangle Drop, 1986, pierced, $15 – three graduated beads in gold or silver; **Gala Dangle**, 1988, pierced, $15 – silver or gold loop with rhinestone accents

Back: **Dramatic Drape**, 1987, pierced $15 – silver or gold curtain drape; **Sweet Mesh**, 1994, pierced $15 – lustrous pearl in gold mesh circle; **One Fish, Two Fish**, 1992, pierced $15 – extremely rare openwork gold fish with lapis eyes; **Sculptured Drop**, 1987, pierced $15 – long silver or gold pointed drop; Center: **Pearly Cluster Hoop**, 1995, pierced $15 – dressy pearl hoops entwined in gold; **Fan Twist**, 1987, pierced, $15 – pleated gold twisted fan; Front: **Roman Riches**, 1987, c/p $15 – large hoops reminiscent of Corinthian column scrollwork; **Golden Weave**, 1986, c/p $10 – large square basket weave design; **Basic Hoops**, 1996, pierced, $15 – traditional gold hoops; **Peacock Dangle**, 1994, c/p $10 – gold bird with amethyst accents

Back: **Metallic Splash**, 1992, c/p, $10 – gold or silver threads intertwined with white vinyl; **Metallic Collage**, 1988, c/p, $15 – classic dome with confetti colors in blue or gold; Center: **Beaded Hoop**, 1993, pierced, $10 – classic gold bead hoop; **Dogwood Flower**, 1992, clip, $20 – pearlized pink or white in gold; Front: **Textured Hoops**, 1992, c/p, $15 – gold hoops with beaded texture; **Angelica**, 1992, c/p, $15 – lacy gold with milky-white moonstone

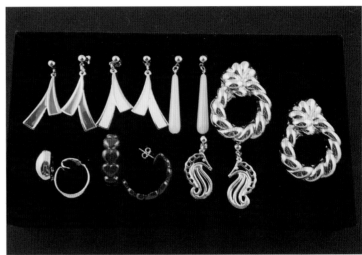

Brushstroke, 1993, c/p, $15 – cast gold dangle in blue or white enamel; **Sleekly Elegant**, 1990, pierced, $15 – rose quartz or lapis drops in gold setting; **Bold Twist**, 1993, c/p, $10 – bold gold wreath in knotted rope design; **Small Classic Hoop**, 1989, c/p, $15 – gold wedding ring hoop; **Hearts Around Hoop**, 1991, c/p, $10 – red epoxy enamel or gold hearts; **Dangling Seahorse**, 1990, pierced, $15 – gold openwork seahorse

Evening Glamour, 1994, clip, $25 – gold filigree with multi-colored faceted stone accents can be worn without the drop

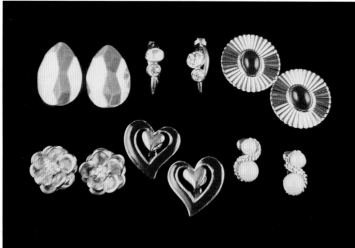

Back: **Add-a-Look**, 1990, pierced, $15 – rhinestone studs, ribbed gold teardrop, and shiny silver teardrop to be worn several ways; **Floral Expressions Convertible**, 1993, pierced, $15 – gold flower with pearl centers can be worn with flower jackets, leaves jackets, or the pearl center alone; Center: Convertible Heart; **Loop-a-Hoop Convertible**, 1979, pierced, $15 – extremely rare shiny silver and gold rings can be taken apart; Front: **Lace Heart**, 1981, pierced $15 – gold heart on silver lace jacket can be worn without the lace jacket

Golden Facets, 1985, c/p, $10 – faceted sparkler; **Double Hoop Crystal**, 1998, c/p, $15 – double hoop accented with sparkling crystals; **Midnight Moon**, 1986, c/p $10 – large ribbed gold circle with carnelian or onyx center; Front: **Faceted Petals**, 1993, c/p $10 – pastel petals in gold; **Double Heart**, 1989, c/p, $15 – outside hearts are translucent enamel in red or sapphire and inside hearts are gold; **Classic Twist**, 1991, c/p, $15 – gleaming gold braid swirls around two pearls

Back: **Hobby Horse Earrings**, 1981, pierced $10 – polished gold rocking horse; **Dancing Reindeer Earrings**, 1980, pierced $10 – two special deer from Santa's sleigh; **Elephant Earrings**, 1981, pierced $10 – openwork gold elephant; Center: **Teddy Bear Earrings**, 1978, $10 – gold bears; **Pretty Posies Earrings**, 1980, pierced $10 – gold baskets with pink enamel posies; **Coupled Hearts Earrings**, 1980, pierced $10 – textured and shiny gold hearts; **Coral Blush Earrings**, 1980, pierced $10 – plastic coral rosebud in silver stud; Center: **Delicate Daisies Earrings**, 1977, pierced $10 – colorful daisy in gold setting; **Heart of My Heart Earrings**, 1978, pierced $10 – shiny gold or silver heart inside a larger heart; **Double Fun Earrings**, 1986, pierced $10 – plastic ice cream cone; Front: **Daisy Rainbow Convertible Earrings**, 1980, pierced $10 wooden flowers with yellow plastic center; **Flight of Color Convertible Earrings**, 1979, c/p $15 – colorful butterflies with gold body; **Oyster Cove Earrings**, 1981, pierced, $15 – pearl stud with shell or hoop jacket

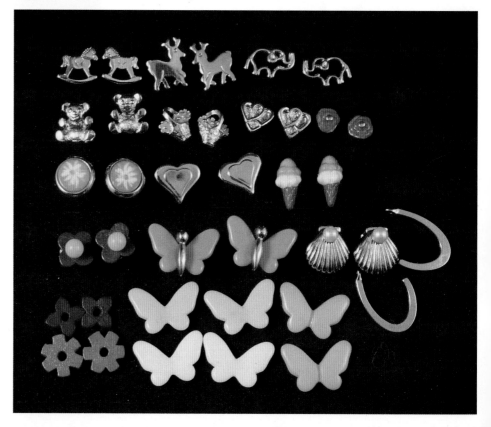

Golden Swirl, 1982, pierced $15 – traditional gold circle goes with everything; **Leafspray**, 1978, pierced $20 – extremely rare gold cut-out leaf motif; **Starfish**, 1984, pierced $10 – extremely rare tiny dimensional gold starfish design which was so popular that Avon brought it back in a larger size with matching pieces in 1987; **Sculptured**, 1995, pierced, $10 – matte finish hoops to wear alone or with drops in gold or silver, also had a matching pendant; **Strawberry Sparkle**, 1995, pierced, $15 – ruby rhinestone studded berries dangle from gold leaves; **Faux Marcasite Hoop to Hoop**, 1994, pierced, $15 – fantastic marcasite circles; **Mickey & Friends Earrings**, 1990, pierced, $10 – gleaming gold Mickey Mouse studs; **Ribbon Sparkle**, 1987, pierced, $15 – gold circle accented with gleaming rhinestone; **Cultured Pearl**, 1980, pierced $15 – large pearl stud set in gleaming silver; **Sterling Silver Knot** aka Genuine Sterling Silver Knot, 1995, pierced, $15 – dainty love knots; **Simply Stated Hexagon**, 1978 - $15 – extremely rare sterling silver hoops; **Sterling Silver and Genuine Amethyst**, 1995, pierced, $15 – genuine amethyst in sterling silver filigree; **Sterling Silver Textured Square**, 1987 - $15 – large silver square

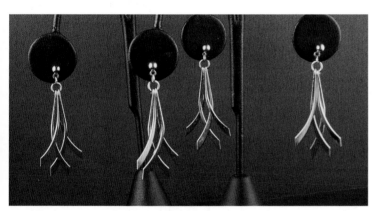

Windchimes, 1987, pierced, $20 – breezy dangles in silver or gold swing and sway

Pearlized Pastel, 1989, c/p, $15 – blue or pink shell motif with gold accents; **Apple Harvest**, 1994, pierced, $10 – red overlay apples with gold accents; **Day Into Evening**, 1990, c/p, $15 – wear gold swirl alone or add polished gold dangle embellished with rhinestones; **Grape Cluster Drop**, 1996, c/p, $10 – gold grapes; **Golden Knot**, 1987, c/p, $15 – textured and smooth gold; **Glitter Flame**, 1988, c/p, $15 – gold flame setting with fiery silver or fiery red insets

Chandelier, 1994, pierced, $15 – showers of gold chains with faceted clear beads accents; **Faceted Shower**, 1992, c/p, $15 – crystal clear chandelier dangles of faceted beads hanging from gold filigree cap; **Dangling Daisy**, 1994, c/p, $15 – gold flower with faceted crystal center

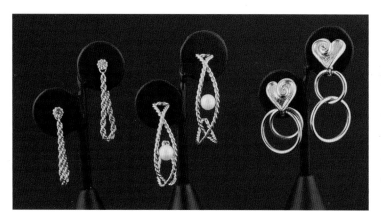

Sparkle Ropetwist, 1993, pierced, $10 – classic rope with
rhinestone accent; **Twisted Wire Hoop**, 1994, pierced, $10 –
twisted gold rope with pearl accent; **Heart to Heart Hoop**, 1996,
c/p, $15 – gold heart to wear alone or with hoops

Color Fun, 1993,
pierced $10 – gold
hoops with pearl and
blue glass dangle with
red bead accents

Back: **Rhinestone Fantasy**, 1991, pierced, $20 – crystal-studded
gold swirls; **Golden Sparkle**, 1996, c/p, $15 – dazzling crystals
with gold frames; **Pave Accented Pear Drop**, 2005, pierced, $15
– large lemon teardrop dangles; Front: **Icy Facets Dangle**, 1990,
c/p, $15 – gold leaf with rhinestone accent and crystal drop;
Rhinestone Bar, 2002, pierced, $15 – dazzling evening wear; **Two-
Tone X**, 2000, c/p, $15 – gold with pave-look silver inset

Opalescence Twist, 1992, c/p, $15 – elegant cabochons of opal
glass in twist of gold; **Open Heart Drop**, 1995, c/p $15 – large
pearl dangles from a gleaming gold heart; **Dimensional Drop**,
1993, c/p $15 – large pearl in gold ring

Fun Heart, 1993, pierced, $10 – dimensional hearts in red or gold;
Heart Filigree, 1986, pierced $10 – filigree hearts on gold chain

Back: **Precious Purse**, 1991, pierced, $10 – skillfully crafted
handbag in gleaming gold; **Double Loop Doorknocker**, 1996, c/p,
$15 – classic bold gold doorknocker; **Focal Point**, 1986, c/p, $15
– magnificent doorknocker in gold; **Golden Nugget**, 1985, c/p, $15
– right-from-the-mine look in gleaming gold; **Golden Crescent**, 1986,
pierced, $10 – gold fluted wreath; Front: **Classic Texture**, 1981, c/p
$15 – squared off shape of classic earrings softened by a touch of
texturing, **Golden X**, 1998, c/p, $15 – beaded gold in a crisscross
design; **Pink Rosette**, 1998, $10 – nice metallic rose studs

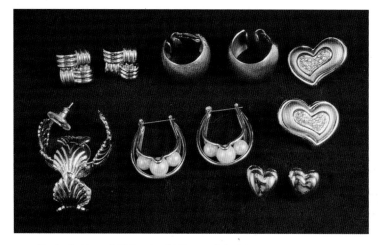

Basic Button, 1996, c/p, $15 – traditional gold square button;
Satin Ribbons, 1978, clip, $15 – elegant large gold satin hoops;
Golden Heart, 1996, c/p, $15 – open hearts of satin matte gold
with pave center and shiny silver bezel; Front: **Shells Around Hoop**,
1994, pierced, $10 – textured leaves in gold; **Captured Elegance
Hoop**, 1993, pierced, $15 – trio of pearls captured in gold cage;
Puffed Heart, 1984, c/p, $15 – gold or silver dimensional heart

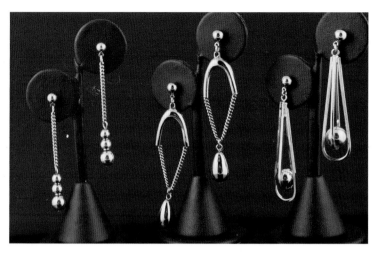

Stylish Swing Dangle, 1994, c/p, $15 – three graduated silver or gold balls on chain; **Suspended Drop**, 1994, pierced, $10 – basic drops in gold or silver; **Sleek Spheres**, 1994, pierced, $15 – sculptured loops enclose an orb in gold or silver

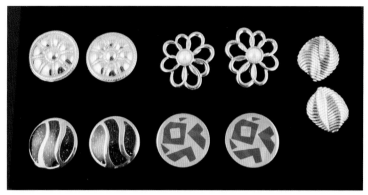

Sculptured Button, 1988, c/p $15 – Roman shield style came in several colors; **Color Sensation**, 1982, pierced $10 – gold circle with fuchsia swirl inserts; **Daisy Bouquet**, 1990, c/p $10 – gold flower head motif with pearl center; **Chroma Graphics**, 1986, c/p $10 – gold circle came with choice of colored inserts; **Sea Treasure**, 1988, pierced $15 – gleaming gold cowrie shell design

Back: **Showstopper**, 1989, $15 – stunning faceted crystal dangles designed to simulate diamonds; **Fanfare**, 1988, c/p $15 – large double fan motif in silver or gold; **Mirror Image**, 1981, c/p $10 – tailored concave round in gold or silver in a futuristic interpretation of Avon's Odyssey cologne; Front: **City Lights**, 1985, c/p $20 – rhinestone studded doorknocker; **Blue Opalesque**, 1991, $20 – look of mysterious blue opal highlighted with marcasite set in silver; **Romantic Treasures**, 1995, c/p $15 – marcasite and blue sapphire hoops; **Sterling Silver Opalesque & CZ Earring Duo**, 2003, pierced earrings $20 – one pair of opal studs and one pair of cubic zirconia studs has matching ring in Ring Chapter

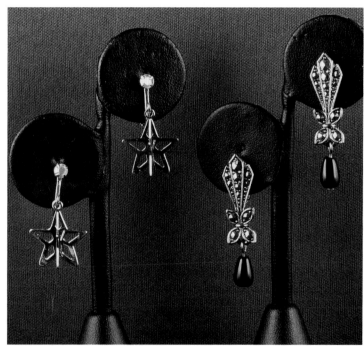

Rhinestone Accent Star Drop, 2000, c/p $15 – dimensional star with rhinestone and crystal accent; **Heirloom**, 1995, c/p, $15 – fan and leaf motif in marcasite with dangling jet black bead accent

Back: **Pleated Crescent**, 1988, c/p, $15 – two intertwined pleated crescents in gold or silver; **Perfect Compliments**, 1987, c/p, $15 – enamel swirls in white, blue, or green; **Golden Brilliance**, 1992, c/p, $15 – button style dazzlers of rhinestones; Center: **Isn't It Romantic Drop**, 1993, pierced, $15 – either pearls or coral hang from gold bows; **Moonlight Lace**, 1988, pierced, $15 – fan earrings with a cream pearl in gold or hematite pearl in antique silver; **Pleated Horn**, 1982, c/p, $15 – silver or gold horn of plenty; Front: **Golden Braid**, 1992, pierced, $10 – bold airy open hoop; **Hoopla Earring Trio**, 1990, pierced, $20 – three pairs of gold or silver hoops boxed together in 3 sizes

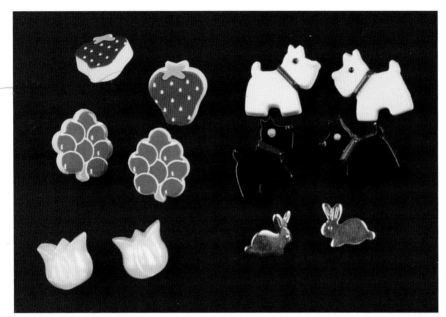

Fruit Punchers Earrings, 1990, pierced, $10 – colorful grape and strawberry; **Playful Plaid Earrings**, 1989, pierced, $10 – Scottie dogs in white and black; **Frosted Tulip Earrings**, 1981, pierced, $10 – tulip bud of pearlized plastic; **Bunny**, 1979, pierced $10 – shiny gold bunny for young adult

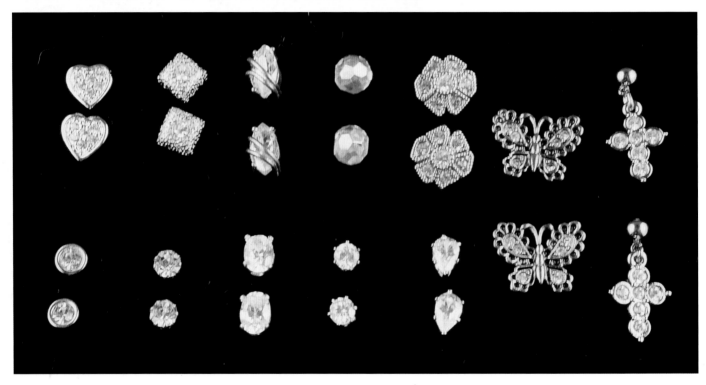

Back: **Heartshine**, 1979, c/p, $15 – heart-shaped cluster of rhinestone chips in a pave setting; **Nugget Sparkle**, 1987, pierced, $10 – gold square with rhinestone sparkler also has a matching pendant; **Crystal Multi-faceted**, 2003, pierced, $15 – aurora borealis sparkler; **Genuine Sterling Silver Wrapped CZ**, 1995, pierced $15 – sparkling stone wrapped in silver has matching ring in the Ring Chapter; **Floral Facets**, 1993, pierced $10 – nice button with multi-colored gemstones; **Brilliant Butterfly**, 1993, pierced, $15 – light antique gold filigree with crystal accents; **Rhinestone Cross**, 1993, pierced, $15 – sparkling crystals in gold setting; Front: **Touch of Glitter**, 1978, $10 – tiny crystal stud; **Facets**, 1988, $15 – rhinestone stud simulates a half carat diamond; **Oval CZ Stud**, 1997, $25 – each stud is 2.8 carats diamond weight equivalent set in gold; **Cubic Zirconia**, 1987, $10 – crystal stud; **Diamond Style CZ Pear**, 1998, $15 – two carats total weight in clear or pink pear-shaped stones

Round Floral, 1999, pierced, $15 – gold earrings with porcelain rose centers; **Golden Glitter**, 1998, c/p, $20 – fluted gold hoops studded with rhinestone accents

194

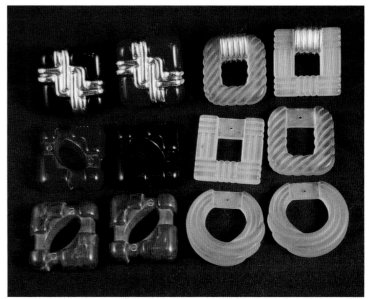

Color Swirl Pierced Earrings, 1986, $15 – shiny gold swirls filled with black, purple, fuchsia, or green enamel; **Color Dangle**, 1995, c/p $20 – bold silver fan with turquoise or black accent; **Doorknocker**, 1996, c/p $15 – white enamel on gold in traditional doorknocker style; **Pink Tulip**, 1994, c/p, $15 – frosted pink petals and transparent green leaves in gold flower pot that moves; **Reflections of You**, 1992, c/p $10 – tiny mirror dangles; **Nautical Style**, 1994, $15 – moonstone fish drop also came with moonstone frog drop; **Classic Baroque Pearlesque**, 2001, pierced, $10 – nice large pearl stud; **Fashion Birthstone**, 1987, pierced, $20 – large birthstone in heart-shaped gold frame; **True to the Heart**, 1994, pierced, $15 – faceted hearts of genuine Austrian crystals in ruby or clear

Convertible Colors, 1992, c/p, $15 – large set in red, black, and blue with gold accents; **Rainbow Ice**, 1987, pierced, $15 – plastic hoops in light blue circles, crystal squares, and pale pink squares

Sterling Silver Genuine Pearl & Blue Topaz, 2000, pierced $15 – stunning blue topaz and pearl sparkler has matching ring in the Ring Chapter; **Faux Amethyst**, 1997, pierced $15 – gold hoops studded with light amethyst crystals

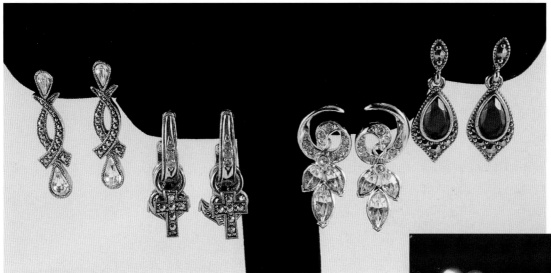

Romantic Essence, 1994, pierced, $15 – faceted crystals and marcaste; **Convertible Faux Marcasite Hoops**, 1994, pierced, $15 – can be worn alone or with the marcasite charms of heart, cross, and anchor; **Spiral Twist**, 1997, clip, $20 – magnificent faceted crystals in rhinestone studded spiral; **Romantic Splendor**, 1994, clip, $15 – silvery marcasite with amethyst stone

Convert-A-Heart, 1986, pierced $10 – gold half heart can be worn alone or with the silver half heart jacket; **Silver Plated Fluted**, 1980, pierced $10 – silver fluted studs; **Roman Holiday Semi-Precious Studs**, 1993, pierced $15 – genuine adventurine or rose quartz balls; **Petite Crescent**, 1984, pierced $10 – tiny gold half-moons

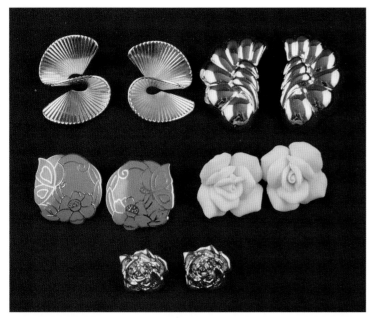

Silver Plated Fan Twist, 1987, pierced $15 – pleated twisted fan is identical to the gold version only in silver-plate; **Stylized Swirl**, 1988, c/p $15 – large sculpted fans to grace your ears also came in gold; **Sophisticated Cloisonne**, 1988, pierced $15 – turquoise circles with gold webbing; **Porcelain Petals**, 1987, c/p $20 – genuine bisque porcelain roses and leaves came in white or pink; **Sculptured Rose**, 1988, c/p $15 – shiny gold roses

Delicate Petals Convertible, 1988, pierced, $10 – rhinestone studs with white flowers and gold jackets; **Skeleton Dance Glow in the Dark**, 1993, pierced, $10 – silver 3-D effect in epoxy enamel; **Lime Slice**, 1982, pierced, $10 – plastic lime wedge; there was also a Lemon Slice in this series

Star Spangle Dangle, 1993, c/p, $15 – globes with white star on blue background suspended from gold wheel with red star center; **Multi-Dangle Star**, 1998, pierced $15, extremely rare red, white, blue, and gold stars on fish wires; **Heart of America**, 1990, pierced earrings $10 – this set is so popular that Avon continues to release it, always with pierced earring; **Americana Star**, 2002, c/p, $10

Halloween Dangle Drop, 2006, pierced $10 – spooky ghost; **Halloween**, 2007, pierced $10 - kitty

Top: **Swinging Cats Hoop**, 1995, pierced $15 – gold kitties sway on gold hoops; **Halloween Spider Web**, 1992, pierced $15 – intricately crafted gold webs with rhinestone accent; **Itsy Bitsy Spider**, 1994, pierced $20 – extremely rare gold and crystal spider; Bottom: **Dangling Witch**, 1994, pierced $25 – extremely rare antique gold witch on broom; **Halloween Drop**, 1999, pierced $10 – trio of Halloween motifs of white ghost, orange pumpkin, and black bat; **Halloween Cat**, 1998, pierced $10 – black cat cut-out face with orange bead accent; **Triple Pumpkin Drop**, 1995, c/p, $10 – bright orange jack-o'-lanterns with cut-out features; **Pumpkin**, 1994, pierced $10 – golden jack-o'-lantern with orange face; **Precious Cat**, 1993, pierced $10 – black cat face with crystal eyes; **Precious Pumpkin**, 1993, pierced $10 – pumpkin shape studded with orange rhinestones – this earring was released again in 1997; all earrings are extremely rare

Halloween, 2007, pierced $10 – choose Spidey or Skully;
Halloween Dangle Drop, 2006, pierced $10 – black bat

Holiday Splendor Collection, 1987, $20 – perfume rollette came in various scents with gleaming gold, faceted pierced earrings

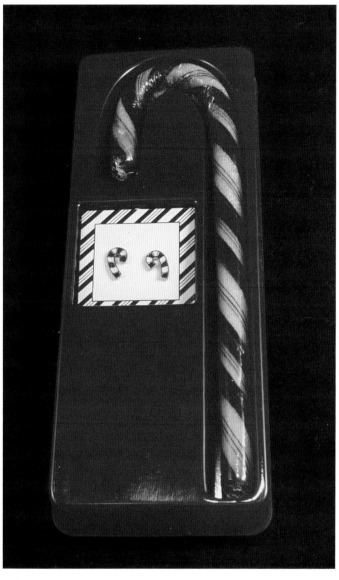

Candy Cane Treat, 1983, pierced, $10 – extremely rare enamel candy canes came with a stick of candy

Back: **Snowman**, 1998, c/p, $10 – pearl stud snowman with gold accents; **Pearly Bell**, 1997, c/p, $10 – pearl bells with rhinestone clapper and gold bow; **Angelic Expressions**, 1996, c/p, $15 – rhinestone and pearl angel; Front: **Angelic Sparkle**, 1996, pierced, $15 – crystal angel; **Pearly Snowman**, 1995, c/p, $10 – dangling pearl snowman with gold accents; **Pearlesque Cluster**, 1989, c/p, $15, gold mistletoe leaves with pearl berries

Festive Snowball Ornament with Pearluster Stud and with **Snowball**, 1987, pierced, $10 – red plastic ornament holds lustrous pearls or textured silver balls; **Happy Holly Days**, 1991, c/p, $15 – cluster of red satin berries; **Snow Petals Convertible**, 1987, pierced, $15 – gold or silver snowflake with rhinestone center in snowflake-decorated heart box

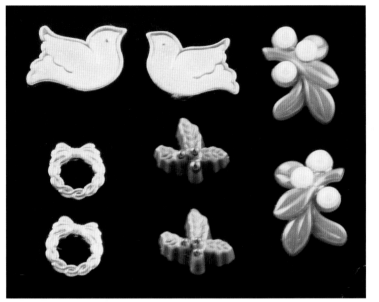

Shimmering Dove, 1988, pierced $10 – iridescent glitter on gold; **Mistletoe**, 1986, pierced $10 – green leaves with pearl berries; **Wreath**, 1982, pierced $10 – tiny gold wreath; **Holly Berry**; 1981, pierced $10 – green leaves with red berries

Back: **Jingle Bell Hoop**, 1992, pierced, $15 – gleaming silver or gold bell suspended from a decorative bow that jingles with movement; **Ring in the Holidays**, 1994, c/p, $15 – gleaming gold bells are bunched with red satin metallic balls that jingle together; Front: **Jingle Bell**, 1991, c/p, $10 – silver bells glisten with sparkling rhinestones; **Jingle Bells**, 1982, pierced, $10 – silver dangling bells with moveable clappers; **Delicate Bells**, 1978, c/p, $10 – gold bell with rhinestone at tip of moving clapper

Back: **Holiday Tree**, 1997, pierced, $10 – green enamel tree with rhinestone and ruby accents; **Colorful Christmas Tree**, 1995, pierced, $10 – gold tree with red and green beads and rhinestone star; Center: **Pearlesque Tree**, 1999, c/p, $10 – gold tree of pearls; **Christmas Tree**, 1998, c/p, $10 – gold tree trimmed in colorful rhinestones; Front: **Sparkling Christmas Tree**, 1989, pierced, $10 – emerald, ruby, and crystal stones in gold tree; **Christmas Tree**, 1986, pierced, $10 – textured gold tree

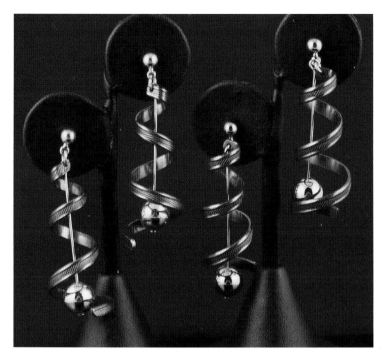

Spiral Confetti, 1993, pierced, $15 – aluminum ribbons with colorful beads in red/gold or purple/silver

Tree Dangle, 1992, c/p, $10 – gold tree with colorful rhinestone ornaments; **Convertible Christmas Tree**, 1990, pierced, $15 – gold filigree tree with rhinestone stud which can be worn without tree; Front: **Trim-A-Tree**, 1988, pierced, $10 – dangle tree that dances with holiday colors

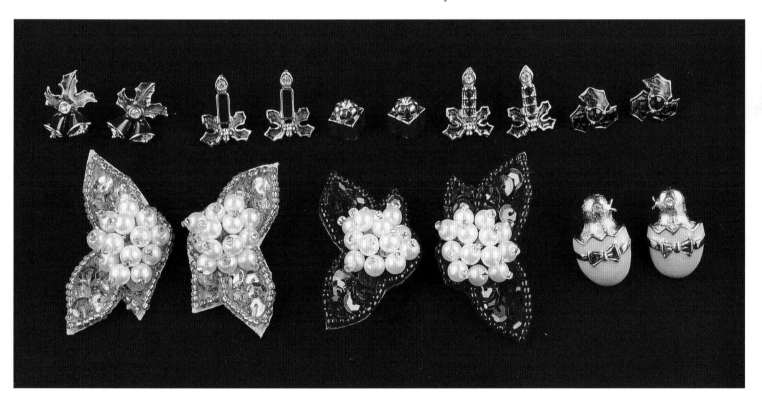

Back: **Holidays**, 1996, pierced, $10 – red bells with green leaves; **Season's Greetings**, 1996, pierced, $10 – glossy red candle and green holly leaves; **Holiday Package**, 1987, pierced, $10 – tiny red boxes tied and bowed; **Sparkling Christmas Candle**, 1993, c/p, $10 – candle of red rhinestones and green epoxy enamel leaves; **Holiday Sparkle**, 1993, pierced, $10 – green holly leaves with ruby berry, released again in 1996; Front: **Sequin Sparkle**, 1991, pierced $10 – gold or red sequin wings with pearl centers; **Easter Elegance**, 1994, pierced $10 – gold chicks with rhinestone eyes in pearly eggshells

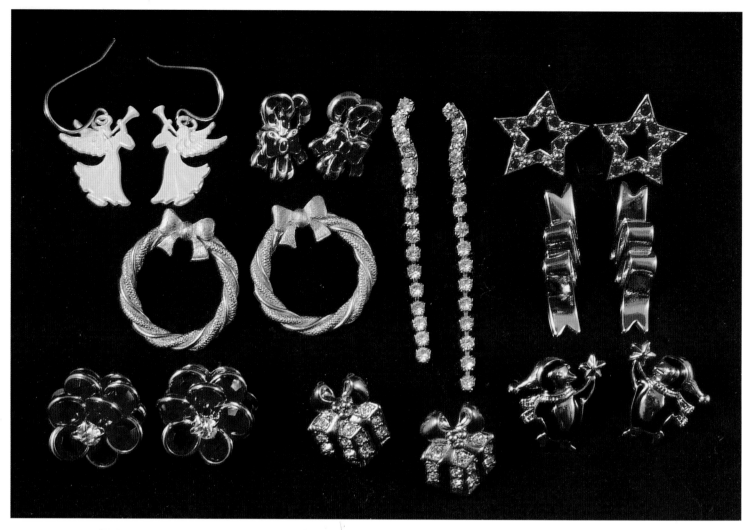

Christmas Novelty, 2001, pierced, angel $10, candy cane $10 – silver angel or enamel candy cane; **Holiday Glamour**, 1987, pierced $15 – sparkling rhinestone dangle; **Sparkle Star**, 1995, pierced, $10 – gold with rhinestones in red, clear, or blue; Center: **Festive Circlet**, 1979, c/p, $10 – wreath in twists of gold; **Festive Ribbon**, 1989, c/p, $10 – classic ribbons in gold; Front: **Faceted Petals**, 1993, c/p, $15 – blue or red faceted petals in gold frame; **Sparkling Package**, 1992, pierced $10 – glowing gold miniature Christmas package; **Penguin**, 1996, c/p, $10 – gold with black glaze

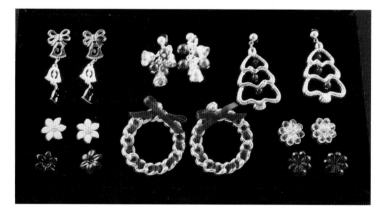

Holiday Joy, 1990, pierced, $10 – dynamite dangles; **Jingle Bell**, 2006 – colorful red and green balls with silver bells; **Deck the Tree**, 1994, $10 – gold tree with red ornaments; **Poinsettia Convertible**, 1984, pierced $10 – gold center with white or red plastic flowers, very rare; **Ribbon Weave**, 1988, pierced $10 – gold wreath with red or blue ribbon; **Convertible Snowflake**, 1986, pierced $10 – rhinestone stud with crystal and ruby jackets, very rare

Festive Sparkle, 1993, c/p, $15 – black or red enamel with rhinestones

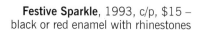

Porcelain Poinsettia, 1992, c/p $10 – gleaming porcelain flower with green leaves; **Snowman**, 1995, pierced $15 – white enamel with red and black trim and bellies that move; **Ornament Dangle**, 1992, pierced $10 – extremely rare red ball or green ball ornament; **Genuine Porcelain Bell**, 1993, c/p $20 – miniature porcelain bell with clappers and gold accents

Toast to New Year's, 1994, pierced $10 – fun champagne bottles; **New Year's Dangle**, 1992, pierced $10 – champagne glasses with pearl stir sticks

201

Bibliography

Avon Products, Inc., New York: Campaigns 1-26, 1965-2004.

Avon Products, Inc., New York: Campaigns 1-14, 2005.

Baker, Lillian. *50 Years of Collectible Fashion Jewelry, 1925 – 1975*. Paducah, KY: Collector Books, 1995.

Brown, Marcia "Sparkles". *Signed Beauties of Costume Jewelry, Identification & Values*. Paducah, KY: Collector Books, 2002.

Brown, Marcia "Sparkles". *Signed Beauties of Costume Jewelry, Volume II, Identification & Values*. Paducah, KY: Collector Books, 2004.

Clements, Monica Lynn and Patricia Rosser. *Avon Collectible Fashion Jewelry and Awards*, Atglen, PA: Schiffer Publishing Ltd, 1998.

Ettinger, Roseann. *Popular Jewelry of the 60s, 70s & 80s*. Atglen, PA: Schiffer Publishing Ltd., 1997.

Lindenberger, Jan & Jean Rosenthal. *Collecting Plastic Jewelry, A Handbook & Price Guide*. Atglen, PA: Schiffer Publishing Ltd., 1996.

Miller, Judith. *Costume Jewelry, The Complete Visual Reference and Price Guide*. New York: DK Publishing, Inc, 2003.

Morris, Betsy. *"If Women Ran the World It Would Look a Lot Like Avon"* Fortune Magazine, 1997.

Rezazadeh, Fred. *Costume Jewelry, A Practical Handbook & Value Guide*. Paducah, KY: Collector Books, 1998.

Taylor, Elizabeth. *My Love Affair with Jewelry*. New York. Simon & Schuster, 2002.

Schiffer, Nancy. *The Best of Costume Jewelry*. Atglen, PA: Schiffer Publishing Ltd., 1996.

Simonds, Cherri. *Collectible Costume Jewelry, Identification & Values*. Paducah, KY: Collector Books, 1997.

Index